T0303171

MUSIC ALIVE!'s

PERCUSSION

MUSIC ALIVE!'s

PERCUSSION!

BY DANIEL GLASS

inTune PARTNERS

Distributed by Hal Leonard Corporation

Published in 2013 by In Tune Partners
582 North Broadway
White Plains, NY 10603

Distributed by Hal Leonard Corporation
7777 West Bluemound Road
Milwaukee, WI 53213

Cover Photos: Stockbyte/Thinkstock; Author Photo: Monica Zane.
Every reasonable effort has been made to contact copyright holders and secure permissions. Omissions can be remedied in future editions.

Printed in the United States of America

Editorial Director: Emile D. Menasché
Book Design: Jackie Jordan

Library of Congress Cataloging-in-Publication Data is available upon request.

ISBN: 978-1-4584-2095-4

intunemonthly.com

DEDICATION

To Christina Faist—For your loving support and wise counsel through every stage of this project. Thanks for believing in me. I love you!

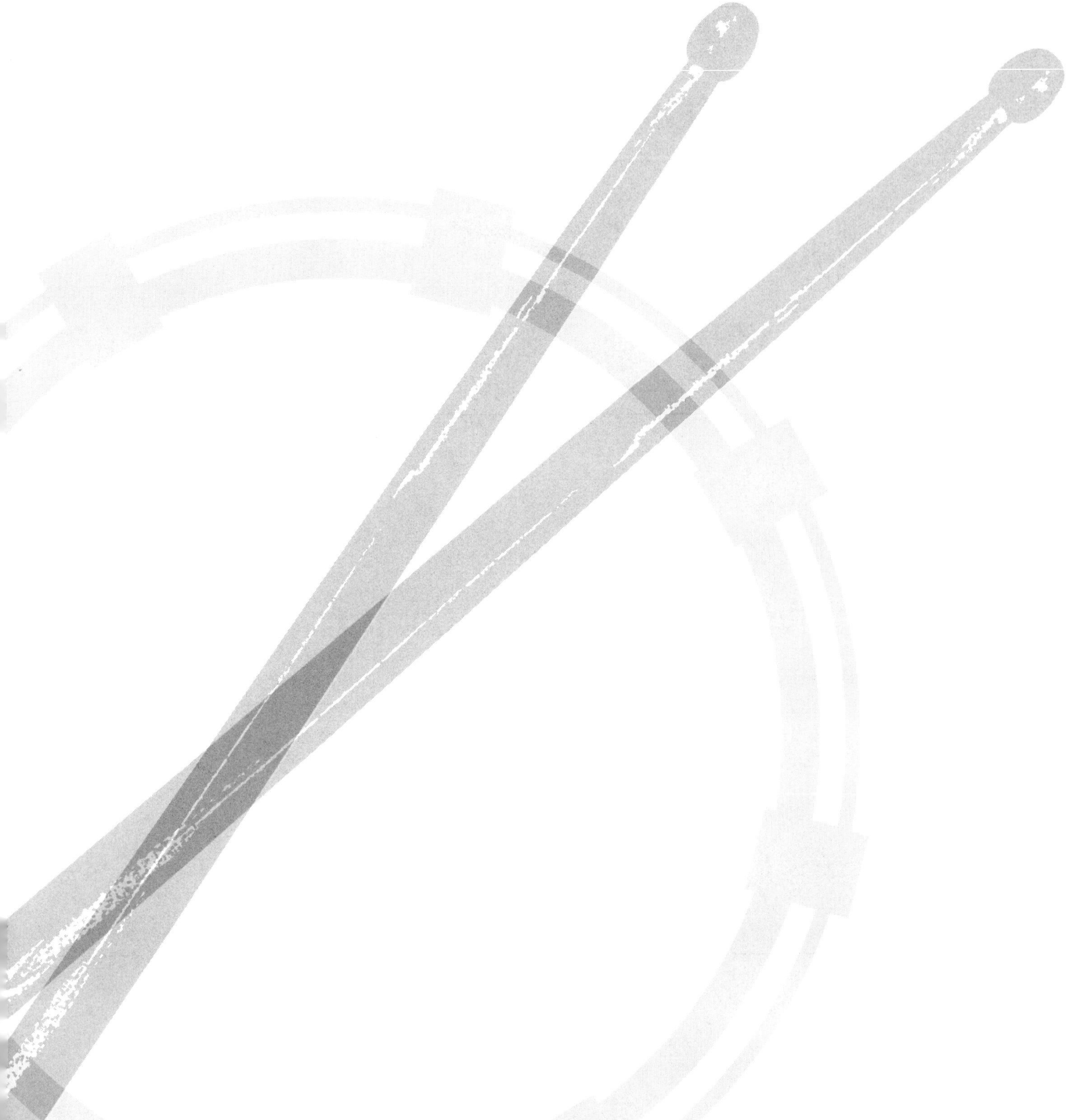

CONTENTS

ON THE DISC

The DVD-ROM that comes with this book includes three types of media—audio files (in MP3 format), video (in QuickTime format), and PDFs. These files can be played/viewed on a computer directly from the disc, or copied to a computer, mobile device, or tablet for easier playback and portability. Each type of media is contained in its own folder.

Audio Folder

Throughout this book, you will see the "listen" icon shown here. It lets you know that there's an audio example on the disc. The files have been named by the track number, and are grouped into folders by chapter. Note that not all chapters have listening examples.

LISTEN!
TRACK 00

Video Folder

In addition to the audio examples, the DVD contains high quality video of the author demonstrating drum set technique.

Resources

The resources folder offers a downloadable PDF poster of the rudiments (courtesy of Vic Firth) along with a list of links of interest to drummers.

All audio examples performed by Daniel Glass, except where noted: **Track 2** Shuffles solo, performed by Daniel Glass. From *The Century Project*. © 2012 by Daniel Glass and DrumChannel.com*. **Track 7** "Grandfather's Clock," performed by Mark Beecher.* **Track 11** "Let It Rip," performed by Danny Raymond. From the DVD *Let It Rip*. © 2008 Tapspace Publications, LLC (ASCAP). Portland, OR. International copyright secured*. **Track 27** "Shadow Behind the Iron Sun," composed and performed by Evelyn Glennie. From the RCA/Victor CD *Thunder Caves*. © 2000*. **Tracks 56** and **57** sample library loops. **Track 58** Brazilian percussion ensemble, performed by Daniel Glass, Excerpted from "Marcella" (written by Melissa Sullivan and Phil Gough). © 2006*

INTRODUCTION

Hello fellow percussion enthusiasts, and welcome to *Music Alive!'s Percussion.* This book is designed to introduce you to the many facets of percussion. It covers a wide range of topics (which we'll explore in detail in Chapter 1), and has plenty to offer whether you're a student, an amateur musician, or someone who merely wants to understand more about the experience of making music.

About the Author

My name is Daniel Glass. I'm a professional musician, author, and educator. I began my love affair with drums at the age of eight, and for the last 22 years, I've been fortunate enough to make a living doing what I love. I'm extremely passionate about my work, and in writing this book. I hope to share that passion with you. In addition to learning how percussion can truly enrich your life, I hope you'll be inspired to pick up one of the many instruments discussed in the following pages.

Like many musicians, I wear a few different hats. As a performer, I've had the good fortune to record and perform with a variety of top-flight acts, including Royal Crown Revue, Brian Setzer, KISS front man Gene Simmons, Bette Midler, Liza Minnelli, and Mike Ness from Social Distortion. I'm grateful to have been voted one of the top five R&B drummers in the world by the readers of both *Modern Drummer*

and *DRUM* magazine.

In 1999, I began researching and writing about the evolution of the drum set. Since then, I've published numerous articles and four books, including the multi-award winning *Commandments of Early Rhythm and Blues Drumming* (co-written with legendary funk drummer Zoro). I also released a large scale DVD entitled *The Century Project*, which looks at 100 years of American music evolution (1865-1965) as seen through the lens of the drum set. In 2003, I started teaching other musicians about what I learned in the course of my research. Today, I present drum clinics and master classes all over the world, including at international festivals like PASIC (the Percussive Arts Society International Convention) and the *Modern Drummer* Festival.

Working on this book has been a great experience. The process of writing it taught me a tremendous amount about a subject in which (I thought) I was already well versed. Wherever possible, I've tried to include experiences and wisdom from my own musical life to help you get the most out of your own percussive journey.

How to Use This Book

Since this book covers a very broad range of topics related to percussion, you can either read it cover to cover in a traditional manner, or skip around between the chapters depending on what interests you. You can also use the book as a reference tool if you need to look up a particular instrument, groove, or style of music.

To help bring the world of percussion to life, the book comes with a DVD-R, which includes audio tracks, video clips, and other graphics that will enhance your understanding of the material being discussed. Finally, while *Music Alive!'s Percussion* is a good overall introduction, it also suggests other resources that will help you dig much deeper into a particular subject.

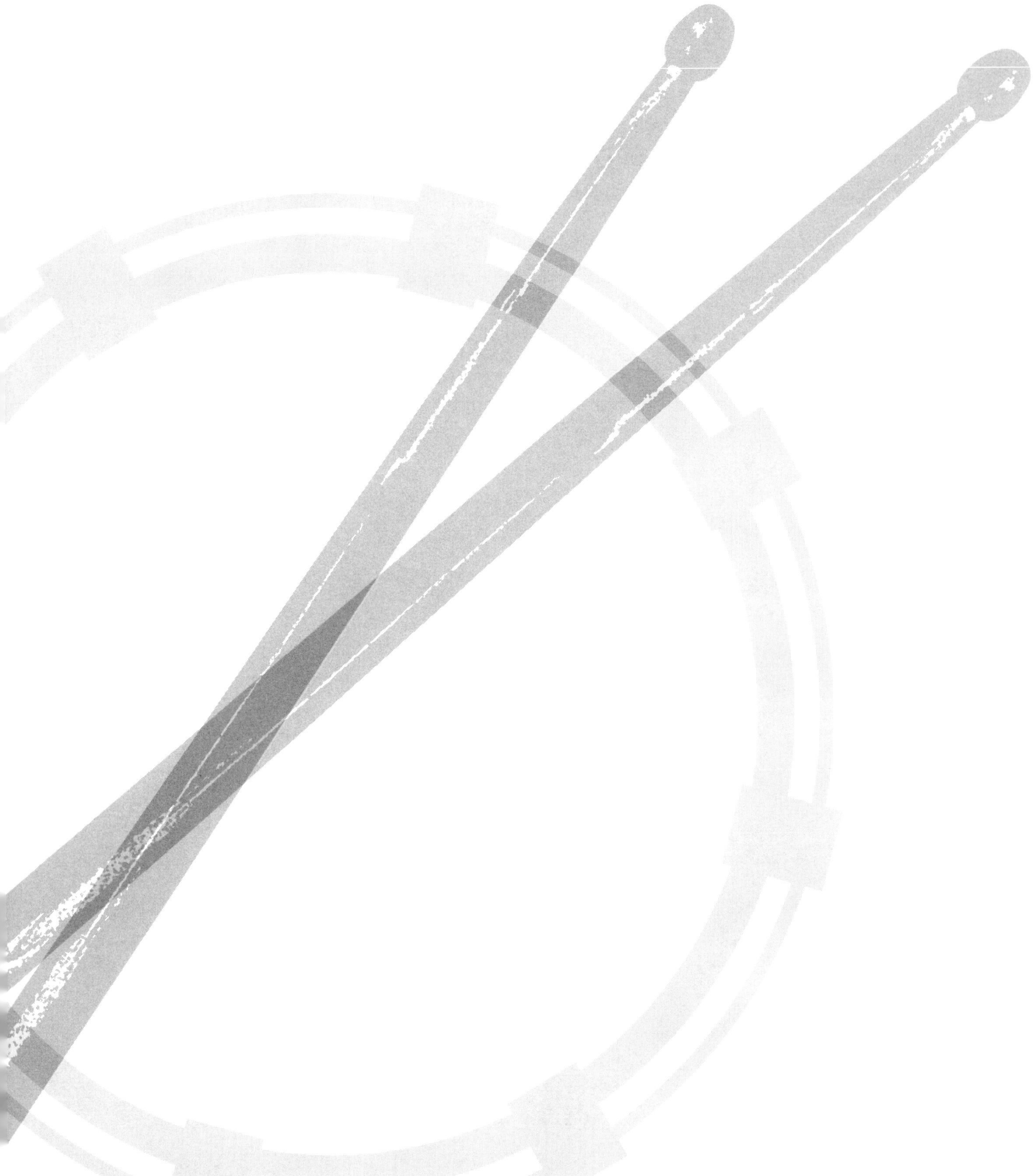

ACKNOWLEDGMENTS

SPECIAL THANKS GOES TO:

The people who helped create this book:

- Designer Jackie Jordan and Editor Emile Menasché at In Tune Partners.
- Mark Cally, who did an amazing job transcribing a multitude of music examples.

The people at the instrument companies who assisted with research or provided media for this project, especially:

- Drum Workshop: Don Lombardi, John Good, Scott Garrison, Juels Thomas, Steve Vega, and Ryan Poyer
- Crescent Cymbals: Michael Vosbein, Kevin Vosbein, and Jeff Ragland
- Vic Firth Drumsticks: Vic Firth, Joe Testa, Neil Larrivee, and Ben Davies
- Aquarian Drumheads: Roy Burns and Chris Brady
- Latin Percussion: Steve Nigohosian, Memo Acevedo, and Marcia Stevenson
- Big Bang Distribution: Bob Kasha and Jonathan Colwell
- D'Addario and Co.: Steve Lobmeier and Marco Soccolli
- Avedis Zildjian Company: John DeChristopher, Paul Francis, and Leon Chiappini
- Remo, Inc.: Remo Belli and Bruce Jacoby
- Yamaha Corporation and Marc Ferris of Giles Communications
- Pearl Corporation
- Adams Percussion
- Roland USA
- AA Meinl
- Alfred Music Publishing
- Ludwig Corporation
- Reloop
- Alternative Mode

- Alesis Corporation
- Tree Works Chimes
- Redmedea
- XLN Audio
- The Early Music Shop

The percussionists and their associates who were kind enough to allow us to include their wonderful performances on the CD:

- Mark Beecher
- Danny Raymond and Murray Gussack at Tapspace Publications
- Dame Evelyn Glennie, Angela Jarrett, Brenda Gillian, and everyone at RCA/Victor
- Melissa Sullivan, Phil Gough, and James Saez

THANKS ALSO GOES TO:

- Mark Beecher and John Beck, for so generously sharing their expertise in the fields of military and classical drumming, respectively.
- Dr. Bruce Raeburn at the Hogan Jazz Archive, Judy Van Zile at the University of Hawaii, Dr. Aaron Glass at Bard College, and Dr. Theodore Dennis Brown at UMass Amherst, for their adroit musical perspective and historical knowledge.
- My teachers: Freddy Gruber, Bruce Becker, and Bob Gullotti, who gave me the tools to manifest my love of drumming history and evolution.
- The William P. Gottleib Collection
- Jose Altonaga and everyone at DrumChannel.com
- Jim Pettit and the Memphis Drum Shop
- Stan and Jerry Keyawa at the Professional Drum Shop
- Scott "Harry" Friedman at Horn Trader Music
- Jose Medeles and Scott McPherson at Revival Drum
- Ed Hartman at the Drum Connection
- O'Rorke's Tavern, Gettysburg, PA
- Isabel Spagnardi, Adam Budofsky, Michael Dawson, Kevin Kearns, Billy Amendola, Michael Parillo, Tracy Kearns, and Sue Hurring at *Modern Drummer* magazine
- Phil Hood, Andy Doerschuk, and Andrew Lentz at *DRUM* magazine

DANIEL GLASS ENDORSES:

- DW Drums, Pedals and Hardware
- Crescent Cymbals
- Vic Firth Sticks
- Aquarian Drum Heads
- LP Percussion
- Ahead Armor Cases
- Power Wrist Builder Practice Sticks
- HQ Percussion
- Pure Sound Snare Wires
- Phat Foot Drum Harnesses

1

PERCUSSION BASICS AND AN INTRODUCTION TO THE DRUM SET

Welcome to the wonderful world of percussion! Although the word has a variety of meanings, when we talk about "percussion" in a musical sense, we are referring to a rich and diverse family of instruments that is nearly as old as the human race. The first music that people ever created was percussive in nature. Scientists have discovered that as far back as 150,000 B.C., our primitive ancestors were using handclaps, stones and primitive tools to beat out rhythms. It's believed that these first attempts at making music arose from a desire to capture the pulse of the human heart.

Today, that urge to create rhythm is still locked in our DNA. Every time you tap your feet, dance along to music, or otherwise express yourself in a rhythmic way, you are essentially acting on the same impulses as those early percussionists!

What Is Percussion?

A percussion instrument can be defined as any object that produces a sound when struck, shaken, rubbed, scraped or made to vibrate. Various categories of percussion include drums, rattles, wooden blocks, cymbals and other kinds of metal plates and bars, all of which make a distinctive sound when struck. That said, one of the coolest things about being a percussionist is that there are no limits on what you can use as an instrument! Percussionists are constantly inventing new ways to play their

IT'S ALL PERCUSSION

1.1 It's all percussion! The percussion family includes a wide range of instruments, including drums, rattles, wooden blocks, cymbals and other kinds of metal plates and bars, all of which make a distinctive sound when struck.

craft, from patting their hands on the surface of water to using their own bodies as an instrument.

Pulse and Rhythm: A Percussionist's "Job #1"

Now that we've established what a percussionist is, let's look at what a percussionist does. The most obvious answer is that he or she "keeps the beat." But what exactly does that mean? When you tap your feet along with a favorite song, you are locking in with an underlying pulse that drives that piece of music. Like a heartbeat, pulse can be found in just about every kind of music in existence—from a rock & roll tune to a Mozart sonata to an Indian Raga. When a percussionist "keeps the beat," they are using their instrument to express that pulse, and create a solid base that other musicians or an audience can easily follow. The steady, repeated patterns that percussionists play when keeping the beat are called "rhythms."

As I mentioned earlier, our relationship with rhythm goes back to the very dawn of humanity. As such, we are all programmed to understand rhythm instinctively. Even an infant, who has no idea what "music" means, will instinctively respond to the rhythm when he or she hears a piece of music.

Throughout history, the purpose of rhythm has always been to tap into that instinct and bring groups of people together to share a common experience. Think about the following: a marching band leading a group of soldiers across a field, an Asian priest using gongs and bowls to conduct a hypnotic ritual, a big band driving a roomful of jitterbugging couples, a rock band leading 10,000 people in a fist-pumping sing-along. In all of these examples, rhythm is being used to grab people's attention, shake them up, and transport them as a group.

DID YOU KNOW?

. . . that there's a dance called the "hambone" that turns your entire body into a percussion instrument? The dance originates from the West African "juba," and is performed by patting and slapping out rhythms on various parts of the body. African American slaves used it during plantation gatherings, because no rhythm instruments were allowed due to fear of secret codes hidden in the drumming. In the mid-1800s, music and lyrics were added, and in 1952, the hambone even became an early rock & roll hit!

The Ways We Use Percussion

We typically think of percussion instruments (Fig. 1.1) as objects that are used in a musical setting, usually for entertainment or dancing. Throughout history, however, percussion has also served many other important functions.

COMMUNICATION

While great for making music, percussion instruments have also been used to help people communicate with each other. In various parts of Africa, for example, two-toned log drums were used to send messages over long distances, similar perhaps to modern devices like the telegraph or telephone. Africans also used "talking drums" and "slit gongs" to tell stories or relay ideas and signals. These instruments imitated the inflections and pitch variations of a human voice, allowing for the creation of very complex and detailed rhythmic messages. You can learn more about "talking percussion" in Chapter 7.

MILITARY

Another important use of percussion has been on the battlefield. Throughout history, commanders have taken advantage of the tremendous volume produced by drums and cymbals to motivate troops, help set a marching pace, and call out various orders or announcements (Fig. 1.2). Percussion was also used as a means of instilling fear in the hearts of the enemy. You can learn much more about military percussion in Chapter 3.

1.2 Civil War military band

RELIGIOUS

As I mentioned earlier in this chapter, rhythm has a hypnotic power that taps into a very ancient part of our human nature. Rhythms can entertain and make us dance, but they can also help us to rise above the turmoil and troubles of everyday life to see the "bigger picture." As such, percussion has played an integral role in religion throughout history. In many primitive cultures, the beating of drums allowed shamans and healers to achieve an altered state of consciousness that helped them communicate with the spiritual world. The Japanese "taiko" drum—estimated to be over 2,000 years old—has been used in Shinto and Buddhist temples as an aid to chanting. In the Western tradition, ancient Jewish prayer services often featured drumming, and the Bible contains several references to the use of percussion in religious ceremonies.

Bringing Percussion to Life

You have obviously picked up this book because in one way or another, you are drawn to percussion and have a desire to make rhythms yourself. The following chapters are designed to help you explore the nuts and bolts of how to do just that. We'll look at some of the main branches in the percussion family tree: classical and marching percussion, world percussion, mallet percussion and electronic percussion. We'll also look at how percussion is used in various styles of music, and introduce you to some of the legendary musicians who pioneered the rhythms and "grooves" that we play today. Finally, we'll dig into some of the technical issues involved with playing percussion, including holding the sticks, striking a drum and more.

The Drum Set: A Good Place to Start

Our journey into the world of percussion begins with an instrument that is probably quite familiar to you: the drum set! This wild contraption—a combination of drums, cymbals, pedals and other hardware—is an integral part of the popular culture that we are used to seeing and hearing every day. Drum sets (Fig. 1.3) can be found on the radio, in music videos, and at most of the concerts we attend. Just about everybody can recognize the name of at least one famous drum set player, and most of us probably know someone personally who plays drum set.

1.3 Drum set

But while you may be accustomed to experiencing the drum set in your daily life, there are a few things you may *not* be aware of regarding this very unique instrument. For example, did you know that compared to most other instruments, the drum set is actually quite youthful by comparison? Violins have been in existence since the early 1500s; guitars can be traced back about 400 years earlier than that. The first drum sets, on the other hand, didn't appear until the 1870s. And while other kinds of percussion are associated with many cultures throughout the world, the drum set's origins are tied to just one place: the United States of America.

In history class, we talk about the U.S. as a place that has brought together people from all over the world and integrated their cultures to create something new. In many ways, the drum set is the musical representation of the American "melting pot" ideal.

The first drum sets were essentially "mash-ups," an unlikely combination of percussion instruments and approaches to playing that really had no business being thrown together. And yet, like America itself, drummers found a way to make these elements work, creating new sounds, grooves, and musical styles. As the drum set evolved during the first half of the 20th century, the gear and playing techniques used by drummers continued to go through many profound and radical changes. Often, these changes were what defined the sound of popular music as a whole.

The fact that the drum set combines and adapts instruments from so many other cultures makes it the perfect tool to introduce you to some of the topics that this book will address. The following section explains a modern drum set piece by piece. Each of these pieces has its own special story to share about the history of percussion. We'll look at the drum set in much greater detail in Chapters 5 and 6.

ANATOMY OF A DRUM SET

A closer look at the drum set reveals that it brings together percussion elements from many different cultural backgrounds. Figure 1.4 identifies the key elements of a drum set, shows the origins of each one, and links to the chapter where you can learn about that element in greater detail.

LISTEN! TRACK 2

Check out this drum set solo, performed by Daniel Glass.

Bass Drum

As the biggest and lowest pitched of the drums, the bass drum is considered the foundation of the drum set. With origins in the Turkish military, it was introduced into orchestral music in the 18th century. The bass drum, along with the snare drum, was the most important element in early drum sets.

1.4 Anatomy of a drum set

Bass Drum Pedal

Invented in the late 1800s, this unique device allowed one person to play both the bass and snare drum at the same time. As such, the bass drum pedal was the key to the creation of the drum set, and gave rise to the term, "kick drum."

Snare Drum

With origins in Europe dating back to Middle Ages, the snare drum was initially used for both military and orchestral purposes. The crisp crack of the snare wires along the bottom head (Figure 1.5) made this drum the ideal for the development of "rudiments," the musical vocabulary used by drummers today. In the earliest years of jazz, drum set players "swung" these rudiments, turning them from marches into dance music.

1.5 Snare wires

Hi-Hat

Created in the late 1920s, the hi hat gave jazz drummers a new way to keep time using cymbals. During the Swing era of the 1930s, the lighter and highly danceable feel provided by the hi hat allowed it to replace the snare drum as the main instrument for timekeeping.

Ride Cymbal

The ride cymbal replaced the hi hat as the dominant timekeeper with the dawn of bebop jazz in the early 1940s. With a diameter of 18-22 inches, rides were larger than earlier generations of cymbals, making it easier for drummers to play with clear stick definition and a wide variety of sonic colors.

Crash Cymbal

Prior to the 1960s, cymbals were generally thin enough that a drummer could ride and crash on the same cymbal. With the rise of rock & roll, however, rides became much heavier. This meant creating a new category of cymbal that would allow drummers to focus specifically on the "crash" that came at the end of most fills.

Tom-Toms

First introduced into the U.S. by Chinese immigrants, early drum set players added tom-toms in the 1920s, finding them useful as sound effects for stage shows and silent movies, and for playing "fill-in's" with dance bands. With the rise of the big bands in the mid-'30s, tom-toms took on a more prominent role, particularly when drummer Gene Krupa showcased them in his work with Benny Goodman's orchestra.

DID YOU KNOW?

. . . that traditionally, drumheads were made from animal hide? Although these heads produced a beautiful sound, they were notoriously temperamental. They would break if struck too hard, and even slight changes in the weather could cause them to go out of tune. "Plastic" heads (made from synthetic material) were perfected in the late 1950s. They were impervious to weather changes and could handle tremendous pummeling, which made the evolution of rock & roll possible.

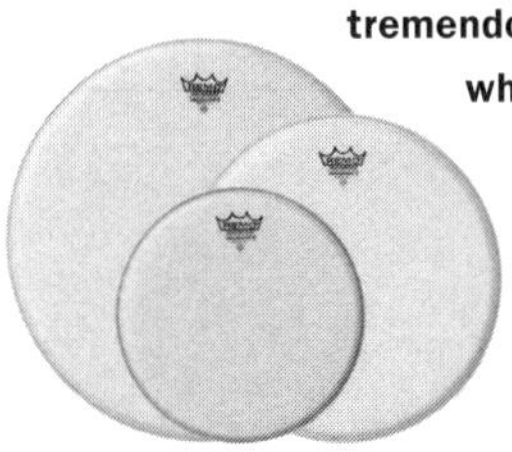

Cowbell

For centuries, shepherds used metal bells hung around the necks of livestock as a means of identifying their herds. Many cultures used these bells for musical purposes as well. The cowbell was likely adapted to the drum set by the first African American jazz drummers in New Orleans and used for playing fills. Cowbells (Fig. 1.7) are an essential part of Latin music and play an important role in rock drumming as well.

Woodblock

Like the cowbell, hollowed out blocks of wood (Fig. 1.8) have also been used as instruments in many cultures. Early drum set players used woodblocks to keep time and as sound effects. The blocks could be played individually, or in pitched sets (sometimes called "temple blocks"). Most of the woodblocks used by drum set players today are actually made of plastic, which makes them more durable.

Tambourine

Another ancient instrument that was adapted for the drum set. Drum set players usually mount the tambourine (Fig. 1.9) to a stand and strike it with a stick, or attach it to the rod of the hi-hat, making it jingle when the two cymbals are brought together with the foot pedal.

1.7 Cowbell

1.9 Tambourine

1.8 Woodblock

Splash Cymbal

1.10 Splash cymbal

A small, thin cymbal (usually 8-12 inches in diameter) that is reminiscent of the type of cymbal first used by drum set players (prior to the existence of ride or crash cymbals). Today, drummers tend to use splash cymbals as sound effects, rather than for riding or crashing.

Additional Percussion

Many other percussion instruments—such as chimes, gong, wind chimes, timpani, and triangle—have all been added to the drum set over the years. Extra percussion plays a big role in situations where drummers a) need a variety of sound effects, or b) need a big set because it adds to the theatrical nature of the music. Drummers famous for including of extra percussion in their setups include Sonny Greer (Duke Ellington), John Bonham (Led Zeppelin), and Neil Peart (Rush). Figure 1.11 shows an array of percussion instruments.

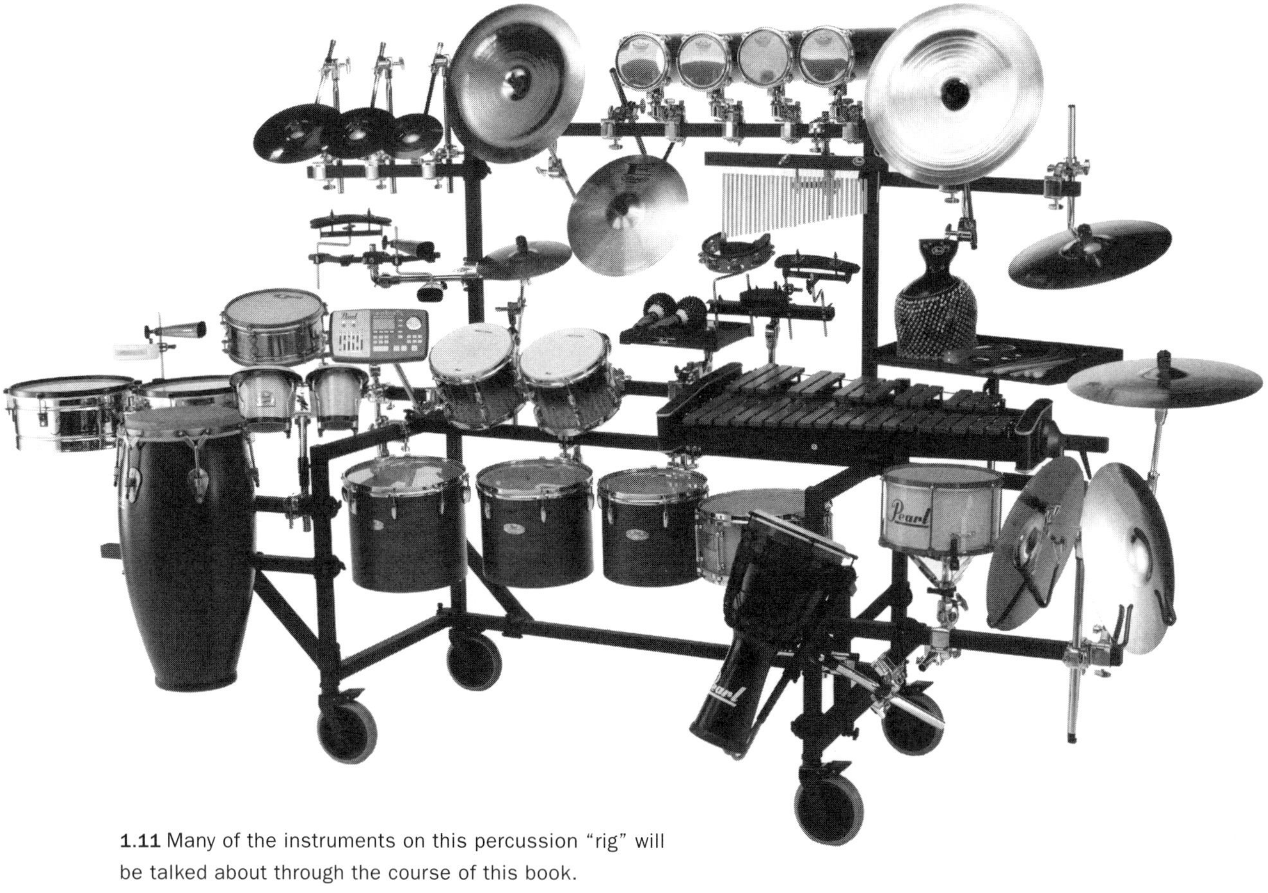

1.11 Many of the instruments on this percussion "rig" will be talked about through the course of this book.

2

2

BASIC NOTATION AND READING

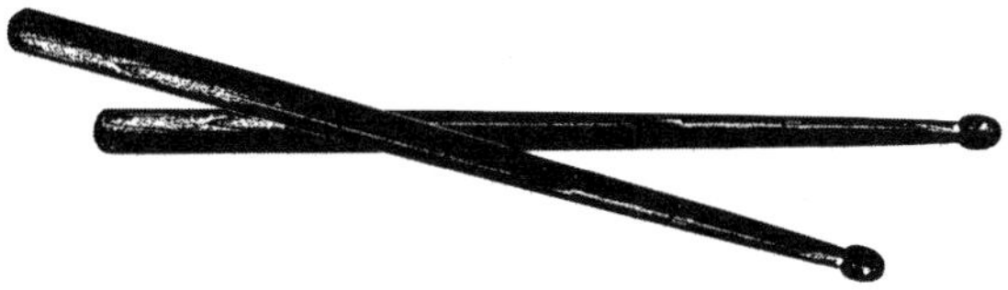

In the last chapter, I noted that the main job of a percussionist is to keep time by playing various rhythms. This chapter will explore the concept of rhythm in great detail, showing how it can be written on a printed page, and how you can learn to read and count it. With this knowledge, you'll be able to understand and play the various musical examples that will be written out in later chapters.

To Read or Not to Read? That Is the Question.

Before we go any further, we should address a basic question that many of us ask ourselves at some point along our musical journey: "Do I really have to learn how to read music?"

The short answer is "no." There's no law that says you have to know how to read music in order to be talented or successful. Some of the world's biggest stars play by ear, meaning they develop a sophisticated understanding of music purely by listening to and memorizing it. For many, learning by ear is more natural (and perhaps more fun) than taking the time needed to learn the basics of reading music.

The great Buddy Rich (Figure 2.1) couldn't read music, but he had such a good ear that it didn't matter.

So why learn to read at all? For one thing, reading allows us to understand music in a visual (as opposed to just an auditory) way. When we can see the music

2.1 Buddy Rich

as it appears on a page, we have another way to remember it, allowing us to learn and recall more quickly.

And although there is a bit of a learning curve up front, the ability to read can save you a lot of time down the road. A good reader can come together with a group of musicians he or she has never met and perform very sophisticated music at a high level, simply by looking at a chart or piece of sheet music. This is how many of my *gigs* (what musicians call jobs) work: We show up and play, with little or no rehearsal necessary!

Think about it this way. When making music, we are communicating ideas, not unlike the way we do when we use language. What if you could only speak a language, but not read and write it? Imagine how that might limit your ability to understand and make yourself understood. Many aspects of life would be affected, from simple tasks like understanding signs or reading a restaurant menu to important ones like applying for a job. Having the ability to read music offers you many more ways to learn and understand what's epxected of you.

So whether you believe that reading music is right for you or not, I encourage you to explore this chapter a bit further. You may be surprised to find how easy it is to learn some of the basics behind reading music. And you will be amazed at how much these can help when it comes to other skills like learning, practicing and performing.

DID YOU KNOW?

... that Buddy Rich, perhaps the most legendary drummer of all time, couldn't read a note of music? Buddy's ears were so big, however (at least musically speaking), that he was able to memorize complicated big band arrangements after just one or two listens.

Notes and Rests: The Building Blocks of Rhythm

In the language of music, the "letters" we use are called notes. A note tells us the pitch we are supposed to play, and how long we should play it. Once we understand how notes are combined on the musical page, we can start to recognize longer and more complex sequences of them. As with the English language, these sequences of notes are known as *phrases*; you might say they are equivalent to sentences and paragraphs.

Just as notes tell us when to play, *rests* tell us when not to play—or to put it another way, when to leave space between notes. Every note duration has a corresponding rest. We will address notes and rests in greater detail later in this chapter.

With some practice, you will eventually be able to scan an entire page of music, understanding not only how the notes are combined, but how fast you'll need to play them (the *tempo*), how loud (*dynamics*), and how to stress certain ones (*accents*). With this information, you can bring the notes to life, giving them character the same way you would use inflections in your voice to indicate whether you're asking a question, or expressing an emotion like happiness or anger.

The Musical Staff

Notes are read in that same way that we read words—from left to right. We arrange notes on a musical *staff*, a set of five horizontal lines (called *ledger lines*) and four spaces. The musical staff offers us a road map for how to understand, interpret and perform the notes on a page of music.

MEASURES AND BAR LINES

Most pieces of music divide the musical staff into units known as *measures* (also known as *bars*). We use measures to organize the notes into a form that makes it easy for us to read. Measures are divided by *bar lines*, and each measure contains a certain number of beats. How many beats is determined by the *time signature*. Figure 2.2 shows a musical staff that features two measures of music separated by a barline.

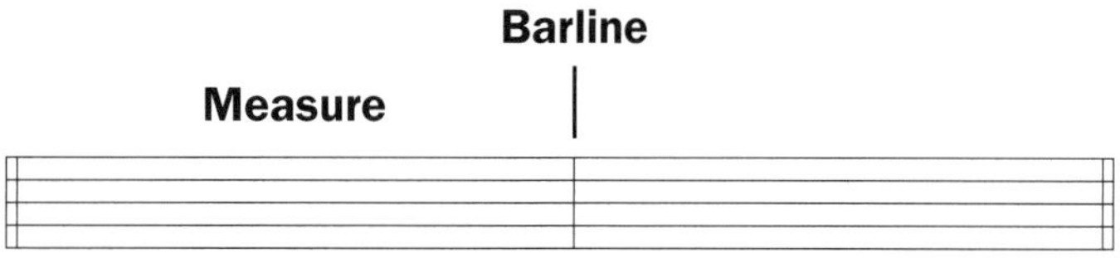

2.2 Musical Staff

PERCUSSION NOTATION

For most instrumentalists, the placement of a note on a particular line or space indicates what pitch is supposed to be played. In percussion, this form of notation holds true for a few multi-pitch drums such as timpani, as well as for mallet instrument like the xylophone, marimba, and vibraphone.

Most percussionists, however, use a special *percussion clef.* Instead of showing various pitches on one instrument, the lines and spaces on the musical staff indicate when to play individual percussion instruments.

For example, a tambourine might be represented by the D line on the staff. All the rhythms that the tambourine plays in a particular piece will be written on that one line. Percussionists across the spectrum—whether they play in a marching drum corps, latin combo or symphony orchestra—all understand and utilize this basic form of notation.

DRUM SET NOTATION

The same concept applies when writing parts for the drum set. In drum set notation, each component of the kit is assigned its own line or space. For example, the hi-hat is usually written on the space just above the staff (like the note G on the treble clef), the snare drum on the third space on the staff (C for treble clef), and the bass drum on the F space below that. The position of each instrument on the staff mirrors the way that a drum set is actually set up; cymbals are placed high up or above the staff, the snare drum and tom-toms are in the middle, and the bass drum and hi-hat (when played with the foot) are on the bottom.

Figure 2.3 shows how the drum set is typically notated on the musical staff. We'll use it as a reference once we start talking about specific drum set grooves in Chapters 5 and 6.

2.3 Common drum notation symbols

Time Signatures and Counting

Music exists in time. Just as we organize our day into hours, minutes and seconds, we can organize music by dividing it into measures and beats that are then *counted.*

We can understand how to count a particular piece by looking at the *time signature,* a two-number combination that's always found at the very beginning of the musical staff. A time signature is read by pronouncing first the top, then the bottom number. For example, this time signature (Fig. 2.4) is called "four/four time."

2.4 4/4 is the most common time signature.

$\frac{4}{4}$

In a time signature, the top number indicates the number of beats that are in each measure. In 4/4 time, there are four beats per measure. The bottom number tells us what kind of note gets one beat. An easy way to understand the bottom number is to simply put a "1" on top of it, and read it as a fraction. In this case, the bottom number in the time signature would stand for 1/4—a quarter note.

If we put it all together, 4/4 time means there are four quarter notes per bar. They are simply counted "1-2-3-4."

4/4, THE "COMMON" TIME SIGNATURE

The vast majority of the music you'll encounter will be in 4/4 time. As a multiple of two, the number four has an evenness to it that is very natural for most people to grasp. Our bodies are designed in a very symmetrical manner—two arms, two legs, two eyes, two ears, etc. Basic human activities like breathing and walking involve two complementary motions ("in and out," "back and forth," etc.). Therefore, it only makes sense that music written in 4/4 seems to fit the rhythm of everyday life.

Because it is used so often, 4/4 is also frequently referred to as *common time*, and is often written with a C in place of the numbers, like the time signature shown in Figure 2.5. 4/4 time and common time are identical.

2.5 Common time symbol C

COUNTING

To help understand how to count like a percussionist, imagine a one-dollar bill as a musical measure. If we split that dollar in half, we have two fifty-cent pieces. If we split it info four equal pieces, we have four quarters. Although each of these coins represents a different monetary value, they all still add up to one dollar.

The same is true in 4/4 time. A note that covers the value of an entire measure is called a *whole note*. It lasts for all four beats (thereby covering the whole measure). We can divide a whole note into two pieces, each called a *half note*. The first of these covers beats 1 and 2, the second covers beats 3 and 4. If we divide each of the two 1/2 notes, we have four 1/4 notes, each receiving one of the four beats.

If we divide again, we get eight equal pieces—*eighth notes*. But since we established the 1/4 note as the pulse (the bottom number in the time signature), we are not going to count any higher than four. Instead, we refer to the notes between the numbered beats as "ands" (signified by an ampersand "&"). A measure of 1/8 notes is counted as follows: "1 and, 2 and, 3 and, 4 and." The 1/8 note that comes after beat one is called "the and of 1." The 1/8 note that comes after beat two is called "the and of 2," and so forth.

We can divide the 1/8 notes in half to create *sixteenth notes*. Now each beat is split into four equal pieces, which are counted as follows, "1 e & a, 2 e & a . . ." etc. All of these examples behave just like the fractions you learn in math; if you add up the individual pieces (four quarters, eight eighths, sixteen sixteenths, etc.), they always equal one, meaning they take up the space of an entire bar. So you can understand the basics of counting, listen to the exercise shown in Figure 2.6 on the CD-R that accompanies this book. It includes a bar with a whole note, followed by a bar of 1/2 notes, a bar of 1/4 notes, a bar of 1/8 notes and a bar of 1/16 notes. To

DID YOU KNOW?

. . . that both "Happy Birthday" and "The Star Spangled Banner" are written in 3/4 time?

LISTEN! TRACK 3

2.6 Whole, 1/2, 1/4, 1/8 and 1/16 notes

𝅝	**Whole note**	=	**4 beats**
𝅗𝅥	**1/2 note**	=	**2 beats**
♩	**1/4 note**	=	**1 beat**
♪	**1/8 note**	=	**1/8 of a beat**
𝅘𝅥𝅯	**1/16 note**	=	**1/16 of a beat**

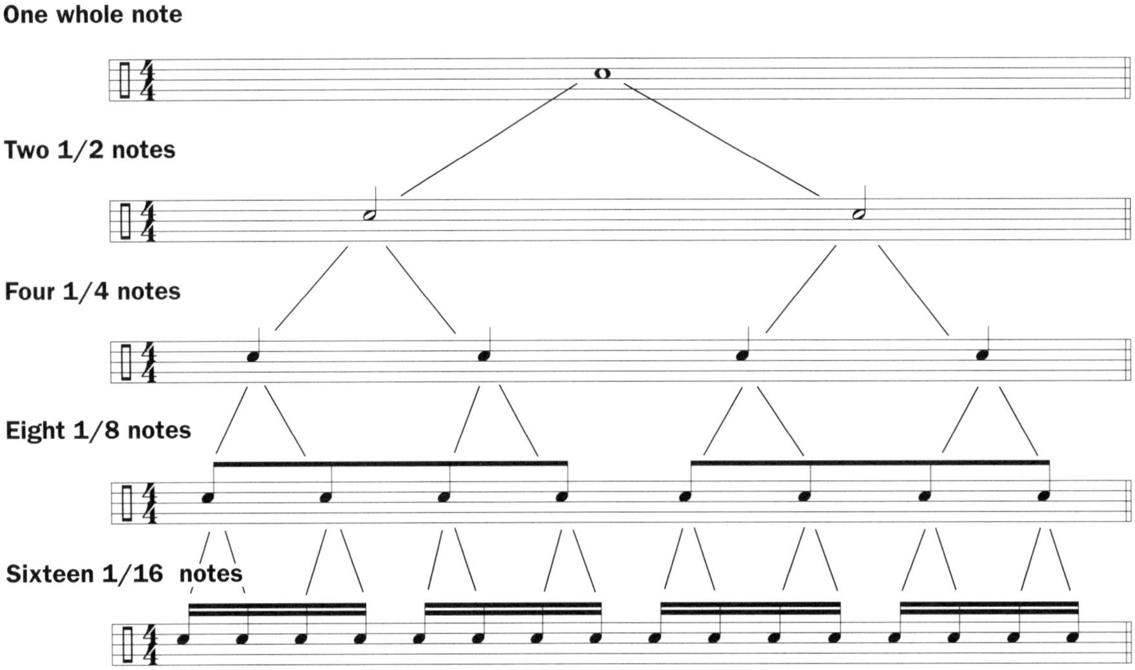

Rests

Rests indicate moments of silence. The most common rests correspond to the notes above.

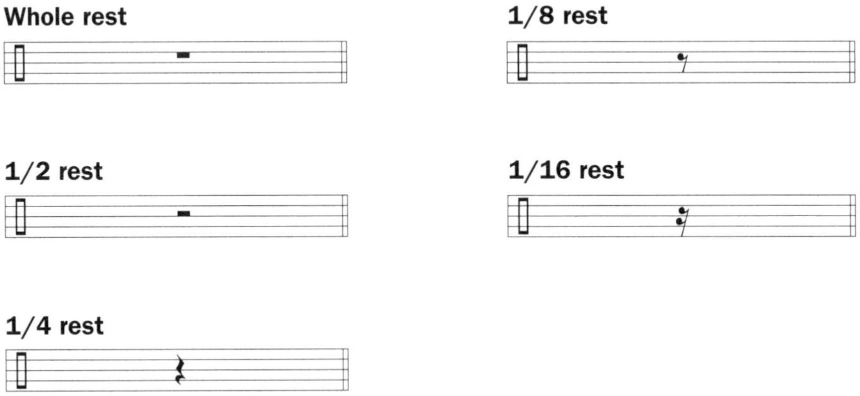

2.7 Rhythmic Notation. This chart shows how a measure of 4/4 time is divided into various note values, and how each one of those subdivisions is counted. It also shows the corresponding rest for each note value.

help you understand how these rhythms fit together around the concept of 4/4 time, each bar also includes the steady pulse of the bass drum playing 1/4 notes.

If you're new to the concept of time signatures and counting rhythm, this all might seem a little confusing at first. However, as we get into some actual musical examples in later chapters, the practicalities of counting will make more sense, and you'll realize that it's actually quite simple. Figure 2.7 shows how different note values relate to one another.

TRIPLETS

In addition to dividing beats into halves, quarters, eighths and sixteenths, you can also divide them into groupings of three. These groupings are known as *triplets*, and they are identified by a small numeral 3 above (or sometimes below) the grouping.

Triplet groups are written to correspond with the other note types we've discussed so far. In other words, we can have 1/4 note triplets, 1/8 note triplets, and so on. A triplet group's duration is equal to two notes of the same value. For example, a 1/4 note triplet spans the length of two 1/4 notes, an 1/8 note triplet spans the length of two 1/8 notes, and so on.

Figure 2.8 offers a good example of how triplets look and sound. The first bar contains four 1/4 notes. It is followed by a bar of 1/4 note triplets. The third bar contains 1/8 notes, and is followed by a bar of 1/8 note triplets. Bars five and six follow the same pattern, only with 1/16 notes and 1/16 note triplets. As in the previous exercise, these rhythms are played against the steady pulse of the bass drum, which plays 1/4 notes.

LISTEN! TRACK 4

2.8 Standard notes (bars 1 and 2) and triplets (bars 2 and 4)

OTHER TIME SIGNATURES

Although 4/4 is by far the most common time signature, it is by no means the only one. Time signatures that divide measures into two, three, and six beats are not uncommon. You'll also find time signatures that divide by odd numbers of beats such as five, seven, nine, and twelve. Not only that, but you'll also find some where the 1/4 note does not represent one beat!

3/4, or "Waltz" Time

Another time signature we encounter on a fairly regular basis is 3/4 (meaning it is composed of three 1/4 notes per measure and counted "1-2-3"). A song written in 3/4 time is sometimes referred to as a "waltz," based on the popular ballroom dance of the same name (and also comprised of three beats). Figure 2.9 shows 1/4, 1/8, and 1/16 notes in 3/4 time.

LISTEN! TRACK 5

2.9

6/8 Time

Another type of time signature has an eight on the bottom, meaning that the 1/8 note gets one beat instead of a 1/4 note. 6/8 time is composed of six 1/8 notes per measure, and is counted "1-2-3-4-5-6" (Fig. 2.10) 6/8 is used in many musical styles.

LISTEN! TRACK 6

2.10

Odd Time Signatures

Other time signatures can include more uneven numbers of beats, like five and seven. These are typically called "odd time" signatures, and are beyond the scope of what we'll be dealing with in this book.

Other Musical Concepts

There's more to reading music than knowing the timing and duration of notes. Notation must also indicate pitch and may include markings that tell you how loud or soft to play and offer other clues about how to make the music more expressive. Figure 2.11 shows the kind of more detailed staff a percussionist might see. As you can see, only a few of the markings are actual notes!

Clef

Just as the time signature tells you how to count, the *clef* tells you what pitches each note represents. The word "clef" is French for "key." The clef symbol is usually placed at the very beginning of the staff. The most common clefs are treble clef (Fig. 2.12), which is used for instruments that have a higher pitch range (like trumpet or violin), and bass clef (Fig. 2.13), used for instruments with a lower pitch range (like

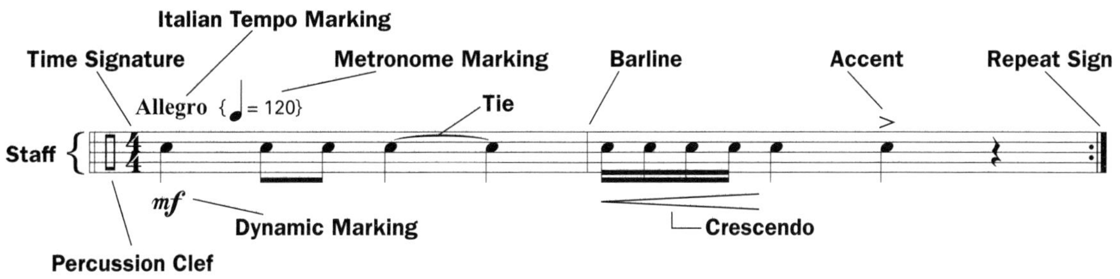

2.11 A musical staff with a range of expressive and other markings

cello or bass guitar). Piano music typically shows two separate parts at once—one in bass cleff (played with the left hand) and one in treble clef (played with the right).

Percussion Clef

As I mentioned earlier, some percussion instruments (for example, timpani and mallet instruments like the xylophone) utilize a variety of pitches. Music for these instruments can be written in treble and bass clefs. But most percussion instruments—for example, snare drum, cowbell, tambourine, etc.—have only one pitch.

2.12  **2.13**  **2.14** 

Music written for these instruments uses a special percussion clef (Fig. 2.14). Each line and space represents a particular instrument rather than a pitch. Most of the musical examples included in this book will use the percussion clef.

TEMPO

Tempo is the Italian word for "time." Written music might include a *tempo marking*, (Fig. 2.15) typically located in the upper left corner above the staff. The number refers to *beats per minute* (BPM). It also shows the note value for one beat. In this case, a 1/4 note. In other words, the tempo is 120 1/4 note beats per minute.

2.15 ♩ **= 120**

A metronome (Fig. 2.16) is used to count time. There are a variety of types, from mechanical devices that play one beat only to digital metronomes that can include accents on the down beat and even play complex patterns.

Specific beats per minute aren't the only way to indicate tempo. In classical music, it is customary to describe the tempo using words. Most of these words are Italian, because many of the most important composers of classical music were Italian, and they wrote in a period before the metronome was invented. These Italian descrip-

2.16 Different types of metronomes

tions of tempo can indicate not only the speed, but also the mood of the piece. For example, *presto* and *allegro* both indicate a speedy execution: presto simply means "faster," but allegro also connotes joy (from its original meaning in Italian). Even after the invention of the metronome, these words continue to be used. Figure 2.17 shows a few key Italian tempo terms.

Grave: slow and solemn
Lento: slowly
Largo: broadly
Adagio: slow and stately (literally, "at ease")
Andante: at a walking pace
Moderato: moderately
Allegro moderato: moderately quick
Allegro: fast, quickly and bright
Vivace: lively and fast (quicker than allegro)
Presto: very fast
Prestissimo: extremely fast

2.17 Here are some of the most common Italian terms used to describe tempo, listed from slower to faster.

DYNAMICS

Dynamics is the musical term for how loud a piece of music should be played. As with tempo, dynamic markings are based on Italian terms, and are used universally in notating just about every style of music (classical, jazz, rock, etc.). The two basic dynamic indicators are shown in Figure 2.18.

p or piano, meaning "soft".
f or forte, meaning "strong" (or for our purposes, "loud").

2.18

But there are many different shades of "soft" and "strong." Figure 2.19 shows the terms for quietest to loudest. These markings are usually placed below the staff.

ppp	pianeissimo possibile ("softest possible")
pp	pianissimo ("very soft")
p	piano ("soft")
mp	mezzo-piano ("moderately soft")
mf	mezzo-forte ("moderately strong")
f	forte ("strong")
ff	fortissimo ("very strong")
fff	forteissimo possibile ("loudest possible")

2.19

Crescendos and Diminuendo

If a piece of music gets gradually louder, it is called a *crescendo*. A crescendo is indicated either by the symbols shown in Figure 2.20, or by the abbreviation *cresc.* Figure 2.20 also shows symbols telling you to make the music gradually softer: the *diminuendo* (or a *decrescendo*), also indicated by the abbreviations *dim. or decresc.*

2.20 A crescendo mark (left) and a diminuendo mark (right)

Accents and Ghost Notes

If a particular note is to be played louder than all the others, an accent mark is placed above it. If a note is to be played softer than all the others, then it is written in parentheses and called a ghost note. Figure 2.21 shows how they're written.

2.21 Accent (left) and ghost note (right)

Grace Notes

A *grace note* is an unaccented note that gets attached to a louder note, and is typically played just before or after it. In percussion, grace notes are used in specific rudiments, such as a *flam* (Fig. 2.22) or a *drag* (Fig. 2.23). For a more detailed explanation of rudiments, check out Chapter 3.

2.22 Grace notes in a flam rudiment

2.23 Grace notes in a drag rudiment

Tied Notes

A *tie* is a curved line connecting the heads of two notes. A tie indicates that they are to be played as a single note with a duration equal to the sum of the individual notes' note values. In Figure 2.24, the two 1/4 notes that are tied together would have the value of a 1/2 note.

2.24 The tie tells us to play the two 1/4 notes as a single note with the same duration as a 1/2 note.

Dotted Notes

If a dot is added after a note, it indicates that the note should be held for one and a half times its value. For example, a *dotted quarter note* is held for the length of a 1/4 note plus an extra 1/8 note, totaling three 1/8 notes (Fig. 2.25). Writing a dot makes it easier to read than using a lot of ties. As you can see, a 1/4 note with a dot after it is easier to look at than either a 1/4 tied to an 1/8 note or three 1/8 notes tied together. All three are equivalent, but the first is the simplest for our eyes to "digest."

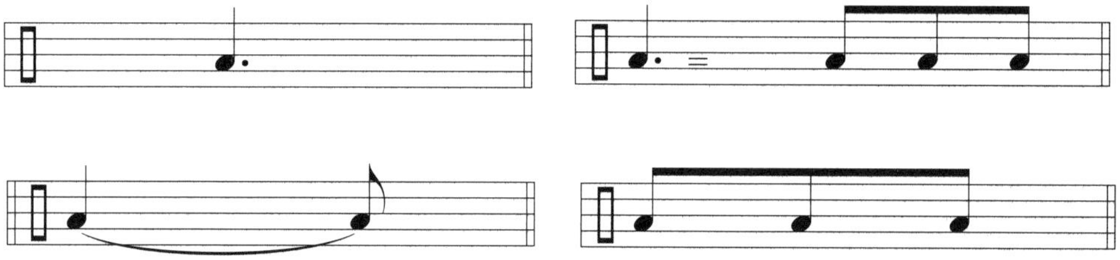

2.25 A dotted 1/4 note (top left) has a duration of one and half beats. As you can see, it's much easier to read than the other three measures shown here, even though they all indicate the same note duration.

Repeats

If a musical passage of multiple measures is to be repeated, then those measures are bracketed by what are called *repeat signs* (Fig. 2.26).

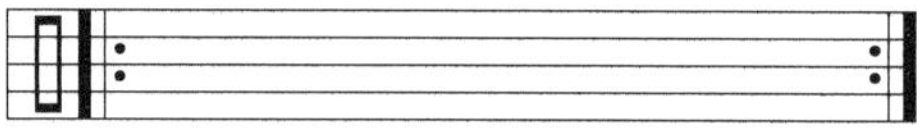

2.26 Repeat signs

If a single measure is to be repeated, then the measure (or measures) following it includes this symbol (Fig. 2.27).

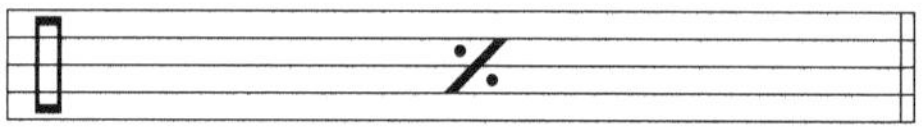

2.27 The repeat one measure sign

If a two-measure phrase is to be repeated, then the measure (or measures) following it includes this symbol (Fig. 2.28).

2.28 The number above the repeat sign indicates how many measures to repeat.

Moving On

While advanced players may encounter some unusual addition symbols, you've already seen everything you need to know to read almost any piece of music. Reading takes practice, but like anything else, the more you do it, the better you'll get at it. Eventually, you may even be able to "hear" the music in your head just from looking at it on the page!

3

MARCHING PERCUSSION AND RUDIMENTS

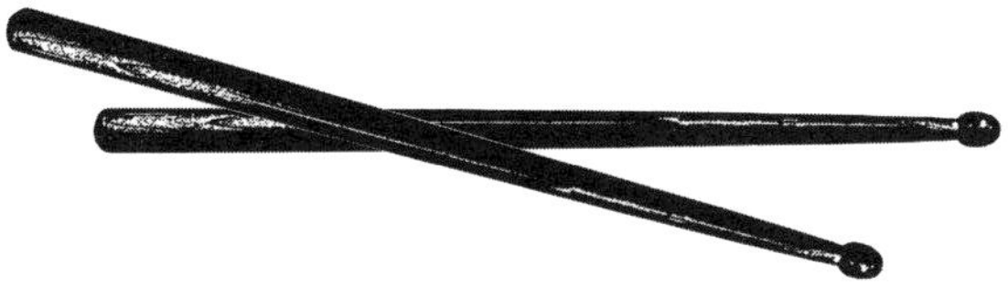

Today, we often think of drums and percussion as instruments used for the purposes of entertainment. Throughout history, however, one of the most important functions of the percussionist was military. Drummers performed many vital functions, and the rhythmic building blocks they created (known as *rudiments*) would eventually form a foundation that's still used by today's marching and concert bands.

In this chapter, we'll look more closely at the military/marching percussion section, focusing on the various instruments and their functions. We'll also pick up the sticks ourselves, explore the various ways to grip them, and get a taste of the rudiments.

Drums and the Military

Okay, here's a not so trick question: When it comes to taking up an instrument, why are many of us attracted to percussion? Answer: Because percussion instruments (particularly drums and cymbals) are LOUD and imposing. Many percussionists (myself included) get a huge amount of satisfaction from knowing that we make music by hitting stuff and creating lots of volume. (It's also pretty cool that we can drown out most other instruments if we like!)

But while making noise on drums and other percussion can be lots of fun, the loudness of these instruments is also the basis for one of the most important historical functions of a percussionist: to help run an army. Before the days of radios, loudspeakers and walkie-talkie's, drums were widely used to send messages to large groups of soldiers. By listening to specific rhythmic patterns (known as *cadences*) played by company drummers like the ones shown in Figure 3.1, a soldier knew when to get up in the morning, when to go to bed at night, when to eat, when to report for duty, and when to attack.

3.1 Civil War-era drummers

The steady pulse of cadences also assisted soldiers in marching from place to place in an orderly fashion. And on the battlefield, drums were the only instrument loud enough to rise above the din to pass along commands, help bolster a soldier's courage, and hopefully strike fear in the hearts of the enemy. In many cultures, drummers were so important to the conduct of war that it was considered highly dishonorable to knowingly strike or wound a drummer in battle.

DID YOU KNOW?

... that although we usually think of a marching drum as being worn and played by the same person, military cultures throughout history have transported the drums in many different ways? For example, ancient Chinese battle drummers stood on horse-drawn chariot-like devices. During the spread of Islam in the seventh and eighth centuries, drummers sat astride horses carrying pairs of kettledrums. And 16th century Japanese picture scrolls show a soldier carrying a drum on his back with two comrades on either side beating it.

The Dawn of the Marching Band

While many nations have used drums and other percussion for military purposes, the model for the kind of military marching bands we see today originated during the Turkish Ottoman Empire. In the late 13th century, the Turkish sultans organized groups of musicians—known as *mehters*—from their personal guard units. Often quite large, these mehter bands (Fig. 3.2) incorporated drums of several different sizes, hand held cymbals, trumpets and fife-like instruments. All of these instruments were loud and easy to transport so that they could march with the army into battle. The thunderous, crashing sound of the mehter was designed to fill the Ottoman soldiers with strength and courage, while at the same time unnerve the enemy.

3.2 A modern version of the traditional Turkish marching band, known as a mehter. The instrumentation used by the mehters was very similar to modern marching percussion. From left: nakers (small kettledrums), zils (hand held cymbals), kos (large kettledrums) and dawuls (bass drums).

Taking their lead from the Ottomans, European armies began adding marching bands in the 16th century. Military drummers in France and Switzerland were the first to develop the special sticking combinations we now call rudiments. And because Swiss soldiers were mercenaries who fought for many different countries, they helped make the rudiments standard in other countries, too (Fig. 3.3). This established the basic vocabulary that remains at the heart of what drummers study and practice to this day. We'll take a closer look at rudiments later in this chapter.

3.3 Traditional Scottish marching bands always include bagpipes.

John Philip Sousa and the American Military Band

The spread of European colonialism in the 1700 and 1800s brought the military band concept to many other parts of the world, including India, Asia, and South America. Marching bands were also introduced into Britain's North American colonies, which would soon become the United States. During the Revolutionary war and into the 1800s, the American military band structure was not very sophisticated, relying on fife and drum corps that were modeled on their European counterparts. With the perfection of valved brass instruments in the 1830s, however, the size, sound and style of military bands began to evolve. Trumpets, cornets, and tubas began taking on a much more dominant role, leading to a new offshoot known as the *brass band.* Brass bands began to assume a more cultural role outside of the military, playing dances, concerts and patriotic events.

3.4 John Philip Sousa and his band in 1893

These changes in the structure and function of the military band allowed the United States to start establishing its own brass band tradition by the late 1800s. This charge was led by John Philip Sousa (1854-1932), a composer and conductor whose patriotic marches have become as synonymous with the United States as baseball and apple pie. Even though Sousa (Fig 3.4) died nearly 80 years ago, we still hear his music everywhere, particularly in

DID YOU KNOW?

... that the large marching tuba known as a Sousaphone (Fig. 3.5) was designed in the 1890s by John Philip Sousa himself? His goal was to create an instrument that would project sound upward and over the band, whether its player was seated or marching.

3.5 The sousaphone.

military settings like parades and on the 4th of July. Just about every American military, marching and concert band plays Sousa marches like "The Washington Post" or "The Stars and Stripes Forever." And Sousa's "Semper Fidelis" is the official march of the United States Marine Corps.

Like a classical music composer, Sousa invested his marches with beautiful melodies and unusual harmonies, transforming them into something beyond mere parade music. In doing so, he elevated the status of the military band into that of a major concert attraction (performing over 15,000 concerts throughout his career). In an age before the invention of sound recordings or radio, Sousa's band was a sensation, and he became the face of American popular culture around the world. John Philip Sousa's 1893 composition "The Liberty Bell" was used by the British comedy troupe Monty Python as the theme music for their 1970s TV show.

The Influence of African American Military Bands

It's impossible to talk about the evolution of American popular music without discussing the major contributions made by African Americans. Starting in the 1600s, Africans were first brought to North America as slaves, and as such, they were largely stripped of their native instruments, dances and other customs. Despite having their cultural identity taken from them, African slaves and their descendents managed to bring their own ideas to the European-based music and dances that already existed in this country. By the early 20th century, African American influence would emerge as a driving force behind nearly every style of pop music to come out of the United States, including ragtime, jazz, swing, bebop, rhythm & blues, rock & roll, soul, funk, and hip-hop. We'll look more closely at many of these styles and their origins when we discuss the drum set in Chapters 5 and 6.

Before the U.S. Civil War, it was customary for Southern plantation owners to have their slaves provide musical accompaniment at social functions like dances. Why? Because the African-style treatment of European music was apparently very popular with the dancers.

Unlike the rest of the slave-holding South, the city of New Orleans, Louisiana, had a somewhat more permissive attitude toward African culture, and during much of the 1800s, an area called Congo Square (Fig. 3.6) was designated where slaves and their descendants could perform traditional African music and dances one day

3.6 Congo Square drummers and dancers

a week. This tradition of openness was one of several reasons that New Orleans would become the birthplace of jazz in the early 20th century.

In the free North, the army employed black drummers in both the Revolutionary War and the War of 1812. The early 19th century saw the formation of the first all-black brass bands, and by mid-century these bands were commonly seen at dances and other social functions in the Northeast. During the Civil War (1861-1865), a conflict fought to end slavery, African American bands marched for both sides, again applying their own distinctive take on the U.S. military band tradition (Fig. 3.7).

3.7 African American marching band, early 20th century

At the dawn of the 20th century, African American piano players were instrumental in creating an exciting new style of music called ragtime. Black bandleaders like James Reece Europe integrated the rhythms of ragtime into the military band setting. Working with the famous dancing team of Vernon and Irene Castle, Europe helped make dances like the cakewalk and the foxtrot hugely popular. This established the brass band as the setting for what would emerge in the 1920s as jazz.

DID YOU KNOW?

... that the Royal Hawaiian Band is the oldest and only full-time municipal band in the United States? Operated by the City & County of Honolulu, the Royal Hawaiian Band has been entertaining Hawaiian residents and visitors since its founding in 1836 by King Kamehameha III.

The popularity of bandleaders like John Philip Sousa and James Reece Europe allowed the brass band to carve out a new identity in American culture, one that was no longer part of the military, but still included many of the traditions, such as marching in formation and wearing military-style uniforms. The rise of the modern marching band coincided with the rise of American football, which had been gaining in popularity at universities since the late 1800s. Bands began to perform at games, using the grid of the football field to create formations and patterns, all of which led to the first halftime show in 1907.

Marching Bands Today

3.8 The Boston Crusaders drum corps in action

Today, the marching band has evolved into a highly sophisticated organization, one whose activities often go well beyond parades and football games. Some marching ensembles don't just play at sporting events—they compete against one another, performing repertoires that can range from classical music to Sousa marches to jazz, modern rock, pop and funk.

Marching ensembles rooted in military bands called *drum & bugle corps* put the percussion section on center stage on a football field.

Modern drum corps competitions (Fig. 3.8), governed by such organizations as Drum Corps International and Drum Corps Associates, showcase incredible technical skills, dizzyingly intricate formations, corpsmen marching in odd time signatures, and a stunning repertoire.

3.9 The show *Drum Line Live* captures the unique and funky style of African American marching bands.

The African American marching band tradition has continued to evolve as well, displaying a distinctive (and very funky!) style (Fig. 3.9), as well as a fiercely competitive scene among America's Historically Black College and Universities (HBCU's), such as Howard University. Winter Guard drumlines (Fig. 3.10) also compete in a range of divisions that include school and extra-curricular groups.

3.10 Winter Guard International's Vegas Vanguard

Today's marching percussion instruments have evolved as well, often made of space age materials and design elements that allow players to achieve ever more complex rudimental combinations.

Many of today's marching bands include what's called a "pit" (or "front ensemble"), an additional percussion section made up of non-marching members who play hand percussion, mallet instruments, timpani, and even drum set.

But bands continue to play a key role in the modern military setting as well. Military musicians carry on in the tradition of

DID YOU KNOW?

... that there's a special magazine just for participants and fans of Drum Corps International (DCI)? It's called—not surprisingly—DrumCorps International Magazine.

their predecessors by marching in parades and accompanying all manner of important ceremonies and events.

Overall, marching and concert bands have played a huge role in the lives of Americans over the last century. School band programs often serve as a young person's first exposure to music, and have introduced generations of kids to the benefits of playing an instrument. Beyond that, being part of a school band program teaches commitment, discipline, and teamwork. It's also a lot of fun and can offer kids a place to belong during the sometimes turbulent years of middle and high school.

Instruments Used in Marching Bands

Here are some of the percussion instruments you're likely to find in a marching ensemble today. Many of them are modern updates based on instruments that are centuries old.

SNARE DRUM/FIELD DRUM

The snare drum is one of the oldest types of drum, with roots going back to the Middle Ages (around the 14th century). Its design is based on a small drum called the tabor (Fig. 3.11), which was worn around the neck, and sometimes played at the same time as a fife. The strands (or snares) that stretch across the bottom head are what give the snare drum its name; they provide a rattle-like "snap" when struck. The snare strands help to focus the sound of the drum, and when the rim and the head are struck simultaneously (known as a "rim shot") they can increase the volume significantly. In military drumming, the snare drum is sometimes also referred to as a *field drum*.

3.11 The tabor, ancestor of the modern snare drum

Within a military percussion unit, the snare drum is usually considered the lead instrument. The crisp, punchy attack provided by the snares helps it stand out and makes it well suited to playing complex cadences and solos.

Before the existence of radio and electronic communications, the snare drum was the primary means of communicating orders to soldiers. American troops were awakened each morning by an alarm clock of fife and drum playing the well-known cadence "Three Camps." Troops were also called for meals by certain drum pieces such as "Peas on a Trencher" or "Roast Beef." A cadence called "The Tattoo" was used to signal that all soldiers should be in their tents.

LISTEN! TRACK 7

"Ancient" rudimental drumming expert Mark Beecher performs a traditional military cadence known as "Army 2/4."

The first snare drums were designed in the same way that drums had been for thousands of years: A head made of animal skin was stretched onto a wooden shell and held taut so the drumsticks could rebound off it easily. The original snare wires, like other stretchy musical accessories such as guitar and violin strings, were made from animal gut. As technology

3.12 Anatomy of a snare drum

advanced, however, drummers found that snares fashioned from metal cables were more durable and gave a crisper and more consistent sound. Today's snare wires are usually coiled, which allows them to lie more evenly against the bottom head.

In the 1800s, new technology gave drummers the ability to add more tension to the drumhead, allowing them to play faster and more complex rhythms. Metal tension rods were used to hold the head in place, and the snare itself was attached to a metal *strainer*, which meant a drummer could adjust the sound of the snare from a loose rattle to a tight snap. Modern snare strainers usually include what's called a *throw-off*, which allows the drummer to release the snares away from the bottom head completely, giving the drum a tom-tom type sound.

Figure 3.12 shows the various parts of the snare drum, including the rims, lugs, tension

3.13 Different types of snare drums. Top row (L to R): rope-tensioned military snare drum, 1920s Ludwig Black Beauty, modern marching snare. Center (L to R): orchestral concert snare, piccolo snare, popcorn snare. Bottom (L to R): acrylic snare, snare shell made from a wood and metal combination, vented snare.

rods, and snare strainer mechanism (a.k.a. the throw off). Many of these parts, along with a tool called a *drum key*, are involved when changing and tuning a drumhead. For more on tuning, see Chapter 6.

Snare drums can be made from a variety of materials. The most common of these are wood, metal, and various acrylics. Snare drums typically measure 14 inches across, but their depth may vary depending on the use. Marching snare drums can be a foot in depth or more, while snare drums used for orchestral and drum set playing are typically about 5-6 inches deep.

Piccolo snare drums are much shallower, measuring about 3-4 inches in depth. Snare drums with abnormally small diameters are often called "soprano," "popcorn," and "firecracker" drums. They have diameters as small as 8 inches, and are often used for higher-pitched special effects, or they may be added to a drum set as a second snare. Other specialty snare drum shells may be built from combinations of materials (wood and metal, for example), or they may be "vented," meaning they have extra holes cut into them. Figure 3.13 shows a variety of snare drums.

DID YOU KNOW?

. . . that many cultures alter their drums to give them the raspy quality of a snare? "Rattle drums," which are played in India and Tibet, get their rattle from pellets placed inside the drum. And the first tom-toms to be used on drum sets were actually Chinese ethnic drums that included a built in rattling device.

BASS DRUM

The bass drum is the largest in the drum family, and therefore has the deepest and boomiest tone. Because of its large size, bass drum patterns are typically very simple and straightforward. In a military setting, the bass drum is used to mark or keep time. This means the bass drum literally sets the pace that soldiers follow as they march. Bass drums are typically played with soft mallets, giving them a dull "thud" that fills up the lower end of the sonic spectrum. Modern marching bands usually include bass drums of several different sizes, each of which has a distinct pitch. This allows the bass drum section as a whole to play fairly intricate patterns between the drums.

TENOR DRUM

In addition to the snare drum, a traditional military or marching band may also incorporate tenor drums. These are about the same size as a snare drum, but do not have snare wires underneath, giving them the tonal quality of a tom-tom. The role of the tenor drum is to fill up the middle pitch range between snare drums and basses. Like the bass drummer, the tenor player is typically a timekeeper, and therefore has much simpler parts than the snare. Tenor players also typically use mallets instead of sticks. These are typically hung from the wrists with cords, enabling the player to twirl or *flourish* the mallets between strokes. For a tenor drummer, the flourishing routines can be just as integral to the performance as the notes themselves.

MULTI-TENOR DRUMS

In more contemporary-style marching bands, the single tenor drum has largely been replaced by *multi-tenor drums* (or "tenors" for short). These are essentially a collection of tom-toms of various sizes and pitches, mounted on a rack and carried by one person. Multi-tom rigs typically include anywhere from three to six drums, and each is known by its own nickname ("tri-toms," "quads," "quints," etc.).

3.14 Jersey Surf's marching percussion section: snare, bass drums, multi-tenors and cymbals

The drums themselves are very different from traditional marching tenors; they are much shallower, with only a single head, and a much higher pitch. The different sized drums in a tenor rig allow for intricate melodic combinations, and the smaller sizes and highly tensioned heads allow multi-tenor players to create lightning fast combinations between drums. Multi-tenor parts are often as rudimentally complex as those played by the snares. Figure 3.14 shows a a range of marching drums in action.

CYMBALS

Cymbals have existed since man began working with metals. The word cymbal is derived from the Latin word cymbalum, which means "cup." Many early cymbals did actually resemble a cup or bowl (Fig. 3.15). Over time, however, the instrument began to flatten out to its current shape. Today, the *cup* (or *bell*) only refers to the raised section in the center of the instrument. When struck, the bell produces a higher "pinging" pitch than the rest of the cymbal.

3.15 Early Greek cymbal, c. 500 B.C.

In early military settings, the purpose of cymbals was straightforward: to strike fear in the heart of the enemy by creating a tremendous clash that could be heard across the battlefield. In a modern marching band, the cymbals function in a similar way, but their explosive sound is more integrated into the music as a whole.

As in classical music, marching cymbals are played in pairs and held by a leather wrist strap that is strung through a hole in the middle of the cup. The cymbals can be struck together in any number of ways to create a variety of sonic effects. For example, they can be openly crashed to produce a loud, ringing tone, or they can be *choked* together to produce a more rhythmic "chick" sound. Cymbals are often used to punctuate or accent certain rhythms within a cadence. In many cases, they provide an extra punch to the basic beats played by the bass drum.

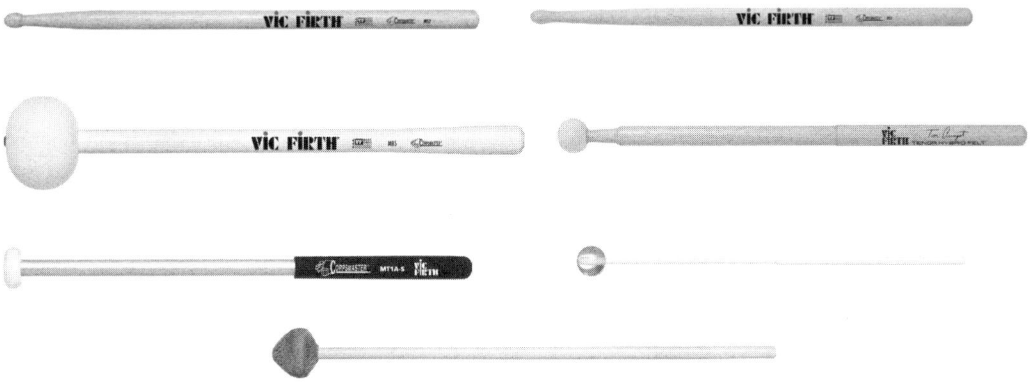

3.16 Tools of the Trade From L to R: Snare sticks, bass drum beater, tenor mallets, keyboard mallets

Playing the Snare Drum

When we set out to play the drums, many of the elements that we learn—from holding the sticks to striking the drum to creating rudimental patterns—can be traced back to a military tradition. Now that we've looked at some of the history around this subject, let's pick up the sticks and start bringing that tradition to life! Figure 3.16 shows an array of sticks, beaters and mallets used by today's marching/military percussionists.

THE GRIPS

When you pick up the sticks for the first time, you might think that it's okay to hold them any way that feels natural, as long as you're able to make music. This is not entirely the case. While we certainly want our drumming to feel easy and natural, there is a very particular way that the sticks must be held in order to achieve that effect. We refer to this method of holding the sticks as a *grip*.

3.17 The author at work. Maintaining a relaxed but consistent "grip" allows a drummer to get the maximum out of the sticks while doing a minimum of work. One way to tell if a drummer has this ability is to look at a photo of him or her in action. If the drummer's hands appear still, but sticks are a blur of motion, then chances are that he or she has what we call "good hands."

The word "grip" seems to imply that we're supposed to clutch the sticks tightly. But in truth, the opposite is the case. If our rhythms are to feel steady and relaxed, then our hands, arms and bodies have to be relaxed. So, while it's certainly necessary to hold on to the sticks, the real trick is to do it in a way that allows physical forces like rebound and gravity to do most of the job for us. Figure 3.17 shows me demonstrating a proper grip.

When playing the snare drum (and the drum set as well) most drummers hold sticks in one of two ways: the *traditional grip* and the *matched grip*. Prior to the 1960s, almost all drummers played the traditional grip, which traces its roots back hundreds of years to European military bands. The rise of rock & roll, however, brought with it amplified instruments and vocals. As a result, many drummers switched to the matched grip in an effort to get more volume (not to mention a bigger motion) from behind the set. So, although the matched grip is the newer of the two grips we are discussing, it is by far more popular.

Deciding which grip to use is totally up to you. Drummers use both traditional and matched grip in every musical situation, and unless you are in a marching band that requires you to play one way or the other, there is no right or wrong approach. The only requirement is that the music sounds and feels good.

We'll take a look at each grip in more detail in the next section.

DID YOU KNOW?

... that in 1964, when drummer Ringo Starr appeared with his band the Beatles on the Ed Sullivan TV show, the band made such an impact that an entire generation of drummers changed their grip from traditional to matched practically overnight?

THE MATCHED GRIP

The matched grip (Fig. 3.18) gets its name because both sticks are held the same way, making them a "matched" pair. As I've mentioned, the goal with any grip is to hold the stick in a way that is very natural, so that your hand and wrist are relaxed as if simply hanging at your side.

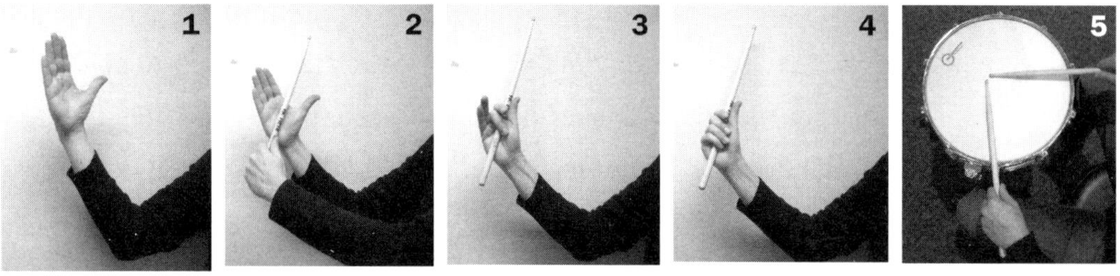

3.18 You can set up the matched grip by following these steps:

1. Starting with your arm hanging at your side, lift your forearm straight up so that you are looking at your palm.
2. Place the stick into your palm at a 45-degree angle, so that the butt end comes out the fleshy part of the palm.
3. Now, lightly grip the stick between the thumb and first finger, and use the middle finger to hold it against the palm. Keep your focus on these three fingers, as they constitute the main part of this grip. Note: Don't "wrap" the index finger around the stick; keep it straight and relaxed. Stretch the thumb flat and use it to press the stick into the index finger.
4. Lastly, bring the back two fingers onto the stick, lightly securing it in the fleshy part of the palm.
5. Once the stick is "housed" in this grip, turn your arm over so you are looking at the top of your hand and your elbow is slightly away from your side. When both sticks are held in this manner they will cross each other at a 90-degree angle.

PLAYING A GRACE NOTE AND GETTING A REBOUND

Now that you're holding the sticks properly, let's start putting them to work on a drum or practice pad. Whether you're sitting or standing, the drum should be about the height of your belt line. Since we're just getting started, keep the drum or pad completely level.

We'll start by creating a grace note, one of the key building blocks of the rudiments. A grace note is quieter than a regular stroke—it's really more of a tap—and therefore it is played a little bit differently.

Without altering your grip in any way, lift your right wrist and then let it fall, allowing the stick to strike the head. The downward part of this motion should be a release, simply controlled by gravity. Think of it as a tree falling in the forest. Once the stick has struck the head, let it bounce back slightly and then, in essence, "catch" it by squeezing lightly with your front three-fingers (the focal point of your grip). The idea of the stick naturally bouncing off the head is called a *rebound*, and it's one of the keys to successfully developing good hand technique.

Using just one hand at a time, let's put the "lift and drop" motion we just explored into a musical context. If you have a click track or metronome, set it to play 1/8 notes at a tempo of around sixty beats per minute (BPM). This means you will be counting in 1/8 notes ("1-and-2-and-3-and-4-and"). As you count, drop the wrist on beats 1, 2, 3 and 4, and lift on the "ands," as shown in Figure 3.19. Now, try playing grace notes with alternating hands, maintaining the "lift and drop" motion as you go from side to side (Figure 3.20). Finally, play the exercise (Figure 3.21) in such a way where you lift one hand while dropping the other. Remember, the "work" you do should be in the upward direction. Your drops should remain nice and relaxed. Resist the urge to drive the stick downward.

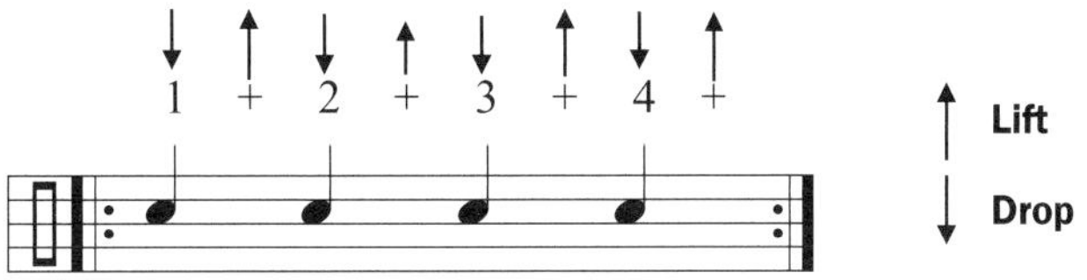

3.19 Play on the downbeats, lift on the "ands."

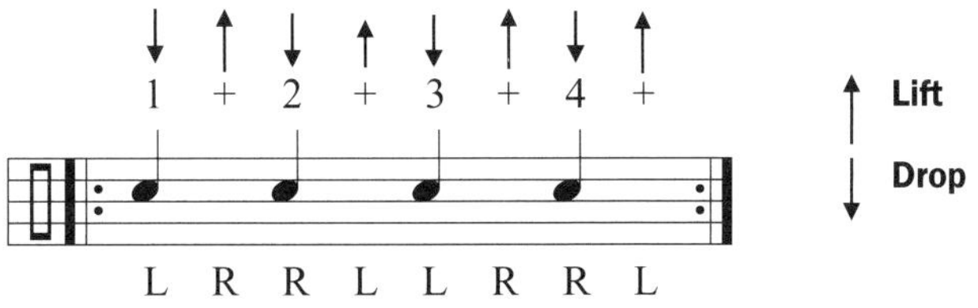

3.20 Alternate hands while playing downbeats.

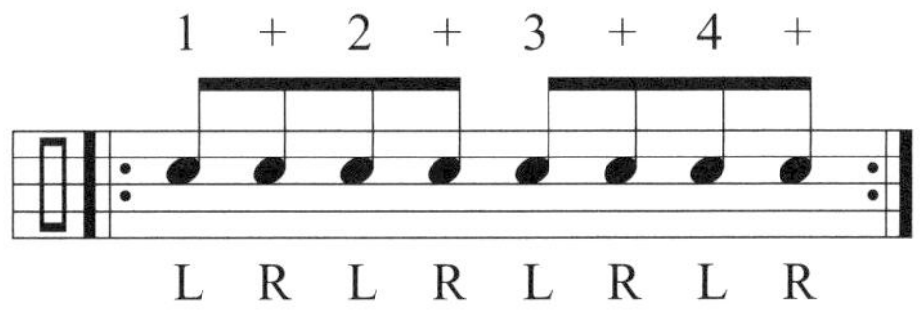

3.21 Alternate hands to play 1/8 notes.

CREATING A STROKE

As we just explored, a grace note is really just a tap that's achieved by lifting and dropping the stick. Now let's add a little more downward force and create a proper stroke.

The motion of playing a stroke in the matched grip is very similar to knocking on a door. When we knock, we don't bury our hand into the surface of the door. We strike the door and immediately bounce off the surface to bring our hand back. Each knock is a complete motion that begins and ends in the same neutral starting position.

The same is true with a drumstick. Although we're now applying more downward force, the goal is not to drive the stick into the head, but to use the energy generated by that force to allow the stick to come back to us, thereby setting up the next stroke. Many drummers refer to this technique as "pulling the sound out" of the drum.

Now that we've developed our lift/drop techniques, let's put it to work in a rhythmic context. The exercises in figures 3.22–3.24 are made up of various combinations of 1/4, 1/8 and 1/16 notes (refer back to Chapter 2 if you need a refresher on what these are all about). As you play each exercise, remember to count aloud, and always alternate your hands as indicated by the L (left) and R (right) markers.

LISTEN!
TRACK 8

3.22

LISTEN! TRACK 9

3.23

LISTEN! TRACK 10

3.24

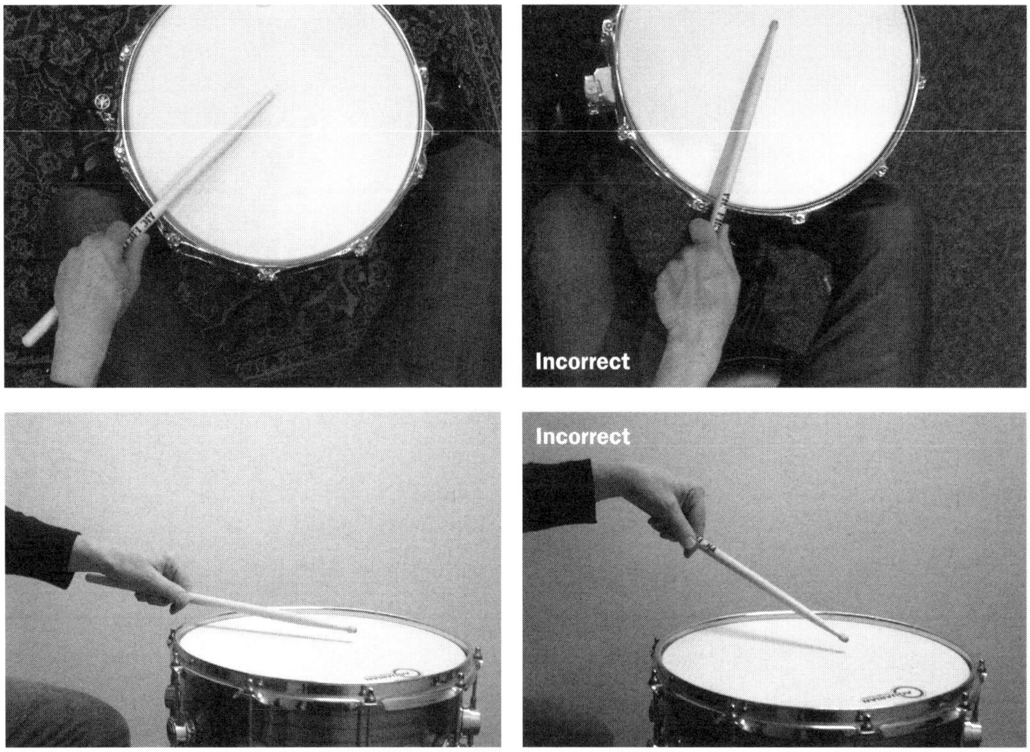

3.25 Top and side view of the correct (left) and incorrect (right) neutral position

Some Do's and Don'ts

When playing these exercises, make sure that your hand returns to the "neutral position" at the end of each stroke. As I mentioned earlier, "neutral" means your wrist should be straight and flat, as it would be if it were hanging at your side. Don't twist the wrist in an outward or downward direction, or try to make the stick point straight ahead. Every time you force your wrist into an unnatural position, you are adding tension. And I can't stress this enough: Tension is every musician's worst enemy! Figure 3.25 shows both correct and incorrect positioning.

3.26 A Revolutionary War-era drummer shows the traditional grip.

TRADITIONAL GRIP

The traditional grip was created by European military snare drummers, primarily out of necessity because of the way they wore their instrument (Fig. 3.26). Typically, the snare drum was slung over the right shoulder by a strap, and hung at a slant in front of the drummer. With the drum positioned this way, it would be very awkward to play using the matched grip, so drummers devised an alternate grip that would allow them to walk and play simultaneously.

Today, marching snare drums are carried on sophisticated harnesses, allowing them to be played flat. Still, the majority of marching bands and drum corps choose to utilize the traditional grip.

Setting Up a Traditional Grip

Figure 3.27 shows the steps needed to create a traditional grip.

3.27 Steps for setting up the traditional grip

1. Hold your left forearm out with the palm open and the thumb up, as if you are going to shake someone's hand.
2. Place the stick in the crook between the thumb and first finger and hold it in the place. This area is where the stick is actually gripped in the traditional grip.
3. Now fold your ring finger and pinkie underneath the stick, creating a bridge on which the stick can rest. Keep these fingers lightly pressed against the hand at all times.
4. Finally, lay the first and middle fingers over the top of the stick, so that the first finger touches the base of the thumb, creating a loop.
5. When both hands are set in the traditional grip, the elbows are held slightly outward and—as with the matched grip—the two sticks should cross each other at a 90-degree angle.

TAPS AND STROKES IN TRADITIONAL GRIP

When playing taps and strokes in the traditional grip, the "lift and drop" concept we addressed previously is the same. The motion, however, is different. Rather than "knocking on a door," as we did with the matched grip, the traditional grip uses a rotational motion similar to that of turning a doorknob. The "lift" part of your motion turns the knob in a counter-clockwise motion, while the "drop" portion goes the other way.

Using the traditional grip, play Figures 3.22, 3.23 and 3.24 once again; play them as taps first, then as strokes. Remember to focus on the lifts, and let the drops happen naturally.

LISTEN! TRACK 11

Rudimental drumming expert and educator Danny Raymond performs a "corps-style" snare drum solo, demonstrating the power of the rudiments to create some absolutely breathtaking music.

DID YOU KNOW?

. . . that jazz drummers generally prefer traditional over matched grip? There are a couple of reasons why this might be the case. First, traditional grip puts the hand under the stick, allowing it to bounce and rebound more freely. I've also heard it said that traditional grip uses twice the number of muscles as matched grip; perhaps this allows for greater control when playing the often-complex figures found in jazz.

Using the Rudiments

As I mentioned earlier in this chapter, rudiments are the building blocks of a drummer's vocabulary. They consist of a series of sticking patterns that began as military drum calls in France and Switzerland and evolved over several hundred years. Today, rudiments are used by all types of drummers to develop technical proficiency, strength, speed and endurance.

Most rudiments are made up of combinations of single strokes, double strokes and grace notes. Some rudiments have funny sounding names—"paradiddle" and "flam" are two examples. These names are alliterative, meaning they come from the sound made when the rudiment is played. For example, "pa-ra-did-dle," sounds like the four-stroke combination upon which it is based ("left-right-left-left, right-left-right-right"). And a "flam" is what happens when you play a grace note and a louder note in quick succession (the word "plum" also tells you how this rudiment should sound).

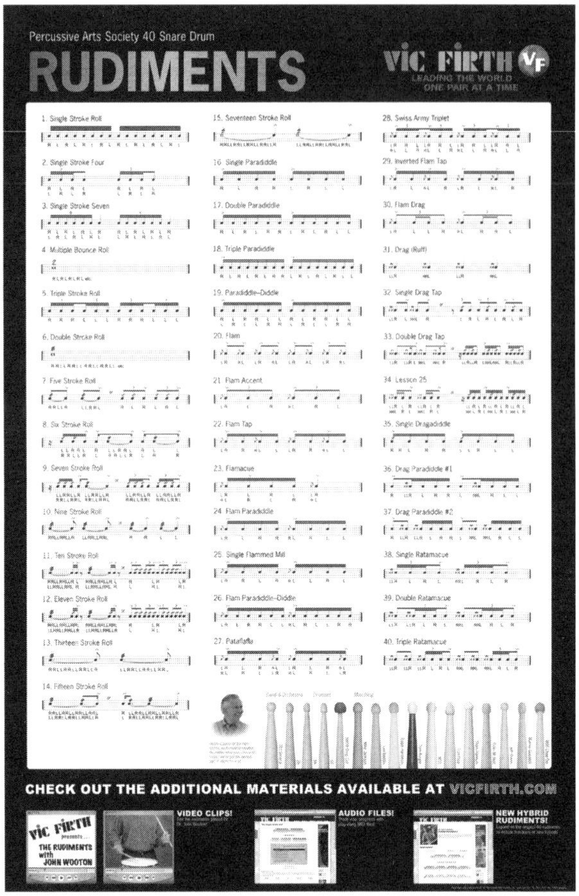

3.28 40 snare drum rudiments. Download and print this poster from the disc.

Swiss and other early European military snare drummers created a basic vocabulary of about 13 rudiments. By the 20th century, that number had grown to 26. Today, with the ever-expanding creativity and competitiveness of the marching band scene, the Percussive Arts Society has officially sanctioned a total of 40 rudiments (Fig. 3.28). In reality, however, there are many more, as modern drum lines continue to come up with their own unique hybrids and variations. You can see and print this rudiments poster in the CD-R that accompanies this book.

A List of Key Rudiments

Let's take a look at some of the most basic rudiments that you are guaranteed to run across when you pick up a pair of sticks. These rudiments are broken into four basic categories: rolls, diddles, flams and drags.

Each rudiment is written over several measures, showing what it looks like at various speeds. As you review these exercises, make sure to listen along to the accompanying track on the CD. You'll notice that even though the speed of the rudiment increases, the entire exercise stays within the context of the time signature (as expressed by the 4/4 pulse of the bass drum). When playing these exercises yourself, be sure to create a similar pulse by setting a metronome to approximately the same tempo.

We'll combine the rudiments into some actual musical pieces in the following chapters. Remember, however, this book is only designed to give you a very basic introduction to the world of drumming and percussion. As such, we can only scratch the surface when it comes to the very broad topic of the rudiments. If you are interested in learning more about rudimental snare drumming, please seek out a good teacher.

ROLL RUDIMENTS

So far, we've looked at how we can play various rhythms (1/4 notes, 1/8 notes, etc.) as a series of strokes. Longer sequences of single or double strokes are often referred to as *rolls*. A roll is generally written as two slashes across the stem of a note. The length of the roll is based on the value of that note. The symbol in Figure 3.29 tells us that the drummer should play a roll that lasts a 1/4 note.

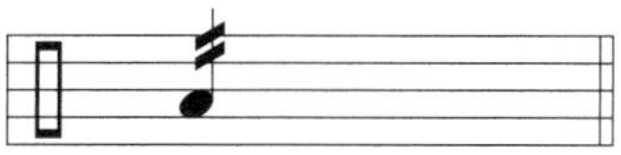

3.29 A 1/4 note roll

Single Stroke Roll

The single stroke roll is the most basic, "nuts and bolts" rudiment of them all (Figure 3.30). Being able to play alternating single strokes smoothly, evenly and at a variety of speeds is one of the keys to being a good drummer.

3.30 The single stroke roll

LISTEN! TRACK 12

Double Stroke Roll

Double strokes (two rights or two lefts in a row) are at the heart of many rudiments, such as the frequently used five, seven and nine-stroke rolls. Playing the exercise shown in Figure 3.31 will help you develop control over your double strokes.

3.31 The paradiddle

LISTEN! TRACK 13

Open and Closed Rolls

Rolls can be played in an "open" fashion, meaning each stroke is clearly articulated, or they can be "closed," meaning the strokes are lightly pressed or crushed into the head, creating a buzzing-type sound. Whether a drummer plays a roll open or closed depends may be mandated by the music, or that choice may be left to the drummer's discretion (Fig. 3.32).

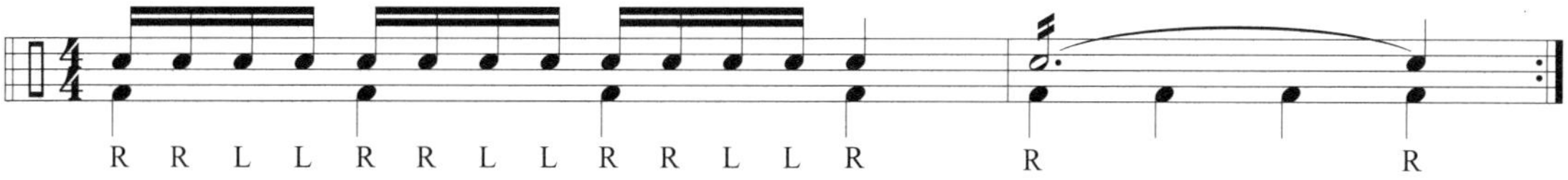

3.32 These roles can be played in both open or closed fashion.

LISTEN! TRACK 14

Five, Seven, and Nine Stroke Rolls

The three rolls shown in Figures 3.33–3.35 (composed of five, seven and nine strokes) are the ones most commonly used by marching drummers. The number of strokes is not only a factor in determining the length of the roll, but also gives the drummer options when it comes to applying the roll to a piece of music. For example, if the music is heavy in 1/8 or 1/16 note runs, five- and nine-stroke rolls may lock in better. On the other hand, if the music is based in triplets, the best choice may be a seven-stroke roll.

LISTEN!
TRACK 15

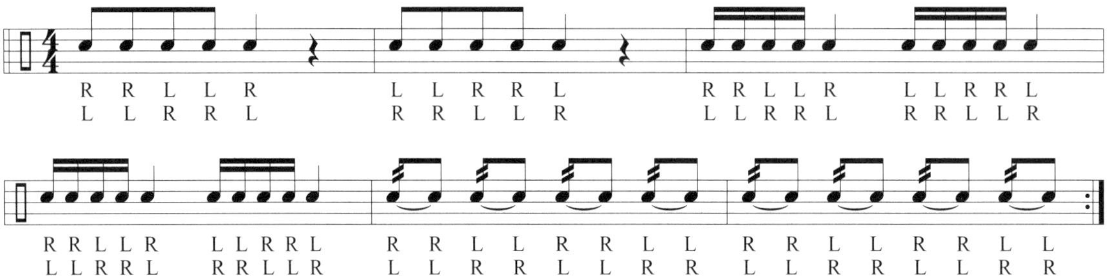

3.33 Five-stroke roll

LISTEN!
TRACK 16

3.34 Seven-stroke roll

LISTEN!
TRACK 17

3.35 Nine-stroke roll

Notice both the five- and nine-stroke rolls begin and end on the same hand, while the seven-stroke roll ends on the opposite hand from which it began.

DIDDLE RUDIMENTS

As I mentioned earlier, the name paradiddle is an alliterative term that actually sounds out the strokes that comprise this rudiment (LRLL, RLRR). "Diddle" is merely another word for double. This particular combination of strokes is an extremely flexible tool that is widely used by drum set players as well as snare drummers.

Single Paradiddle

This is played with two single strokes followed by a double stroke (Fig. 3.36).

LISTEN! TRACK 18

3.36 Single paradiddle

Double Paradiddle

This six-stroke variation attaches two single strokes to the front of a paradiddle (Fig. 3.37).

LISTEN! TRACK 19

3.37 Double paradiddle

Paradiddlediddle

Figure 3.38 shows another six-stroke variation that attaches a second diddle to end of a paradiddle.

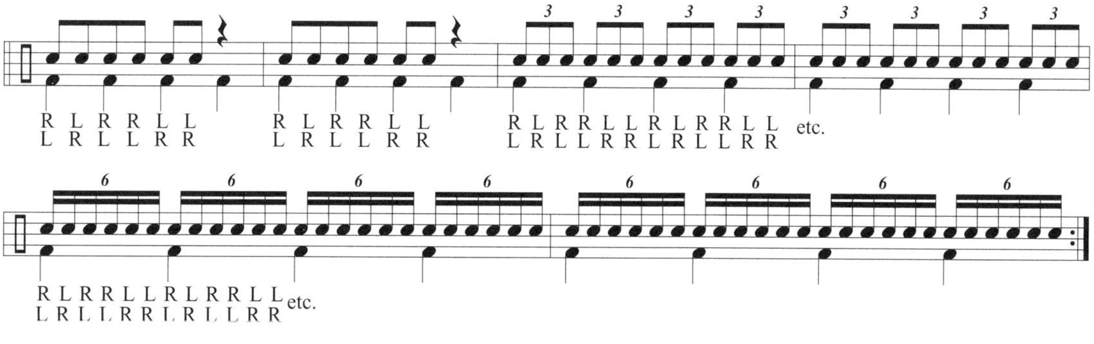

LISTEN! TRACK 20

3.38 Paradiddlediddle

FLAM RUDIMENTS

A flam is a two-stroke rudiment that features a standard stroke preceded by a grace note. When played correctly, a flam should come out sounding like the word "plum."

Flam

A good-sounding flam (Fig. 3.39) is based on a difference in stick height. Lift the stick playing the stroke higher than the stick playing the grace note, and if you let them both drop at the same time, your flam will have the right sound.

LISTEN! TRACK21

3.39 Flam

Flam Tap

Figure 3.40 shows a flam combined with a tap.

LISTEN! TRACK 22

3.40 Flam tap

Flam Accent

You can combine flams with other rudiments to create variations. For example, a flam accent (Fig. 3.41) is simply a grouping of triplets where the first stroke is a flam.

LISTEN! TRACK 23

3.41 Flam accent

Flam Paradiddle

Figure 3.42 shows the rudiment that combines a flam with a paradiddle.

3.42 Flam paradiddle

DRAG RUDIMENTS

A *drag* places two grace notes in front of a single stroke. The name likely comes from the dragging motion used to play the two grace notes in quick succession. As with the flam, a drag may be combined with other rudiments to make new combinations like a drag tap and a drag accent.

Drag

Figure 3.43 shows a drag. To achieve the best sounding drag, follow the same stick height instructions as used in the flam.

3.43 Drag

Ratamacue

The Ratamacue is another rudiment where the name sounds like what's being played. It's shown in Figure 3.44.

3.44 Ratamacue

Moving On

Though they were developed for marching music, the rudiments we just explored, as well as others, are the foundation for almost every type of stick drumming. Many players come back to them again and again as part of their warm-up and practice regimens.

4

4

ORCHESTRAL PERCUSSION

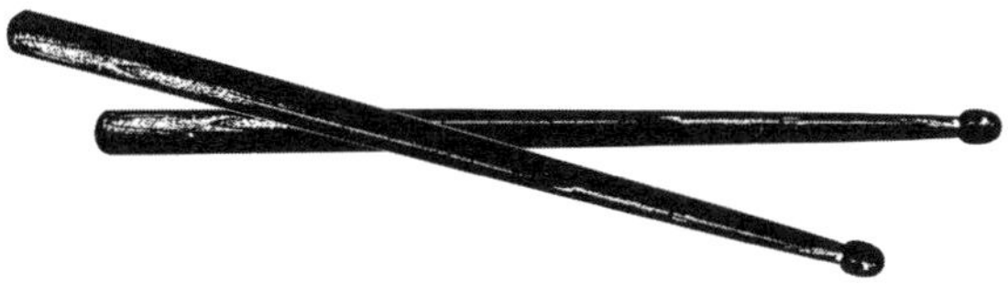

In Chapter 3, we learned that percussion played a key role in the evolution of military music and the marching band. The loud, steady pulse of drums and cymbals helped to transmit orders, keep soldiers marching in unison, and inspire courage on the battlefield.

Western classical music—the focus of this chapter—utilizes percussion in an entirely different way. Unlike military music, classical music is lighter and more delicate in character. As such, an orchestral percussionist's job is not necessarily to create heavy and imposing beats, but to support the other sections of the orchestra (strings, woodwinds and brass) with color and shading.

What Exactly Is Classical Music?

Before we specifically address classical percussion, let's clarify exactly what we mean by the term *classical music*. Typically, it refers to a golden age of European music that lasted from approximately 1550 to 1900. During these years, important orchestral instruments like the piano and violin were invented, and key musical elements like harmony, song structure and technical execution evolved into the form we know today. Music notation was also standardized during this period, allowing the works of important composers to be written down and reproduced so musicians everywhere could play them.

Music scholars usually divide this golden era of classical music into a series of key "periods," each of which is represented by the most important composers who wrote during that time. For example, Johann Sebastian Bach is considered one of the principal composers of the *Baroque* era (1600-1760), Wolfgang Amadeus Mozart emblemized the *Classical* period (1750-1830), and Frederic Chopin is considered one of the great masters of *Romantic* music (1815-1910). Orchestral music composed after 1900 is usually referred to as "modern classical" or "20th century classical" music.

The Role of Percussion in an Orchestra

At the outset of the classical music age, the job of a typical composer was to provide soft chamber music, processionals for church, and songs that would accompany dancing. Percussion, if included at all, provided sparse accompaniment, and parts were written for instruments that were quieter by nature. These instruments included the *tabor* (a predecessor to the snare drum), the *timbrel* (an early version of the tambourine), *nakers* (a small set of metal drums that would evolve into timpani) and the triangle.

4.1 A modern symphony orchestra. Note the large percussion section across the back. Many of the instruments pictured here will be discussed in this chapter.

As orchestras expanded, both in size and in musical direction, ideas about percussion began to change. In the 17th century, timpani became the first "modern" percussion instrument to be included as a standard part of an orchestra. In the 18th century, Turkish music came into vogue, and European composers began to incorporate percussive elements from Turkish military bands—known as *mehters*—into their work (to understand how the *mehter* also influenced marching bands, see Chapter 3).

Over time, snare drum, bass drum, handheld crash cymbals, mallet instruments, and various hand percussion would all be added to make up what we consider to be a modern orchestral percussion section (Fig. 4.1). It was not until the 20th century, however, that composers would begin to truly explore the full potential of percussion, and begin to write for it as a featured instrument.

Over the course of this chapter, we'll take a closer look at each of the main groups of instruments in an orchestral percussion section. We'll focus on the unique design and sound features of each, and discuss how they contribute to the overall sound of the orchestra.

Timpani

Timpani (Fig. 4.2) are large metal drums, usually made of copper and traditionally played in sets of at least two instruments. They are often referred to as "kettle drums," because their bowl shape and metal construction give them the appearance of a big cooking pot.

4.2 A set of four timpani. A pedal at the base of each drum is used for tuning.

Unlike a snare or bass drum, which have no distinct pitch, the bowl-like design of the timpani shells allows them to be tuned to various pitches, often with the use of a pedal that controls the drum's range of notes. Orchestral timpani players typically use a set of four drums of various sizes, allowing them to cover a wide range of notes from low to high. The ability to quickly retune the drums during the course of a performance allows the timpanist to adapt to key changes without changing drums. It is this feature that makes the timpani such a unique percussion instrument, and such a favorite of orchestral composers.

Timpani evolved from war drums that can be traced back to Middle Eastern regions like Egypt and Arabia. Because of their great weight, they were often carried in pairs on horseback. *Nakers*, a Turkish predecessor of the timpani (Fig. 4.3), first came to the attention of Europeans during the Crusades of the 13th century. Throughout the Middle Ages, nakers became something of a status symbol for European royalty; kettledrummers

4.3 Timpani evolved out of Turkish military drums, like the large *kos* (foreground) and the handheld *nakers* (background).

DID YOU KNOW?

. . . that Georg Roth, a German timpani virtuoso, gave a concert in 1798 at which he performed on sixteen timpani with three sticks in each hand?

held a special place in the royal court, and even had their own guild. Secrets of the craft were handed down from master to apprentice, and closely guarded. Although timpinists originally used drumsticks, they eventually switched to soft mallets, which allowed for a warmer, fuller sound.

The first known use of timpani in a classical work was 1675, as part of the opera *Thesee* by Jean-Baptiste Lully. Ten years later, Francois-Andre Philidor composed the first timpani duet, *March for Two Pairs of Kettledrums*. Many popular works featuring timpani have been written since. Two of the most popular include Beethoven's *9th Symphony* (1824), and the opening to *Also Sprach Zarathustra* (1896) by Richard Strauss (better known as the theme to the film *2001: A Space Odyssey*).

Today, timpani can be found in many different types of musical ensembles, including concert bands, marching bands, and even some rock bands—Led Zeppelin drummer John Bonham was famous for his thunderous timpani solos. Modern timpanists have also been known to use their instrument to create a variety of special sound effects, particularly for film scores or more experimental music. Two examples are laying an upside down cymbal on the drum while striking it and running a rubber mallet over the surface of the head.

Other Orchestral Percussion Instruments

Other than timpani, the principal instruments in an orchestral percussion section are snare drum, bass drum, cymbals, and gongs. Like the timpani, these can all trace at least part of their origin to the Turkish *mehter*. Orchestral composers began to include these instruments in their operas and other symphonic works in the late 17th century.

SNARE DRUM

In the last chapter, we talked about the history and construction of the snare drum (Fig. 4.4). This instrument became popular with classical composers with the in-

4.4 The modern orchestral snare drum is an extremely sensitive instrument.

troduction of screw tensioning in 1837. The use of metal tension rods allowed the snare drum to be tuned in a more sensitive manner than had been permitted by the more traditional system of using rope to tune the drumheads. By the mid 1800s, snare drums were being built from brass and other metals in addition to wood, and a shallower version of the instrument was being designed specifically for orchestral players. This smaller size offered a higher-pitched, crisper sound, and gave orchestral snare drummers the ability to to play their rudiments with a wider range of dynamics and tones.

DID YOU KNOW?

... that Ravel's *Bolero* is one of the most well known and demanding pieces that a snare drummer can play in an orchestral setting? *Bolero* begins with a lone snare drummer, who must repeat the same two measures for about 15 minutes, starting at an almost inaudible level, and building to a roar that drives the entire orchestra.

Today, snare drum probably requires the most demanding technique of all the percussion instruments. It can take years to master. The challenge for orchestral percussionists comes not only from playing difficult rudimental parts, but doing so very consistently, and often at a soft dynamic level.

As a solo instrument, the snare drum has also found its place in classical music, particularly in pieces that may have a military theme or sound to them. A great example can be heard in the opening of Sergei Prokofiev's *Lieutenant Kijé* suite.

BASS DRUM

Measuring roughly 40 inches in diameter and 20 inches in width, the orchestral bass drum (Fig. 4.5) is the largest drum of the orchestra. It also has the deepest tone. The

4.5 A collection of orchestral bass drums. These instruments are hung within a frame, which allows them to be tilted at any angle.

predecessor to the bass drum was the Turkish *davul*, a two-headed cylindrical drum that also produced a deep tone. Because of this unique sound, davuls were used extensively in combat as well as in Turkish folk dancing.

In marching and rock music, it's customary to hit the bass drum with a lot of force. But in an orchestra, the instrument is usually played very sensitively. The idea is that the bass drum should be "felt" rather than heard.

HANDHELD CRASH CYMBALS (PIATTI)

In the previous chapter, we learned that handheld crash cymbals played an important role in many cultures as military instruments. In an orchestral setting, these cymbals, shown in Figure 4.6, are known as *piatti,* which is Italian for "dishes" or "plates."

When crashed together at full volume (known as a *clash*), a set of piatti can easily be heard over an orchestra playing at full volume. The loud and explosive nature of

4.6 As in a marching band, *piatti* are played in pairs, and each cymbal is held by a strap threaded through the bell.

piatti initially attracted composers to them because they suggested fury, chaos or a party atmosphere. A skilled cymbal player, however, can also use piatti to obtain an endless variety of dynamic subtlety, color and effect. In addition to a clash sound, it's possible to rub the edges of the cymbals together in a sliding movement (called a *sizzle*), scrape the edge of one along the inside of the other (called a *scrape*), or choke them together (called a *crush*). A cymbal player can also dampen a crash by pressing the cymbals against his or her body.

As with military music, classical music often calls for the crash cymbals and bass drum to be played at the same time. This combination works exceptionally well because it covers both the low and high frequency ranges, making for a very satisfying "thud." (The same idea works in drum set playing, by the way.)

SUSPENDED CYMBALS

Another type of cymbal used in the modern orchestra is the *suspended cymbal,* which is typically placed on a stand so it can be played with sticks or mallets. Suspended cymbals can produce bright and slicing tones when forcefully struck. Or a player can use two mallets to produce a *tremolo* (or *roll*), a wooshy swell that's great for enhancing crescendos (and often reminds listeners of an ocean wave crashing).

Other methods of playing the suspended cymbal include scraping a coin or a triangle beater rapidly across the ridges on the top of the cymbal, giving a "zing" sound.

Occasionally, a composer will call for ancient cymbals or tuned cymbals to be used. Their timbre is very different from piatti or a suspended cymbal—more like that of a small church bell.

GONG/TAM-TAM

Like cymbals, *gongs* and *tam-tams* are large discs made from metal. Although they are similar in appearance, each makes a different sound. A gong has a small dome in the center (called a *nipple*) that produces a single note when struck with a soft beater. A tam-tam has no nipple, and therefore produces a myriad of sounds with no single overruling note.

4.7 Various tam-tams hanging in the "Gong Chamber" at the Memphis Drum shop in Memphis, TN

Gongs and tam-tams originated in the Far East, specifically in China and the Indonesian island of Java. European manufacturers like Paiste (Switzerland) and UFIP (Italy) have also been making very high quality instruments for over 100 years. You can see a selection of them in Figure 4.7.

As with timpani, the big size and sound of gongs and tam-tams made them popular with drummers outside the orchestral setting. Swing drummers like Duke Ellington's Sonny Greer used them during the 1920s and '30s, and rock drummers like

DID YOU KNOW?

. . . that there's an instrument called a "water gong," which is dipped into water as it is struck? The watery dip causes the pitch of the instrument to shift, creating an "otherworldly" effect.

Carl Palmer included them in their setup in the 1960s and '70s. For more on the evolution of the drum set, please check out Chapter 5.

Orchestral Hand Percussion

The following instruments fall under the category of hand percussion, because the percussionist typically holds them while playing. Often, the hand doing the holding is also used to get part of the sound. Many of the instruments listed below are not unique to the orchestral genre, but can be found in a wide variety of musical settings and traditions, including jazz, rock, R&B, and Latin American styles.

TAMBOURINE

Although we typically associate the tambourine with its jingly sound, this instrument is actually part of a family of single-headed hand drums known as *frame drums*. Some of the many ways to play the tambourine include: striking it, shaking it rhythmically, or rubbing your finger across the head to create a vibrating "roll" sound.

4.8 The tambourine on the left has twice as many jingles. The number of jingles affects the sound quality.

4.9 Woodblocks of various sizes

Frame drums in general are used the world over by many cultures (to learn about some of the different varieties, please check out Chapter 7). The tambourine's direct descendant is the *timbrel*, a Middle Eastern frame drum that is mentioned in the Bible. Timbrels were traditionally played by women in dance settings; metal *jingles* (Fig. 4.8) were added to the design during the Middle Ages.

TRIANGLE

The *triangle* is believed to have descended from an ancient Egyptian instrument called the *sistrum*. The name derives from its shape, and the instrument is typically made from hardened steel. When struck with a metal beater the triangle produces a very high-pitched, delicate "ting" sound that can be heard clearly above the orchestra. In addition to single strokes, percussionists can also roll on the triangle by twirling the beater around the inside of the instrument.

WOODBLOCK

The *woodblock* (Fig. 4.9) is an ancient instrument, with origins in Chinese and Korean slit drums. It became a part of the orchestral percussion section in the 20th century. The loud, piercing sound of the woodblock clearly cuts through the sound of the orchestra. It's often used for producing a certain mood (like a clog dance) or for a sound effect (like horses' hooves).

OTHER HAND PERCUSSION

As we'll see a little later on, the 20th century greatly expanded the role of the orchestral percussion section. During this time, many new hand percussion instruments became a part of the percussionist's arsenal, including some (like castanets, shakers, maracas and bongos) from non-Western cultures.

Mallets and Keyboard Percussion

Mallet percussion (also known as *keyboard* or tuned percussion) is the general name given to the pitched percussion family. These instruments are generally laid out like a piano keyboard, and they share the same chromatic tuning (meaning parts can be written for them like any other instrument in the orchestra).

Despite their connection to the piano keyboard, however, mallet percussion instruments have a variety of different looks, and they are made from a variety of materials (usually wood or metal). And where a piano is played with the hands, percussionists use various kinds of mallets to play these instruments (Fig. 4.10). For example, the marimba is played with soft mallets wrapped in yarn, the xylophone with hard plastic or rubber mallets, orchestra bells with metal-tipped mallets, and chimes with a hammer-shaped mallet made of rawhide or plastic.

Beginning with the glockenspiel, mallet percussion began to appear in classical music in the late 1600s. Today, these instruments are featured in a variety of

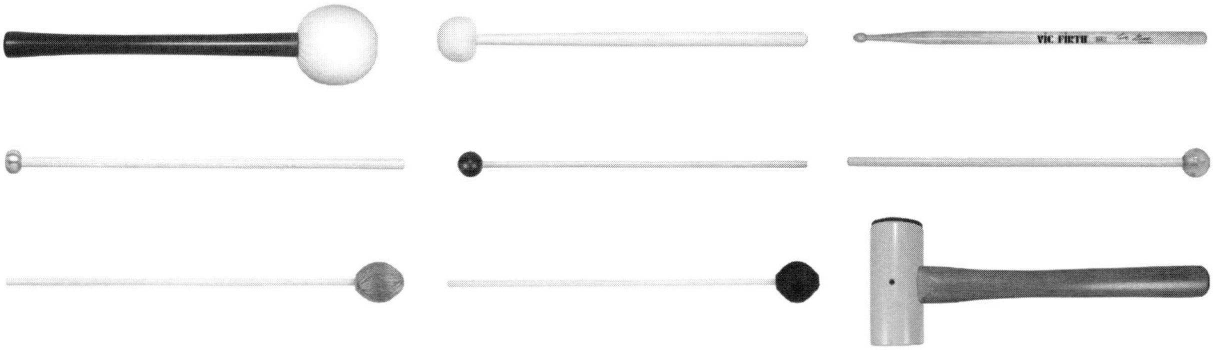

4.10 Tools of the Trade: An array of sticks, beaters and mallets used by today's orchestral percussionist. From L to R: bass drum beater, timpani mallet, drumstick, metal mallet, rubber mallet, plastic mallet, yarn mallets, chime hammer.

well-known pieces, including George Gershwin's *Porgy and Bess*, Aaron Copland's *Appalachian Spring* and Leonard Bernstein's *West Side Story*. Let's look at them in more detail.

GLOCKENSPIEL AND CROTALES

These two instruments, shown in Figure 4.11, are smaller and higher in pitch than the other mallet instruments. Being made of metal, they both have a pure, resonant, bell-like tone that carries over the top of the orchestra, adding brightness and excitement to the sound.

The *glockenspiel* (also known as *concert bells* or *orchestra bells*) has its origins in the European church bell. In fact, the name itself comes from a German word meaning "bell play." In creating the glockenspiel, the idea was to capture the enchanting sound of a choir of bells in a small, compact instrument that could be tuned (and therefore compatible with an orchestra). The rectangular steel bars of the glockenspiel make it possible to achieve this effect.

Well-known classical pieces that use the glockenspiel are Mozart's *The Magic Flute*, as well as Dukas's *The Sorcerer's Apprentice* (which you may know from the soundtrack to the Walt Disney film *Fantasia*). The glockenspiel also shows up in other genres of music ranging from hip-hop to jazz. Percussionist Neil Peart of the rock band Rush used a glockenspiel in several of the band's big hits, including "The Spirit of Radio." The instrument was also featured in Jimi Hendrix's classic rock ballad "Little Wing."

4.11 Glockenspiel (below) and Crotales

Crotales (sometimes called *antique cymbals*) are small, tuned bronze or brass disks about four inches in diameter with a flat top surface. They sound like a small tuned bell, only with a brighter tone and a longer resonance. Like the glockenspiel, crotales are arranged chromatically and are usually played with hard mallets. It's also possible to strike two crotales together, much like a set of finger cymbals. Early uses of crotales in the orchestral repertoire include Hector Berlioz's *Romeo and Juliette* (1839) and Claude Debussy's 1894 work *Prelude to the Afternoon of a Faun.*

XYLOPHONE

The *xylophone* (Fig. 4.12) is an ancient instrument and probably the earliest example of keyboard percussion. The word itself comes from Greek and means "wooden sound." The xylophone's wooden bars are laid out like a piano, typically spanning three and a half octaves. The instrument is played with hard wooden or plastic mallets, which bring out the very short and high-pitched sound made by the bars.

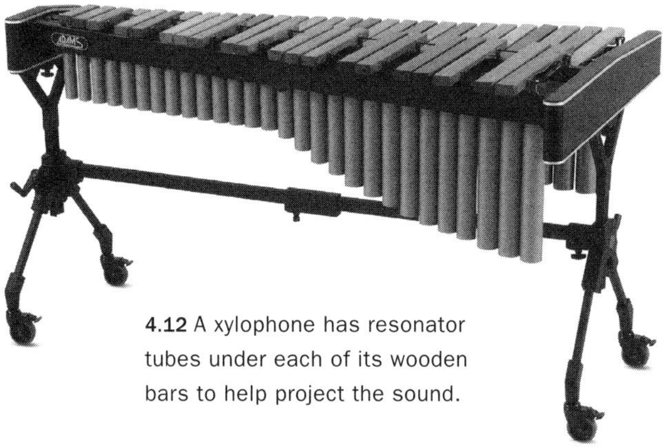

4.12 A xylophone has resonator tubes under each of its wooden bars to help project the sound.

Xylophones have their origins in Asia and Africa, originally descending from instruments like the Ghanaian *balafon* (you can see what a balafon looks like in Chapter 7). Each of the balafon's tuned wooden bars has a gourd placed underneath it, which helps the sound of the bars to project. Modern mallet instruments include a similar design feature—a metal tube found under each bar known as a *resonator*.

The first example of an orchestral xylophone was in the *Danse Macabre*, a spooky piece about dancing ghosts written in 1874 by Camille Saint-Saëns. In this composition and many others, the tight, brittle sound of the xylophone creates a comical or circus-like effect, which has also made the instrument a popular choice for cartoon music (it's all over the opening theme to *The Simpsons*), and in Broadway musicals. The opening to George Gershwin's *Porgy and Bess*, for example, contains a difficult and impressive xylophone part.

MARIMBA

A *marimba* (Fig. 4.13) is a specific type of xylophone that developed in Central and South America. Early accounts of the marimba in Central America date back to 1680, and in the late 1800s it became the national musical instrument of Guatemala.

4.13 The marimba

Unlike the bright, chattering sound of the xylophone, the marimba is known for its rich and beautiful tone, which has helped it emerge as a popular solo instrument. One of the highlights of the 1933 Chicago World's Fair was a 100-member marimba orchestra organized by the legendary virtuoso and marimba designer Clair Omar Musser. In more modern times, performer, composer, and teacher Leigh Howard Stevens (b. 1953) revolutionized the grip and many playing techniques to make the marimba an even more expressive instrument.

VIBRAPHONE

The *vibraphone* is the most recently developed of the mallet percussion instruments. It is also probably better known to the general public than any other. The vibraphone was first marketed in 1922, a time when machines and mechanization were all the rage. Although it looks like a xylophone or marimba, the vibraphone is motorized. Each of its metal bars is paired with a resonator tube that has a motor-driven *butterfly valve* at its upper end. When the valve spins, it creates a shimmering vibrato effect each time the bar is struck. The vibraphone also has a sustain pedal similar to the one used on a piano; when the pedal is up, the bars are all damped and the sound of each bar is shortened.

4.14 Jazz vibraphonist Lionel Hampton wailing with the mallets in 1946

Although the vibraphone is used in orchestral settings, it found its true place in other styles of music. In the late 1920s, the vibraphone's tremolo sound turned a dreamy Hawaiian-style recording of "Aloha 'Oe" into a huge hit. In the early 1930s, jazzman Lionel Hampton (Fig. 4.14) popularized the instrument through his work with Louis Armstrong and Benny Goodman. Hampton probably remained the vibraphone's biggest star until his death in 2002. Other important jazz vibraphonists include Red Norvo, Milt Jackson and Gary Burton—who in the 1960s created a four-mallet approach to playing the instrument that bears his name.

DID YOU KNOW?

. . . that modern percussionists will sometimes play metal instruments like cymbals, crotales, the bars of a vibraphone, and even the chimes with a cello or bass bow? Drawing a bow along the edge of a metal surface produces an eerie, sustained squeal, kind of like the sound made by a car's brakes when it needs new pads.

CHIMES

Part of a family of instruments known as *tubular bells*, orchestral chimes consist of a series of long hollow brass tubes that are pitched in one and a half octaves (Fig.

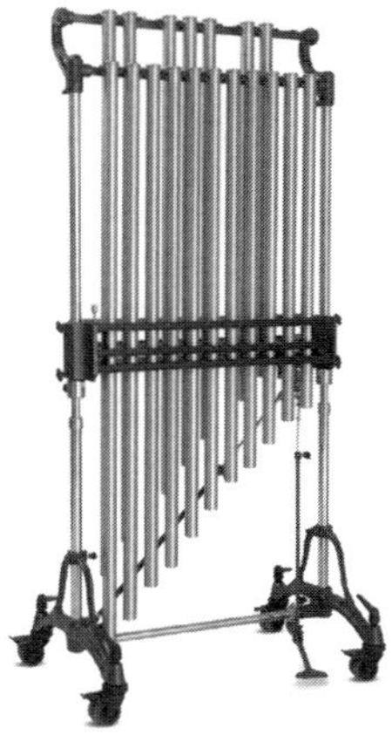

4.15 A set of tubular bells, also known as chimes

4.15). Each tube is typically struck on its top edge with a rawhide or plastic-headed hammer. Often, a sustain pedal is attached to allow the tone of the chimes to ring out. Like the glockenspiel, chimes were created to imitate church bells. They are often associated with Christmas music, such as "Carol of the Bells."

Other instruments in the family of tubular bells include the *mark tree* and the *bell tree*, although unlike orchestral chimes these are not pitched.

PLAYING MALLET INSTRUMENTS

For percussionists who want explore music outside the rudiments and other rhythmic patterns, learning a mallet instrument is a great way to go. Playing a marimba or vibraphone allows you to utilize percussive skills you have already developed (namely, striking something with a stick), while at the same time requiring you to focus on other musical elements like melody, chords and scales.

In general, playing a mallet instrument will give you greater insight into how other instrumentalists approach music, and offer you the opportunity to play in a greater number of musical situations.

The 20th Century's Impact on Classical Percussion

The first decades of the 20th century saw tremendous upheaval and experimentation in the world of classical music. Many composers—weary of the Romantic and Impressionistic motifs that had dominated the art form for more than a hundred years—began exploring new ways to present music. Their primary goal was no longer to write music that was simply pleasant to listen to; rather, they wanted their compositions to capture elements of the highly mechanized, fast paced and chaotic world in which they lived.

These composers pushed the boundaries of music in many different directions. Avant-garde composers like Arnold Schoenberg explored *atonality*, essentially music that lacks a key. Although many listeners found Schoenberg's *12-tone* approach difficult to comprehend, it would become a pillar of 20th century art music. Others began to broaden the definition of what might be considered a musical instrument, incorporating mechanical devices like airplane engines and sirens. George Gershwin blurred musical barriers by combining elements of classical music and jazz in his important 1924 work *Rhapsody in Blue*. Still other composers began to utilize musical motifs from Asia, Latin America and other non-Western cultures.

Percussion had typically played a background role in the classical setting, but composers were now eagerly seeking ways to bring percussion to the forefront. Igor

Stravinsky caused enormous controversy in 1913 with the Paris premier of *The Rite of Spring*, a symphonic ballet that included violent explosions of bass drum and five timpani (played by two players). The original score for George Antheil's *Ballet Mécanique* called for three xylophones, seven electric bells, three propellers, a siren, four bass drums, and a tam-tam. Pretty advanced for 1924 if you ask me!

THE PERCUSSION ENSEMBLE

With a new approach that stressed energy, noise, and technology, the classical stage was set for percussion music to emerge as a stand-alone art form all its own. Thus was born the *percussion ensemble* (Fig. 4.16), a group whose sole purpose is to play music written specifically for percussion. With the percussionist now squarely at the center of the action, composers were freed up to explore all the possible sounds that can be made by percussion. Along the way, they developed new and often complex ways for percussionists to play together.

The first percussion ensemble can be traced to New York City in 1931 with the performance of *Ionisation*, a piece by the avant-garde composer Edgard Varese. *Ionisation* was written for 13 performers who played a total of 39 different percussion

4.16 The Truman State University Percussion Ensemble in 2008

instruments, including three bass drums, two anvils, a trio of gongs and a lion's roar. Other important and forward-thinking composers of 20th century music wrote for percussion ensembles. Here are just a few:

Henry Cowell

Henry Cowell was a revolutionary composer, who pioneered many of the innovations that would become part of 20th century music. In his composition *Pulse*

(1939), each of the six players stands at his/her own "station" of instruments. These are grouped together according to the materials from which they are made: wood (wood blocks, Chinese temple blocks), metal (cymbals, cup gongs), drums, and various "found" industrial elements (pipe lengths, brake drums). In the early 1930s, Cowell envisioned the world's first electronic rhythm machine, called the Rhythmicon, which could produce up to 16 different rhythmic patterns simultaneously. For more on drum machines and other electronic percussion, see Chapter 8.

DID YOU KNOW?

... that *4'33"*, one of John Cage's most famous pieces, requires the performers to sit at their instruments for 4 minutes and 33 seconds—in complete silence?!

John Cage

One of the leading composers of the 20th century avant-garde movement, John Cage was also instrumental in the development of modern dance. *Double Music* (1941), composed by Cage and Lou Harrison, consists entirely of 1/8 notes grouped in twos and threes within a steady 1/8 note pulse, creating a kaleidoscope of small shifts in accent. The timbres of the various instruments (water-buffalo bells, muted gongs, sleigh bells) give the work the jangling, joyous air of a town celebration.

Harry Partch and More Contemporary Composers

Harry Partch was one of the first 20th century composers to experiment with what are known as *microtonal scales*, which break down the traditional Western system of 12 equal intervals per octave into much smaller gaps. Partch's desire to use alternate systems of tuning inspired him to create new instruments that could play his compositions. Some of these instruments were tuned using a system that included an astounding 43 pitches per octave! Partch's custom-made collection included various percussion instruments, with exotic names like the "Zymo-Xyl" and the "Quadrangularis Reversum" (Fig. 4.17).

4.17 The Quadrangularis Reversum, a percussion instrument designed by the composer Harry Partch

More contemporary composers who write for percussion include Steve Reich, who, along with fellow composers like Terry Riley and Phillip Glass, helped create a musical movement known as *minimalism.* Working with tape loops of simple musical patterns, Reich explored what would happen if you gradually moved them in and out of "phase" with one another. The concept translated well to percussion, and many of Reich's "phase" pieces from the 1960s and '70s use drums, bongos, and various mallet instruments to create incredibly intricate yet beautiful layers of sound.

PERCUSSIVE ARTS SOCIETY

Thanks to new developments like the percussion ensemble, the years following World War II became a new golden age for classical percussion. In 1951, the University of Illinois established the first accredited percussion ensemble in an academic setting. Today, percussion ensembles of various sizes and musical styles exist all over the world. Many of these are affiliated with music schools, but some professional groups like Nexus and So Percussion also perform. The repertoire continues to expand all the time; currently, there are more than 500 compositions for percussion ensemble and over 1,000 pieces for solo percussion or for percussion accompanied by instrumental ensemble.

4.18 The author performing a clinic at PASIC in 2009

The Percussive Arts Society (PAS) was established in 1961 as an organization dedicated to stimulating greater interest in percussion among the general public. PAS also exists to promote better teaching of the percussion instruments, and to continually examine the criteria for what it means to be a percussionist in the modern world.

In 1976, PAS held its first International Convention (known as PASIC) at the prestigious Eastman School of Music in Rochester, New York. Today, PASIC is the world's largest annual event dedicated to percussion. The convention includes all manner of clinics, panels, lectures and performances by world-class musicians in every imaginable field of percussion (Fig. 4.18). A typical day at PASIC might feature a performance by an Indonesian gamelan orchestra, a master class on bass marimba, a DCI drum corps demonstrating how to march in 5/8 time, and a red-hot big band concert—all before lunch. If you are interested in percussion, PASIC is truly one of the most spectacular events on the planet, and I think every percussionist should attend it at least once.

PAS also sponsors local chapters in just about every U.S. state. These chapters host exciting events like the "Days of Percussion," which often feature well-known performers. To find out how you can get involved, check out pas.org.

Classical Spotlight: Evelyn Glennie

Evelyn Glennie (Fig. 4.19) is a world-class virtuoso percussionist from Scotland. Since her professional debut in 1985, she has been the first person in musical history to successfully create and sustain a full-time career as a solo percussionist. Evelyn has collaborated with many of the world's top orchestras, and has commissioned 170 works for solo percussion from eminent composers.

All these accomplishments become even more incredible when you consider that Evelyn has been profoundly deaf since the age of 12! Rather than viewing deafness as a disability, she believes it lets the other senses take over, allowing her to experience sound more deeply. In order to "feel" the music better, Evelyn regularly plays barefoot during both live performances and studio recordings. *Touch the Sound*, a documentary film about Evelyn Glennie's perception of sound and musical philosophies, was released in 2004. I highly recommend it! You can learn more about Evelyn Glennie at her website: evelyn.co.uk, as well as listen to her perform the solo percussion piece "Shadow Behind the Iron Sun" on the accompanying CD-R.

Check out Evelyn Glennie's mostly improvised percussion solo "Shadow Behind the Iron Sun," from her CD *Thunder Caves*.

4.19 The phenomenal Evelyn Glennie is a world-class percussionist despite a severe hearing impairment. Because of her tremendous musical accomplishments, she was made a dame (the female equivalent of a knight) in the British honors system in 2007.

5

5

THE DRUM SET, PART I: AN AMAZING JOURNEY (1865-1965)

We first introduced the drum set back in Chapter 1. Figure 1.5 dissected it piece by piece, showing how this unique instrument is actually made up of many parts, which American drummers borrowed and assembled from a variety of different cultural traditions.

In this chapter, we'll take a closer look at the evolution of the drum set. We'll discover where the different pieces came from, and why we play them the way that we do. It's a fascinating story, one that starts with some very humble beginnings in the late 1800s, and winds its way through many of the most important events to occur in America over the last 140 years. Along the way, the drum set underwent many changes, greatly influencing the sound of popular music in the process.

Today, drum sets are played in every country in the world, and used in just about every kind of music. You can find them not only on concert stages and in clubs, but in churches, schools, garages, bedrooms—just about anywhere music is happening.

What's So Great About the Drum Set?

So, what makes a drum set so attractive? For starters, it looks cool … *really* cool. A typical drum set is a big, complex contraption displaying a dazzling array of drums, cymbals, hardware, pedals and other percussive "toys." In a concert setting, you usually find the drummer right in the center of the stage, towering above the other instruments on a special platform (or *riser*). That's pretty cool too.

But drum sets aren't just about look. They're also a lot of fun to play. Few other instruments offer the freedom to bash away to our heart's delight, often with the goal of creating as much sound (or as non-drummers call it, "noise") as we can possibly muster. Watching a great drummer at work can be mesmerizing. It's a choreographed dance of arms and legs, all working together and perfectly synchronized with the music. No wonder that the drum set stands as one of the most popular instruments in the world.

DID YOU KNOW?

... that the drum set is considered to be a single instrument, even though the pieces from which it is composed—drums and cymbals—are also instruments in and of themselves?

Drum sets are extremely adaptable to the personal taste of each player (Fig. 5.1). Instruments like a piano, guitar, violin, saxophone, or trumpet may come in slightly different shapes, sizes and colors. But in general they all have the same number of available notes and the same standard tuning. A drum set, on the other hand, can be assembled in a thousand different ways, and produce a limitless combination of sounds. The sizes and tunings of the individual drums may vary widely, depending on the type of music being played. And other factors like the weight of the cymbals, the diameter of the sticks and the thickness of the drumheads can also contribute to the custom feel of a drum set.

In the Beginning: Why a Drum *Set*?

We learned in previous chapters that drummers had played bass drums, snare drums, cymbals and other percussion for hundreds, and in some cases even thousands of years. However, drummers rarely played more than one of these instruments at a time (perhaps with the exception of timpani). What would inspire a drummer to put several of these instruments together as a *set*?

To answer that question, let's look at the kinds of activities drummers were involved with in the decades that followed the end of the American Civil War in 1865. Electronic media like radio, television, CDs and the Internet did not yet exist. Most entertainment was performed live, and in that setting, there were many opportunities for drummers. Drummers performed in classical orchestras as well as military bands. Nearly every town had its own bandstand, and by the 1890s, John Philip Sousa and others had made the brass band a major concert attraction. Drummers were also involved with theater shows (like vaudeville), traveling shows (like circuses) and dance bands of all types (Fig. 5.2).

The dawn of the 20th century saw the introduction of movies. Since films did not incorporate sound until around 1927, theaters all over the country employed live

5.1 Each of these contraptions is considered a drum set, yet they all have a distinctly different look, sound and feel. From top to bottom: Drum set belonging to the legendary virtuoso Terry Bozio, A modern electronic kit, a "trash" kit belonging to the Brooklyn based band "Electric Junkyard Gamelan."

5.2 New Orleans drummer "Papa" Jack Laine and his Reliance brass band in 1910. Bands of this type performed many functions, including street parades, funerals, concerts and dances. Laine's drum set consists of just a snare drum and a bass drum with an "overhang" pedal.

musicians, who provided what today would be called a soundtrack. The drummers in these orchestras played not only rhythms, but also added various sound effects to enhance the action on the screen.

All of these forms of entertainment placed increasing demands on drummers, not only to come up with more creative ways to be musical, but to also organize themselves in a way that would save money and space (particularly in the crowded orchestra pits of theaters and movie houses). As a result, the first drum sets were likely created out of necessity.

THE BASS DRUM PEDAL

So, if there was a need for a drum set, what actually made such a thing possible? The bass drum pedal. This device allowed one drummer to play bass drum, snare drum and cymbal simultaneously, saving both space and money. A bass drum pedal also permitted a single player to create tightly coordinated grooves that might be hard for group of drummers to play.

Different pedal-like devices began cropping up as early as the 1840s, but the earliest photos of a bass drum pedal date to New Orleans around 1892. Early on, drummers experi-

DID YOU KNOW?

... that at the height of the silent era, movies were probably the single largest source of employment for instrumental musicians in America? In the late 1920s, when "talkies" took over and the Great Depression hit, tens of thousands of drummers were put out of work almost overnight. And you thought drum machines were bad!

mented with a variety of pedal designs (Fig. 5.3) before the freestanding spring-driven type that we use today became standard in the early 1900s.

5.3 One early bass pedal design, called an "over-hang" pedal, was attached to the drum from above.

THE AFRICAN-AMERICAN CONNECTION: NEW ORLEANS AND CONGO SQUARE

We can't talk about the early years of the drum set without discussing the role of African Americans. Drumming has always played a huge role in many aspects of African life. The Africans brought to America during the era of slavery were often prevented from playing their own music, so they and their descendents applied their sense of rhythm to forms of music that were acceptable in America. To help them get through the brutal daily routine of plantation work, for example, they created *work songs* and *field hollers*. These evolved into the blues, one of the cornerstones of 20th century American music. Similarly, African dances and rhythms like the *juba* had a big influence on the evolution of tap dancing, another American art form.

5.4 African slaves were allowed to practice their drumming and dances at Congo Square in New Orleans.

In the city of New Orleans, Louisiana, the attitude toward slavery was a little more open-minded than in the rest of the South. Every Sunday, slaves were given a day off, and they could gather in an area of town known as Congo Square (Fig. 5.4) to play African music and perform traditional African dances. The weekly scene at Congo Square—perhaps akin to what we might call a "drum circle" today—was an incredible spectacle to behold, and actually became a popular tourist attraction. Congo Square helped keep alive aspects of African culture that would prove to be very influential to the later development of American music.

DID YOU KNOW?

. . . that until the 1930s, drummers were generally not allowed to play a full kit when recording? Early studios were very primitive, and the boom of a bass drum or the crash of a cymbal could damage the sensitive recording equipment.

5.5 Buddie Gilmore, a great drummer and showman during the Ragtime era. Notice Gilmore's drum set contains no hi-hat or tom-toms, but includes several Chinese cymbals and a "rack" with various noisemakers.

5.6 Many consider Baby Dodds to be the first important jazz drummer. You can see hallmarks of early drum sets, such as the lack of hi-hats, the large collection of cowbells, and the fact that Dodds is sitting in a regular chair as opposed to a drummer's "throne."

The abolition of slavery in 1865 gave African Americans a greater opportunity to participate in society as musicians. Starting with ragtime in the 1890s (Fig. 5.5), black musicians had a growing influence on many American musical and dance styles. That influence was especially felt in New Orleans, where a new style called jazz came to prominence in 1917.

Jazz was the first kind of music that fully used the drum set in a modern sense. New Orleans drummers like Baby Dodds (Fig. 5.6) and Zutty Singleton developed a technique for keeping time with all four limbs while spontaneously improvising on multiple instruments. Every drum set player today—whether playing jazz, funk or punk—still follows this approach.

Bring on the Traps: The Drum Set Grows

Today, we tend to think of "drummer" and "percussionist" as two different jobs, each with its own category of instruments and skills. The earliest drum set players, however, were often expected to fill several roles, including those of dance band drummer, orchestral percussionist, and sound effects artist—so they needed a wide variety of sounds, which they found in some new instruments that were arriving with immigrants from faraway places.

IMMIGRANT CONTRIBUTIONS TO THE DRUM SET

The dawn of the drum set happened during a period of mass immigration into the United States. Between the years 1880 and 1920, more than 20 million people came to America from many different countries and cultural backgrounds. These immigrant groups brought their cultural heritage with them—including their language, dress, cuisine and of course, their musical instruments.

Early drum set players drew inspiration from many of these ethnic instruments, and began to use them as noisemakers and sound effects for their work in theater and films. These additions to the basic bass/snare setup became known as "traps," short for "contraptions" or "trappings." Immigrants who brought many of the most important traps came from the following areas.

Europe and Asia Minor

5.7 A Greeko cymbal

The Greeks have been making cymbals for thousands of years, and immigrants from that nation contributed to the drum set in the form of what are called *Greeko cymbals* (Fig. 5.7). These small discs (about 3 inches in diameter) have a clear, high-pitched tone that made them a perfect complement to cowbells, woodblocks and other traps.

A family from Turkey started Zildjian, the best known and most popular cymbal company in the world. Zildjian's legacy as a cymbal maker can be traced back to 1623, when the family started producing instruments for the Turkish sultans. Over 300 years later, in 1929, Zildjian opened a factory in America (Fig. 5.8); the high quality of cymbals quickly made them a favorite among drum set players.

5.8 Cymbal smiths work at the original U.S. Zildjian factory

The modern bass drum pedal (Fig. 5.9) was first patented by the Ludwig family, German immigrants who would go on to create one of the most storied drum companies on the planet. Immigrants from Germany also founded two other legendary American drum companies: Slingerland and Gretsch.

Immigrants from Ireland founded the Rogers Drum Company.

5.9 The design of the modern bass drum pedal was first patented by the Ludwig family in 1909.

China

Many of the most popular traps used by early jazz drummers were ethnic instruments brought by Chinese immigrants, who came to America in vast numbers starting in the mid-1800s. These instruments included temple blocks, woodblocks, gongs, cymbals and the first tom-toms (Fig. 5.10), which were quite small and often painted with ceremonial designs like dragons.

5.10 Unlike a modern tom-tom, a Chinese tom-tom was not tunable. The head was "tacked" on, meaning that if you broke it, you had to buy a whole new drum.

Chinese cymbals (Fig. 5.11) typically had a flanged edge (making them look like they'd been popped inside out), and a very "trashy" sound. Today, cymbals of this type are still referred to as "China" cymbals.

5.11 A Chinese cymbal of the type used by early drum set players.

Africa

Because Africans were brought to America against their will as slaves, we would probably not consider them "immigrants" in the traditional sense. Once in the U.S., however, the contributions made by those of African descent had a huge effect on the sound of American music. Music styles from ragtime to rock & roll to hip-hop have been pioneered by African Americans, and many instruments that drummers use today, from cowbells to conga drums, trace their roots back to Africa. To learn more about African percussion instruments, please see Chapter 7.

THE FIRST FILLS

Drummers who worked at theaters and movie houses used their traps to create sounds and rhythms that would add life to the action on the stage or screen. A tom-tom, for example, could catch the "bump-and-grind" motions of a dancer; temple blocks could imitate the sound of horses clopping down the street; a slide whistle could enhance the comic effect of a gag like someone slipping on a banana peel.

The ability to "nail" all these effects, often while simultaneously keeping time, was considered an art, and drummers who could do it well were in high demand (and well paid). Figure 5.12 shows just such a professional in action. His massive setup centers on a drum rack, which supports several cymbals, tom-toms, and a trap table holding sticks, a tambourine and a set of Chinese temple blocks. The toms are still similar in design to Chinese ethnic instruments—the heads are tacked on, and only tunable on top. In addition to a drum set, trap drummers often played many standard orchestral percussion instruments. This fellow is using chimes, bell lyre, vibraphone, gongs, tambourine and a full set of timpani.

Traps also became indispensable to drummers who played dance music; they used the noisemakers to "fill in" the spaces between various sections of timekeeping. In essence, traps allowed early drummers to develop the concept of "fills" that are so much a part of the way we play today.

BRUSHES

One problem faced by early drum set players was how to play in a way that didn't drown out the other musicians. Remember, at this time a drummer typically shared the stage with light acoustic instruments such as clarinets, cornets, banjos and tubas. Since amplifiers did not yet exist, it would be very easy to drown out these instruments with the large marching instruments that made up the core of the drum set.

5.12 A theater "trap drummer" at work in the late 1920s

Early drum set players began looking for a quieter alternative to sticks, hitting the drums with light everyday objects such as whiskbrooms and flyswatters. By the mid-1920s, drum companies were making a kind of stick that used a soft fan of wire and began marketing them as *brushes*. Within 10 years, brush playing had flowered into a unique art form all its own, and today is a staple of jazz and many other styles of drumming (Fig. 5.13).

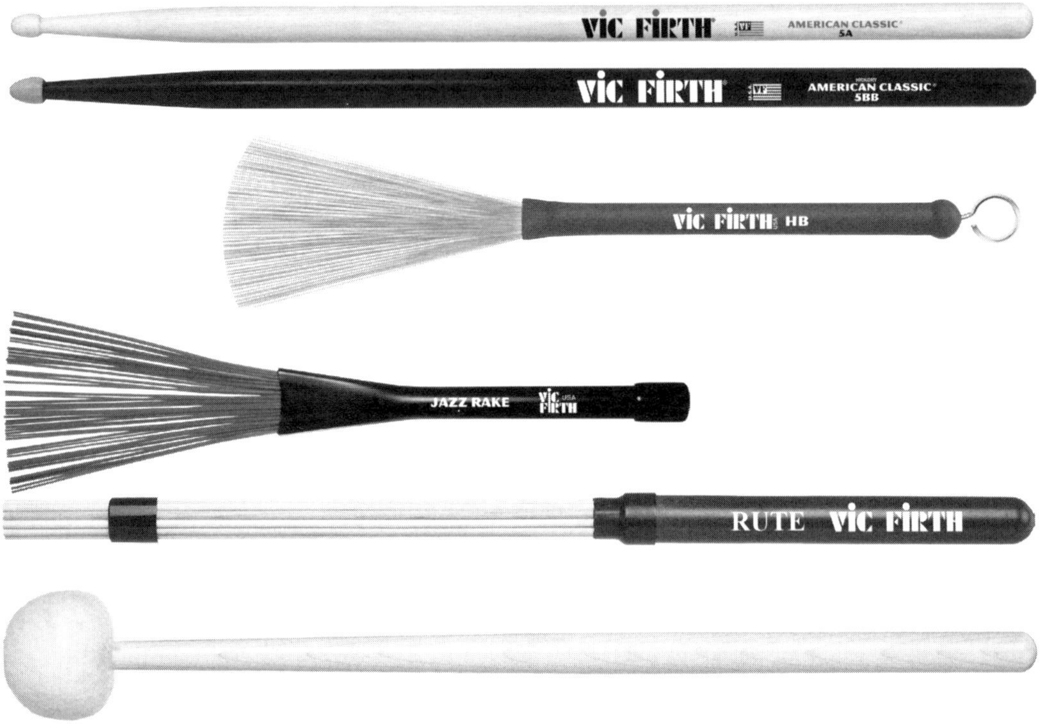

5.13 Here's an array of beaters that you're likely to find in the stick bag of a drum set player. From top to bortom: Two drumstick varieties, wire brushes, plastic brushes, a "rute" stick (for quiet playing) and mallets.

The Big Band Era

As jazz evolved and became more acceptable in American society, the concept of a jazz band began to expand as well. A traditional New Orleans band included just a few horns (sax, trumpet, trombone) that mostly improvised their parts. Bands of the 1920s, however, began to organize larger groups of horns into sections, each of which played specific parts that were written out. These bands, which often included 10 or more members, also updated their instrumentation, in particular replacing the tuba with the string bass. This allowed the feel to move away from the "two-beat" march feel of early jazz, and toward a more danceable "four-beat" feel.

Big bands exploded into the mainstream in the 1930s (Fig. 5.14). The upbeat, danceable sound of big band jazz—now known as *swing*—caught on via radio, a new, cheap form of media that offered escape to a population struggling with the economic depression. The Swing era reached its peak in the early 1940s, when the

5.14 Acts like the Bob Crosby big band (featuring drummer Ray Bauduc) were the rock starts of their day.

big band sound became the soundtrack to World War II.

For drummers, the Swing era brought with it a new kind of freedom. To mirror the sophistication of big band arrangements, drummers wanted to create a lighter, more fluid feel over which the rest of the band could float. A new device called the hi-hat replaced the snare drum as the primary timekeeper, and a steady "four-beat" pulse on the bass drum drove dancers into frenzy.

Some swing drummers weren't content to be anonymous timekeepers. Leading the charge was Gene Krupa, drummer with Benny Goodman's groundbreaking big band (Fig. 5.15). Krupa was the first true superstar of the drums. The instrument's first important soloist, he inspired a fascination with drumming in the public mind that endures to this day and paved the way for future drumming superstars like Buddy Rich, Ray McKinley and all that followed.

5.15 The legendary Gene Krupa, trying out some Zildjian hi-hats in the late 1930s. The diameter of these cymbals is several inches smaller than the kind we use today.

THE HI-HAT

As jazz bands got bigger and louder, cymbals became a more important part of the drum set (Fig.

5.16). The hi-hat, first introduced at the end of the 1920s, let drummers bring a lighter touch to their timekeeping, and helped the rhythm section create a smooth, washy pulse that flowed along effortlessly. While many drummers were just beginning to grasp how to use the hi-hat, Count Basie's "Papa Jo" Jones emerged as the first master of the instrument in 1936.

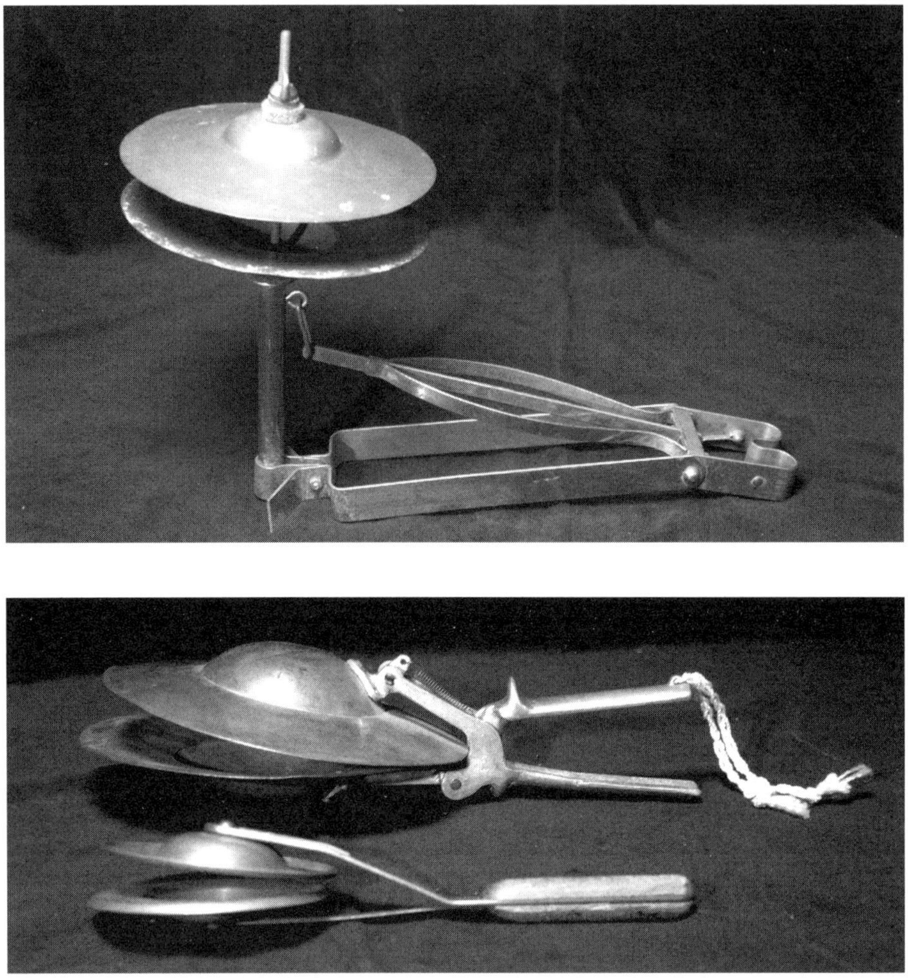

5.16 Time-keeping devices known as the "low boy" (top) and "hand sock" cymbals (bottom) were used in the 1920s until the hi-hat was perfected in the early '30s.

SEPARATE TENSIONED TOM TOMS

Gene Krupa was more than a flamboyant entertainer. He also made some important contributions to the evolution of the drum set itself, particularly regarding tom-toms. Since its introduction to the drum set as a Chinese folk instrument, the tom- tom had grown in size, but changed very little in design. The heads were still tacked on, making tom-toms fragile and difficult to tune (see Figure 5.12). With his newfound star power, Krupa was able to influence the Slingerland drum company to produce tom-toms that could be tuned from both top and bottom, the same as a snare or bass drum.

In 1936, Krupa added a large floor tom to his set up, and featured it on Benny Goodman's "Sing, Sing, Sing," one of the most memorable anthems of the Swing era. As a result of this success, tom-tom-based features and solos began to show up in every band's repertoire. By the early 1940s, drummers were almost always playing fills on tom-toms instead of traps.

DID YOU KNOW?

... that by listening to one special CD, Benny Goodman's *The Carnegie Hall Concert*, you'll understand why the big bands of the 1930s were the first rock stars? His drummer Gene Krupa still amazes listeners here in the 21st century.

DOUBLE BASS

Many drummers today include two bass drums in their kits (a setup that's especially popular with rock and metal players). But the double bass kit actually dates back to the late 1930s and legendary swing drummer Louie Bellson (Figure 5.17). While still in high school, Bellson began designing prototype versions of double bass kits in woodshop class. He also began experimenting to see how such a setup could work in a musical setting. In 1952, while a member of Duke Ellington's big band, Bellson recorded the first solo feature for double bass. It's called "Skin Deep," and was written by Bellson himself.

Although the twin bass drum setup may look cool, it adds to the amount of gear

5.17 The legendary swing drummer Louie Bellson in the 1940s, showing off a massive double bass kit that includes seven tom-toms with "dual tension" tuning

that a drummer must carry around, so many drummers today prefer a double pedal (Figure 5.18), which allows them to play double bass patterns on a single drum.

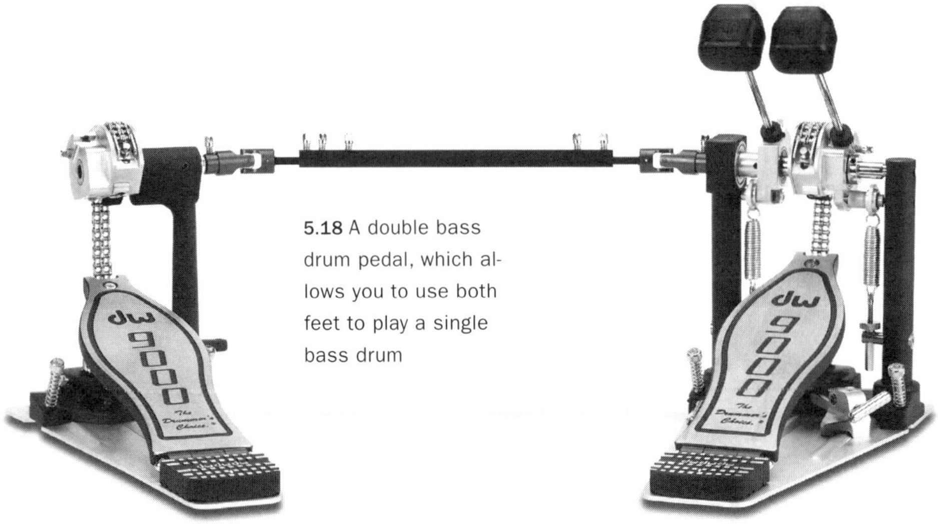

5.18 A double bass drum pedal, which allows you to use both feet to play a single bass drum

THE DRUM CONSOLETTE

Today, we're accustomed to seeing drum sets accompanied by lots of heavy-duty hardware. Each cymbal typically has its own stand, and very often tom-toms and even accessories like hand percussion are individually mounted. This is a relatively new phenomenon, dating back to the 1960s, when loud rock & roll became more dominant, and owning a car became an option for the average person. Before that, most working drummers had to use public transportation to get to their gigs—and had to be able to carry their entire drum set with them!

One obvious way to address this issue was to mount everything—all traps, cymbals and tom-toms—on the bass drum. During the Swing era, this idea was expanded to incorporate rack systems called *consolettes* (Fig. 5.19). Like a modern drum rack, the consolette could hold drums, cymbals and traps (except the hi-hat) and could be rolled on and off stage with ease.

DID YOU KNOW?

. . . that there's always been a close relationship between drummers and dancers? Many of the things we play with sticks and brushes started as an attempt to imitate the footwork of dancers (particularly tap dancers). Many famous drummers started as dancers or had dance experience. The list includes Buddy Rich (who was a child star in vaudeville), bop master Philly Joe Jones, and the great Steve Gadd, who appeared on The Mickey Mouse Club as a tap dancer.

Bebop and Straight Ahead Jazz

Bebop evolved from swing in the mid-1940s. It grew out of a desire by African American musicians to create jazz music that was no longer specifically tied to dancing, but rather that functioned as a unique expression of the black experience. Bebop included complex melodic lines, expressive solos and more interaction between the musicians. The music took jazz in a more artistic direction and established the "straight

5.19 Chick Webb, a highly influential swing drummer and bandleader in the 1930s, was famous for his "rolling consolette," which held all drums and cymbals and could easily be rolled on and off stage.

ahead" blueprint we still follow today.

To adapt to this new style, bebop drummers made some changes to the drum kit. Drummers like Max Roach (Fig. 5.20) dramatically reduced the size of the bass drum, using it more like a tom-tom than a timekeeper. The primary instrument for

5.20 Bebop drummers like Max Roach used larger cymbals and smaller drums.

timekeeping became a larger, mounted cymbal known as a *ride*. And bebop drummers increased the diameter and thickness of their hi-hats, allowing for a louder "chick" sound when played with the foot on beats two and four. These changes in the setup allowed bebop drummers to "float" over the rest of the band and gave them greater freedom to "comment" on what other band members were playing.

The 1950s: Rhythm & Blues and Early Rock & Roll

The 1950s saw more big changes in popular music. By then, big bands had lost much of their impact and bebop, while elevating jazz to an art form, had moved it away from being dance music. Thanks to amplification, smaller combos of three to six members could use electric guitars and basses to play as loud as a big band (Figure 5.21). "Rhythm & blues," an African American style with a great dance beat, became popular among younger listeners, and by the mid 1950s, it would blend with country music and other influences to morph into rock & roll.

5.21 Saxophonist Louis Jordan was the king of rhythm and blues in the 1940s. He distilled the concept of a big band down to a small group, and utilized a powerful shuffle groove to set the stage for what would become the "big beat" of rock & roll in the 1950s.

SHUFFLES AND BACKBEATS

Now that they were playing with amplified instruments, drummers no longer had to worry about being too loud for the rest of the band. This gave them a new freedom that played an important role in the transition toward rock. The shuffle rhythm (discussed in greater detail in the next chapter) dominated the sound of R&B and early rock & roll, and for the first time ever, a drummer could play a *backbeat* (a heavy snare hit on two and four) through the length of an entire song without having to worry about drowning out the other musicians.

CRASH CYMBALS

Though there were fewer radical changes to the drum set than in previous eras, some important developments did occur in the 1950s. First, drummers settled on a bass drum diameter of 22 inches, which remains the standard today in most pop music settings. Second, because rock and R&B were so much louder than previous music styles, a entirely new type of cymbal evolved that was designed to be "crashed" at the end of fills (vs. being "ridden" during the timekeeping process). Crash cymbals are now a standard part of most drum sets.

PLASTIC DRUMHEADS

Probably the most significant innovation to emerge during the early Rock era was the synthetic (or "plastic") drumhead. Since the appearance of the very first drum thousands of years ago, heads had always been made from natural materials like animal hide. While these heads sounded great, they were notoriously unpredictable. Even slight changes in temperature or humidity would cause the heads to shrink or expand. As a result, drummers would often have to retune many times throughout the course of a single show. Plastic heads were able to withstand all kinds of weather conditions, and as a result were given names like "Weather King," and "Weather Master" (Figure 5.22).

In addition to being more sonically consistent than their predecessors, plastic heads were also much more durable, particularly when it came to withstanding the hard hitting style of rock drummers, and the very rigorous conditions under which they toured. Without plastic heads, rock & roll may never have evolved as it did.

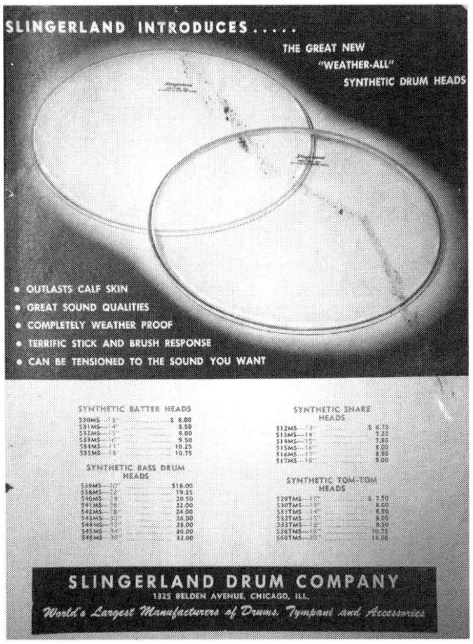

5.22 A 1960s ad from the Slingerland drum company for their synthetic (plastic) drumhead, called the "Weather-All"

Perhaps the most important change brought on by the switch to plastic heads had to do with the sizing of drums. In the era of animal hide, drum companies from different countries used a variety of measuring systems (Imperial, metric, etc.) when sizing the diameters of their shells. However, when the American company Remo achieved dominance in the plastic head market, they stipulated that all their products would be manufactured in inches. If a drum company wanted to outfit its latest line with the cool new heads, it had no choice but to do the same. Today, all drums are sized in inches, no matter what their country of origin, allowing for the marketing of drums (and heads) on a global scale.

The Beatles: The Drum Set Blueprint Is Finalized

Our journey through 100 years of drum set evolution ends in 1965, with a phenomenon known as the *British Invasion*. The "invaders" consisted of a wave of English rock bands that crossed the Atlantic to become extremely successful in America. This wave was led by the Beatles, the first English rock group to gain worldwide prominence, and the band responsible for turning rock & roll into the truly international phenomenon that it is today. The Beatles weren't the first rock band to write and perform its own material, but they were among the first to add outside elements

5.23 A Ludwig Oyster Black Pearl drum set from the early 1960s, otherwise known as the "Ringo kit"

to rock's basic R&B and country underpinnings. Along the way, they established a new generation of young musicians who saw that it could be possible for anyone to do the same.

RINGO AND THE MATCHED GRIP

Thanks to the Beatles' global popularity, the band's drummer, Ringo Starr (real name: Richard Starkey), changed the face of drumming. How did he manage this? By using the matched grip. While this might not seem like much of a big deal in today's world, it's important to understand that prior to the 1960s, the traditional grip was the *only* grip used by most drummers. One might switch to matched grip for a moment if extreme volume was needed, but virtually no one used it as a primary grip until Ringo. A generation of aspiring drummers would follow his example. From that point on, the playing field tilted in the other direction, and the matched grip became the more popular of the two.

The mass switch from traditional to matched grip was the

DID YOU KNOW?

... that Ringo Starr didn't just influence drummers, but influenced the fortunes of drum makers, too? After millions of Americans watched him play his Ludwig drum set (Fig. 5.23) on Ed Sullivan's television show in 1964, Ludwig instantly became the most popular drum company in the world. To keep up with demand, the factory operated 24 hours a day for several years. The drum set pictured is one of many vintage kits included in *Daniel Glass presents The Century Project*, a DVD that focuses (like this chapter) on the evolution of the drum set.

final step in solidifying a blueprint for the drum set that still holds true today. By 1965, all the major pieces of the modern drum set (hi-hat, toms, ride cymbal, crash cymbal, etc.) were in place, as was the way that we play the instrument in a popular music setting. Although kits have gotten bigger and smaller, and some drummers have incorporated a variety of "bells and whistles" like additional percussion, specialized cymbals and electronic drums over the years, this basic blueprint has actually changed very little.

Moving On

Having looked at the evolution of the drum set, the next step is to actually get behind a kit and start playing. In the next chapter, we'll get into the nuts and bolts of setting up the drums, as well as some pointers on related issues like changing heads and tuning. We'll also explore the basics behind some of the most popular styles you're likely to encounter on your own journey as a drum set player.

6

6

THE DRUM SET, PART II: SETTING UP AND PLAYING IN VARIOUS STYLES

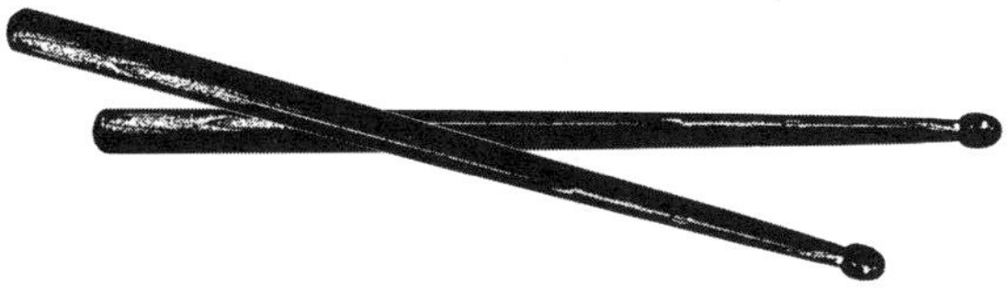

While Chapter 5 looked at the evolution of the drum set, it's now time to get behind the kit yourself and start playing! We'll look at some basics regarding set up and tuning, and then turn our attention to a few of the more common styles of music you're likely to encounter as a drum set player. These styles include rock, blues, jazz, hip-hop, country, Latin and reggae.

Setting Up

When you watch a drum set player at work, the basics of what's involved seem pretty self-explanatory: Sit down, pick up the sticks, and start wailing. Until, that is, the moment you actually sit behind a drum kit yourself. Suddenly, there are a lot of questions that demand answers: How high do I sit? How much should I angle the various drums and cymbals? Does it matter how close or far I'm sitting from the pedals? And finally, how do you tune this thing?

Unfortunately, there are no "correct" answers to any of these questions. How you set up and tune the drums is a matter of personal taste. Some drummers set up a certain way because they want the kit to "look cool," or because they want to imitate the way their favorite player does it. That's all well and good, but if a) the way you're sitting feels awkward, b) it's hard to reach a certain part of the kit, or c) it physically hurts you to play such a set up, then chances are pretty good that your playing will be affected negatively. In general, a good rule of thumb to follow is: If you feel comfortable behind the drums, your playing will sound comfortable to others. The same goes for tuning. A set of well-tuned drums can make your experience a lot easier, while poorly tuned drums can actually make you sound worse.

Sitting

Traditionally, a drum set player sits on a stool, which is also known as a "throne" (after all, the drummer is king or queen of the stage, right?). In setting up your drum set, think of your throne as a kind of a home base. In other words, get comfortable on the throne first, and then bring the rest of the kit to you.

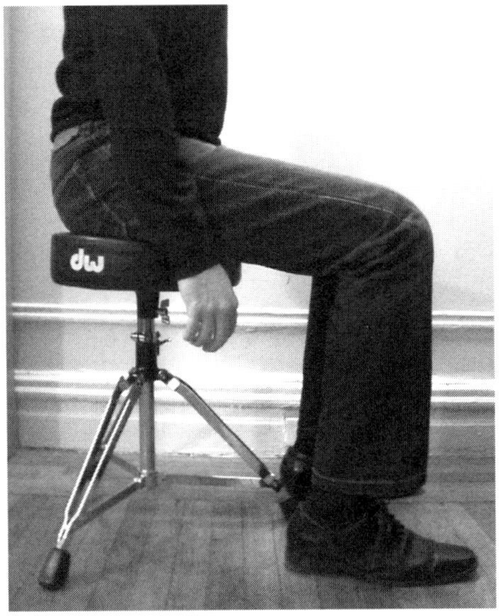

6.1 Proper sitting position. Ankles, knees and hips should be bent at 90-degree angles.

Obviously, how high you sit will play a key factor in determining the height of all the other components in the kit. A good starting point is to sit so that your ankles, knees and hips are all bent at 90-degree angles (Fig. 6.1). You can always adjust from there, but in general, most of us can stay pretty well balanced when seated in this position.

ADJUSTING THE KIT

Once you've found a comfortable height to sit at, it's time to surround yourself with the remainder of the gear. The hardware on a typical modern set is designed to let you to place each drum and cymbal at the exact height or angle you desire. While this is convenient, it may also be a bit confusing for a novice.

A good rule of thumb is to make sure that you can reach each drum and cymbal with ease, simply by reaching out your arm toward it. If you find your arm is fully extended, you are excessively "reaching," your neck is craning out, or your back is hunched over trying to reach one of these instruments, then you should probably rethink your set up.

WHAT IF YOU'RE LEFT HANDED?

About 10 percent of the world's population is left-handed, and that includes yours truly. When I got my first drum set, I figured that since I wrote, ate and threw a ball with my left hand, I must set up the drums "lefty" as well. Essentially, a left-handed setup is a mirror image of a standard set up in terms of where the drums and cymbals are placed (Fig. 6.2).

Interestingly, my "lefty" status always prompts the following question: "Does set-

6.2 A lefty drum set up (left) is the mirror image of a more typical right-handed set up (right).

ting up your kit left-handed affect your ability to play?" The answer is, absolutely not—a lefty drummer can do everything a right-handed drummer is capable of. That said, there are a few potential downsides to playing lefty. Since the positioning of the hands and feet are reversed in a lefty set up, all the coordination between the four limbs are reversed as well. This means that when a lefty drummer sits at traditional "righty" kit (and vice versa), playing even the most basic rhythms becomes very difficult. Since we live in a right-handed world, this issue will likely crop up almost every time you want to play another drummer's kit, or if you're one of several drummers sharing the chair in a big band, for example.

HOLDING THE STICKS

When playing a drum set, you can use either the traditional or the matched grip. If you're a beginner, it's probably easier to start with the matched grip, because both hands will be using the same motion to strike the drum. For all the details about these two grips, please see Chapter 3.

Tuning the Drums

Tuning a drum is something of an art form, the finer points of which are best learned from someone who has experience rather than through a book. That said, here's some basic guidelines when it comes to changing heads and tuning your drum set.

Like many instruments, a drum can be "tuned." But whereas other instruments are usually tuned to a specific pitch, the goal in tuning a drum is to create an ideal amount of tension on the heads so that the instrument has a beautiful resonance. A well-tuned drum should also give you a nice response when you strike it (in other words, your stick will bounce back easily).

The device used to tune a drum is called a *drum key*; the key turns what are called *tension rods*, special screws that are evenly spaced around the rims of the drum.

When we add tension to these rods (by turning the key in a clockwise motion), the the head gets tighter and the pitch of the drum goes up. When we decrease tension (counter-clockwise), the head loosens and the pitch goes down. You can see what drum keys and tension rods look like in Chapter 3—see Figure 3.12.

Every drum has a certain range of pitches at which it really "sings." Your goal as a drum tuner is to home in on that range. If the head is too tight, the drum will sound "choked" and not ring at all. If the head is too loose, the drum will sound "dead," kind of like you're hitting a cardboard box.

Both the top and bottom heads serve a particular function in the tuning process. We tune the bottom head for sound; as such, it should be tuned first and used to find the optimal pitch range as described above. The top head is tuned for response. If it's well-tuned, the stick will comfortably rebound off it. While there's no rule that says it has to, the bottom head generally ends up being at a slightly higher pitch than the top.

A FEW WORDS ABOUT DRUMHEADS

You may not realize it, but the type of drumhead you put on your kit can greatly affect the way it sounds. A high quality head and good tuning can make a cheap drum sound like a million bucks. Conversely, the most expensive drum kit in the world can sound like junk if it's not well tuned.

Often, we decide what kind of heads to use based on the music that we play. For example, a jazz drummer might choose a thinner head so the drum will be more sensitive and ring longer. If you play heavy metal, you'd probably use a thicker head to bring out the lower overtones of your drums and make them sound more "thuddy." In an effort to appeal to the many different kinds of drummers out there, drumheads are produced in dozens of varieties (Fig. 6.3), including *clear*, *coated*, *multi-ply* (models that have more than one layer of plastic), and even heads that use oil between two layers to control their resonance.

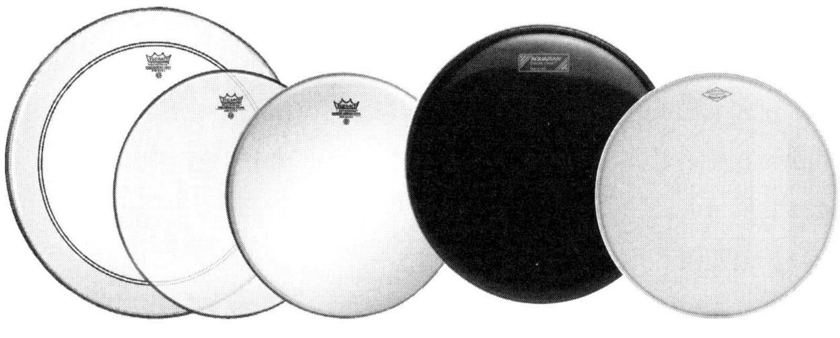

6.3 Drumheads come in a wide variety of sizes, textures, thicknesses and colors.

WHEN SHOULD YOU CHANGE THE HEADS?

Drummers may change their heads for several reasons. One is to get a different sound out of the drums. A much more likely reason, however, is that the heads are worn out from being played. As you might imagine, the ultimate nightmare for any drummer is to break a head—especially the snare or kick—right in the middle of a gig. To avoid such a disaster, it pays to regularly check on the condition of your heads. You'll know it's time to put on a new head when the drum starts to lose decay and vibrancy when you hit it. Other signs that you need to replace the head include rattling, a loss in tone, and physical defects like excessive pits, dents or small tears.

You'll find that the heads that need changing most often are the tops of the snare and tom-toms, as well as the batter side of the bass drum (the side facing the pedal). Bottom heads and the front head of the bass drum don't get hit very often, so they rarely need to be changed. However, you should still keep an eye on them in case they get damaged to a point that it affects the sound of the drum.

PUTTING ON A NEW HEAD

When you change and tune a drumhead, it's easiest if you start by setting the drum on your throne. Doing so will mute one side (the head resting against the cushioning of the throne), allowing you to clearly hear the head you're working on.

Removing the Old Head

Start by removing all tension rods with your drum key, turning counter-clockwise. Pull off the rim and the old head. Lay the new head onto the shell of the drum and rotate back and forth to make sure it's sitting evenly.

Mounting the New Head

Tighten all the tension rods by hand (twisting clockwise with the thumb and forefinger) until they are about even all the way around. Next, using your drum key, tighten each rod one full turn (about 360 degrees). You should do this in a "crossover" pattern (Fig. 6.4), going from one side of the drum to the other. This will keep your head sitting evenly on the shell, which is very important if you want the drum to sound its best.

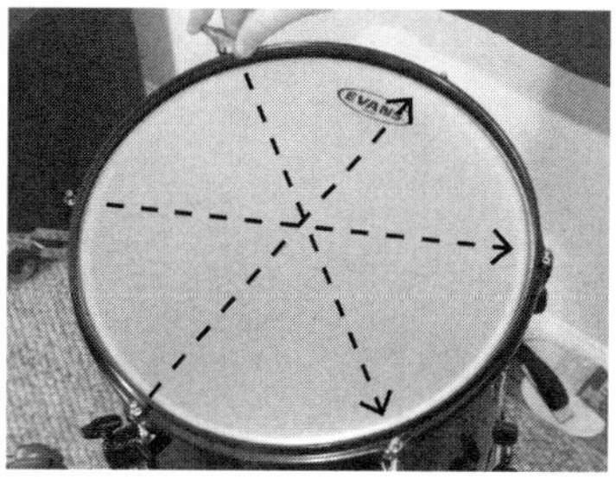

6.4 When putting on a new drumhead, tighten the tension rods in a "crossover" pattern, so the head tightens evenly against the shell.

Stretching the Head

After all tension rods have been tightened in this manner, check the head to make sure there are no uneven areas or wrinkles in the surface. If there are, tighten the closest tension rod until they've been smoothed out. Next, press down hard with the palm of your hand in the center of the head and around each lug (don't worry, the head can take it). This will stretch the head, which is another important part of the tuning process. Tighten each lug another 360 degrees with your key, then stretch again. Once the head has been properly stretched out, it will hold its tuning much longer (Note: Bottom heads for snare drums are generally much thinner than the heads on other drums, so if you have to change that particular head, don't stretch it in the manner described above. You could put dents in it or even break it).

Making Adjustments

Now comes the most important part—fine-tuning the head to make it sound as good as possible. This is the point where the art form of drum tuning really comes into play. Tap the drum with a stick while using the key to tighten or loosen the tension of the head until you start to hear a clear, consistent tone emerge from the drum. If the head is sitting evenly against the shell and has been stretched well, you should start to hear that tone pretty quickly.

Listening

Once you have tuned the bottom head and found the ideal pitch range for your drum, follow the same steps for the top head. After you've stretched it and found a good tone, hold up the drum and solidly strike the top several times. Listen for overall sound and notice how well the stick rebounds. Now, mount the drum on a stand and strike it again, being careful to listen from the side rather than from above. The drum has a very different sound depending on where you are in relation to it.

Fine Tuning Tips

If you've tuned your drum well, you should hear a strong, resonant tone coming from it, whether you're listening from above or from the side. If the drum sounds boxy, has no distinguishable tone (which might sound like many different tones colliding with each other), or a tone that "dips" in pitch when you strike it, go back and try again. I very rarely get a drum tuned the way I like it without a bit of tweaking. But with some practice, you'll soon have a much greater understanding of how to make your drum set sound its best.

Drum Set Notation

Many of the grooves we'll explore in this chapter will be written out in music notation. If you don't read music, or need a brush up, Chapter 2 offers a general explanation of notation that should be all the preparation you need to follow along.

In drum set notation (Fig. 6.5), each component of the kit is assigned its own line or space. For example, the hi-hat is usually written on the first space just above the staff, the snare drum on the staff's third space, and the bass drum on staff's first space. The position of each instrument on the staff mirrors the way that a drum set is actually set up; cymbals are placed high up or above the staff, the snare drum and tom-toms are in the middle, and the bass drum and hi-hat (when played with the foot) are on the bottom.

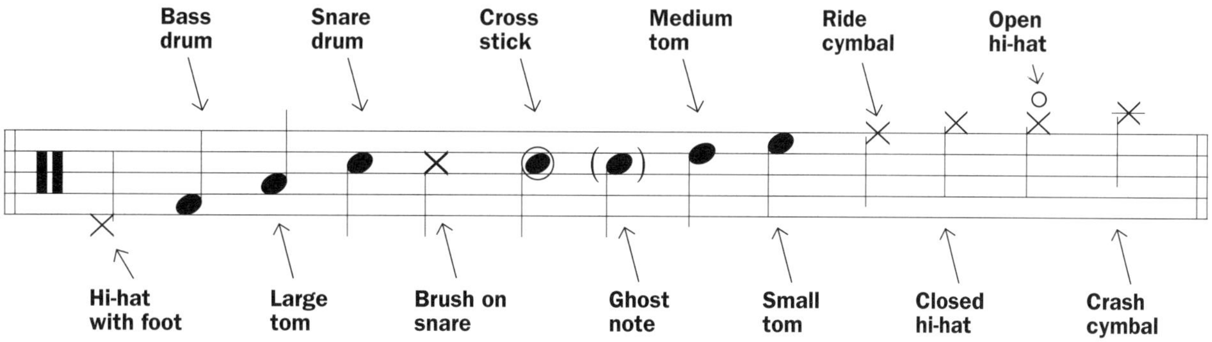

6.5 In typical drum set notation, each drum has its own position on the staff.

Drum Set Styles

Now that you're up to speed on notation, it's time to explore some well-known styles of music you're likely to encounter as a drummer. We'll learn a little about the history of each style and see how the drum grooves give it a distinctive sound. We'll also look at some important players from each genre, including masters who pioneered the way it's played, and some of the younger "cats" that are making waves today. Remember, the information included here is only a general overview. For more resources, please check out the "Resource Guide" included in the CD-R that comes with this book.

Rock & Roll

When learning to play the drum set, rock & roll is a great place to start. It's a style that most of us grow up hearing every day, and from a rhythmic perspective, the grooves are fairly simple and easy to understand.

Rock emerged in the 1950s when artists like Chuck Berry, Little Richard, Bill Haley and Elvis Presley began to "flatten out" the swinging grooves of rhythm & blues, and give them a more aggressive edge. The electric guitar quickly became the dominant instrument in rock, and as the Beatles, the Rolling Stones and Jimi Hendrix ushered in the more experimental styles of the 1960s, the music became a lot louder, heavier and more diverse.

By the early 1970s, rock was branching out in many different directions, from *progressive rock* bands like Genesis and Yes, to *heavy metal* groups like Black Sabbath and Led Zeppelin, and more *avant garde* artists like the Velvet Underground and Frank Zappa. The late '70s and early '80s saw the rise of *punk*, a more stripped down version of rock, as well as *new wave*, which explored the new frontier of electronic instruments. Since that time, rock has continued to diversify, adding new directions of its own, as well as combining with other styles like Latin, Jamaican reggae and ska, hip-hop, and others.

THE BASIC ROCK GROOVE

Since rock tends to be loud and heavy, the key to playing a good rock groove is to focus on the lower register of the kit, namely the bass drum and the snare (Fig. 6.6). A basic rock beat in 4/4 time has the hi-hat playing on all the 1/8 notes, the kick drum on beats 1 and 3, and the snare drum playing accented hits (otherwise known as *backbeats*) on 2 and 4. When written out, the groove looks like Figure 6.6.

LISTEN! TRACK 28

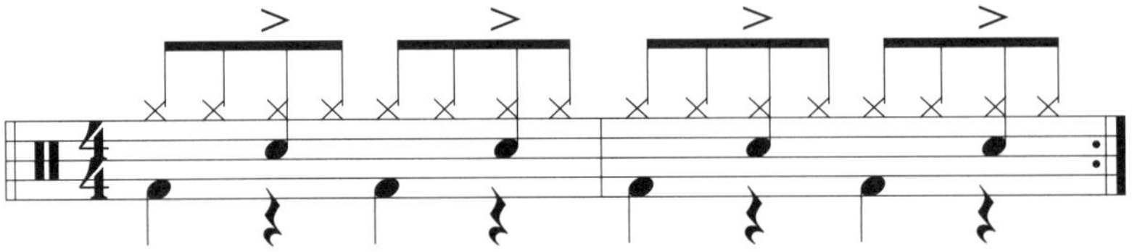

6.6 A basic rock groove

Once you've got the basic coordination down, it's time to hone in on some specific issues that have to be considered whenever you learn a new pattern or style of music on the drum set.

Striking the Drums

Although hitting a drumhead with a stick seems relatively straightforward, it's important that you do it in a way that allows the tone of the drum to come through. Other than making sure the drum is in tune, the best way to ensure this is to allow the stick to *rebound* (bounce back) off a snare drum or tom-tom.

The same goes for the bass drum; let the beater ball of the pedal rebound slightly off the head after each stroke. By utilizing the concept of rebound, you will allow the drum to ring as it's designed to do. This may also help prevent injury, which sometimes results from excessively "burying" the stick or beater ball into the head.

Locking In

One of the biggest challenges in playing the drum set is the process of coordinating all your limbs to work together. When practicing your basic rock groove, ask yourself the following questions: On beat 1, am I hitting the kick and hi-hat at exactly the same time, or are they slightly off? The same goes for beat 2, where the hi-hat and snare have to be in sync. If the timing on each instrument is not identical, then you haven't fully "locked in."

Limb Independence

While it's important to lock in, it's also vital to get each limb to play its part independently of the others. In other words, if you were to change what one of your limbs was doing, would the others be able to continue their rhythmic flow uninterrupted? One way to double check your level of limb independence is to make one of the elements silent. Using the groove we just learned as an example, try playing the snare part on your leg, instead of on the drum. Now, focus on the hi-hat and see if the consistency or volume of your strokes changes every time you play the snare part. If it does, you need to continue working on making those two limbs "independent" of each other.

VARIATIONS ON THE ROCK GROOVE

Once you've got your basic groove down, the next step is to add some variations in the bass drum pattern, shown in Figures 6.7—6.10.

LISTEN! TRACK 29

6.7 Rock Variation 1

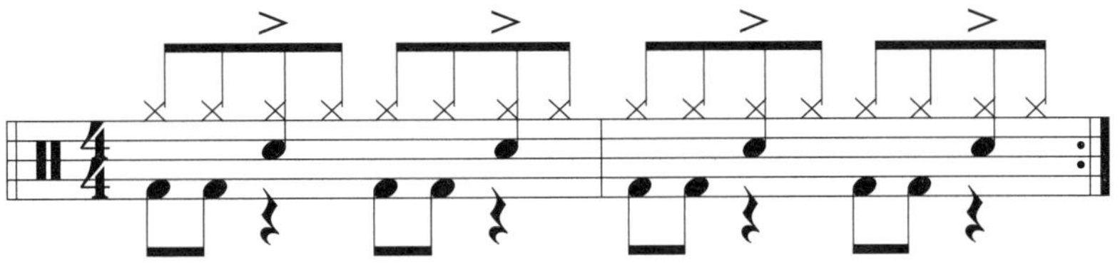

LISTEN! TRACK 30

6.8 Rock Variation 2

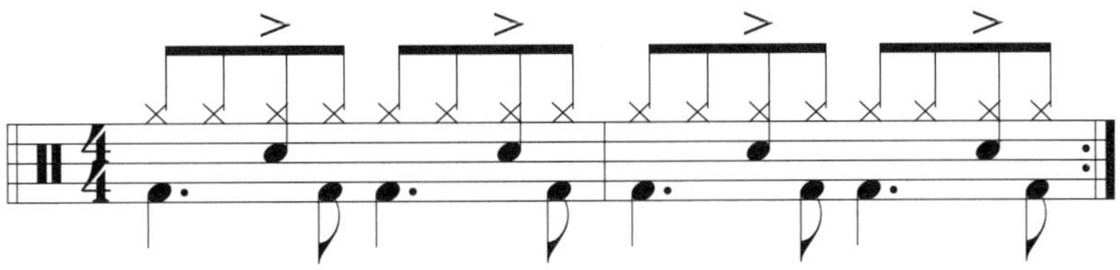

LISTEN! TRACK 31

6.9 Rock Variation 3

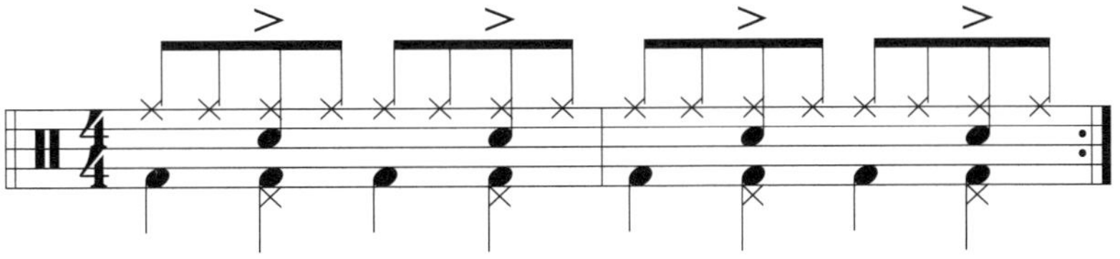

LISTEN! TRACK 32

6.10 Rock Variation 4

You can also experiment with playing the hi-hat part on the ride cymbal, and use your foot to close the hi-hat on beats 2 and 4 along with the snare.

Fills

Playing the drum set not only involves keeping steady beats, but adding various transitions known as *fills*. Fills are short musical passages or rhythms that a drummer uses to lead a band from one part of a song into another—from the verse into the chorus, for example. As opposed to the repetitive nature of a groove, fills offer the drummer an opportunity to be creative, and many great songs can stake their claim to fame because of interesting drum fills.

Keith Moon (Fig. 6.11) was one the greatest rock drummers of all time. Playing with the classic British band the Who, Moon seemed to continuously play fills on every part of his enormous drum set. Yet he somehow managed to keep good time as well. Not an easy feat for any drummer!

6.11 Keith Moon

A good drummer can play fills on any part of the drum kit, but most of the time they are played on the snare and tom toms. Rock drummers generally use 1/8 and 1/16 note combinations as the basis for a fill, and conclude by hitting a crash cymbal on the first beat of the next measure. In each of the following examples (Figures 6.12–6.14), play three bars of the basic groove followed by the fill.

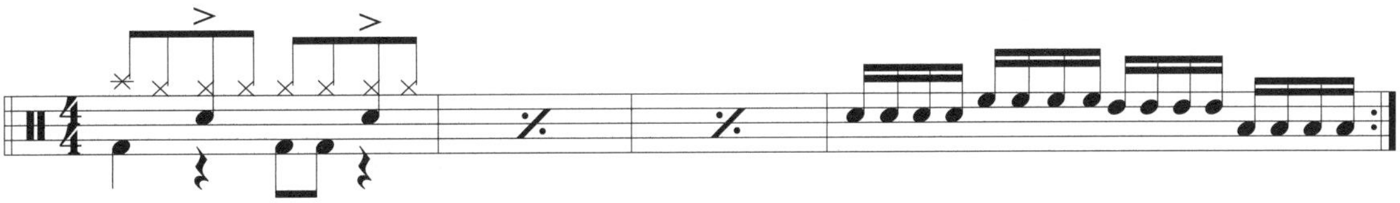

6.12 Rock Fill 1

LISTEN! TRACK 33

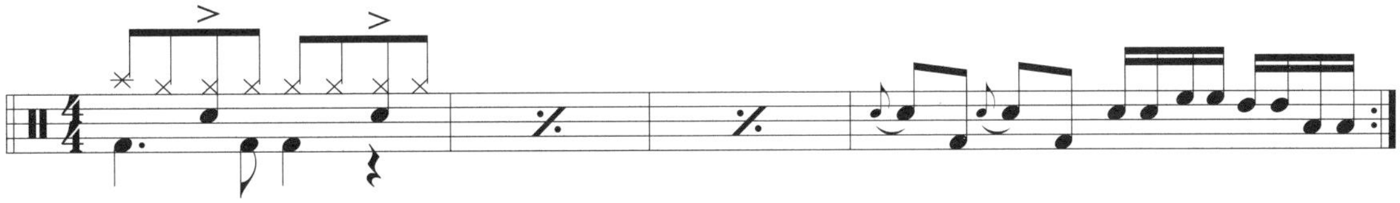

6.13 Rock Fill 2

LISTEN! TRACK 34

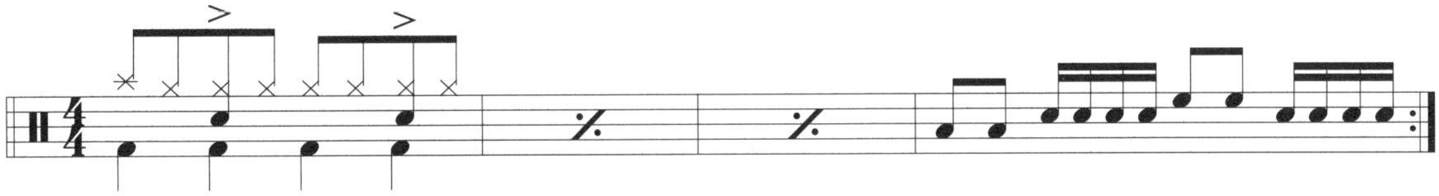

6.14 Rock Fill 3

LISTEN! TRACK 35

ROCK MASTERS

- Charlie Watts (Rolling Stones)
- Ian Paice (Deep Purple)
- John Bonham (Led Zeppelin)
- Steve Gadd (Studio Legend)
- Neil Peart (Rush)

WHO'S DOING IT TODAY

- Josh Freese (Nine Inch Nails, Studio)
- Travis Barker (Blink-182)
- Abe Laboriel, Jr. (Paul McCartney)
- Danny Carey (Tool, Fig. 6.15)

DID YOU KNOW?

. . . that the Phil Collins 1981 song "In the Air Tonight" contains one of the most recognizable drum fills of all time? The fill—an explosion of tom toms which happens 3:16 into the song, has been used in many advertisements, as well as film and television soundtracks. It's also been sampled countless times, and is even referenced by boxer Mike Tyson in the film "The Hangover."

6.15 Danny Carey, drummer for the progressive metal band Tool, is known for his incredible technical ability, which integrates the use of odd time signatures and polyrhythms into the rock setting.

Blues and R&B

Blues is a traditional style of music that traces its roots back more than a hundred years to rural African Americans. Although the term "the blues" refers to a feeling of sadness, blues music can transmit a wide variety of emotions. Because it was traditionally played as folk music, early forms of the blues generally didn't include drums. That is, until the mid-1930s, when the great Count Basie (Fig. 6.16) and his orchestra made the blues an integral part of the big band craze. Since that time, blues has been at the heart of many kinds of popular music styles, including all those we've talked about thus far.

In 1949, *Billboard* magazine officially coined the term "Rhythm & Blues" to encompass a wide variety of African American music styles. Since then, R&B has come to mean a number of different musical styles originating in the African American community.

In the 1950s, Chicago blues artists like Muddy Waters and Howlin' Wolf brought the music to new levels of popularity, and their sound was a big influence on '60s "British Invasion" icons like the Rolling Stones as well as blues-rock artists like Eric Clapton, Led Zeppelin, Jimi Hendrix, and Fleetwood Mac. Never out of the spotlight for very long, blues music experienced a major resurgence in the 1980s with the popularity of Stevie Ray Vaughn, George Thorogood and the Fabulous Thunderbirds.

Unlike rock, which is based in a straight 1/8 note feel, the groove at the heart of

6.16 Count Basie's big band, featuring the legendary "Papa Jo" Jones on drums, made the blues an essential part of American popular music.

many blues and R&B tunes is a triplet-based feel called a *shuffle* (Fig. 6.17). Another common blues feel is called the 12/8 (Fig. 6.18), because it expresses all 12 triplets in a bar of 4/4 time.

A more contemporary approach to playing a shuffle is based on what is called a *halftime feel*, (Fig. 6.19) which moves the placement of the backbeat from beats 2 and 4 to beat 3. In the early 1970s, R&B drummers found that by playing a shuffle in this manner, they could open it up give it a roomier feel. Great examples of a half-time shuffle include Stevie Wonder's "Superstition" and "Babylon Sisters" by Steely Dan. The halftime feel is the basis for styles like funk and hip-hop, which would go on to dominate the R&B scene over the next four decades.

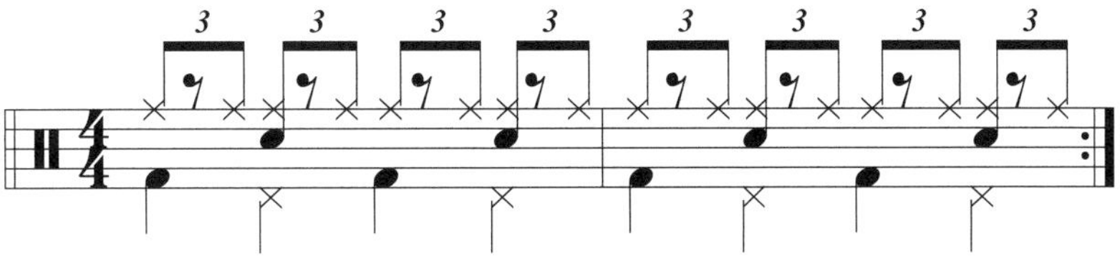

LISTEN! TRACK 36

6.17 A typical blues shuffle

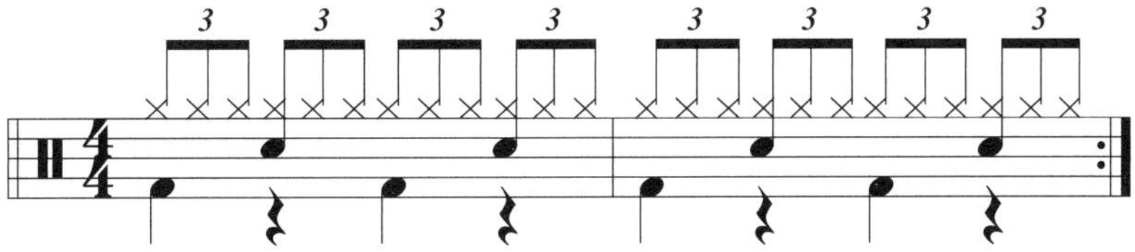

LISTEN! TRACK 37

6.18 The bluesy 12/8 feel

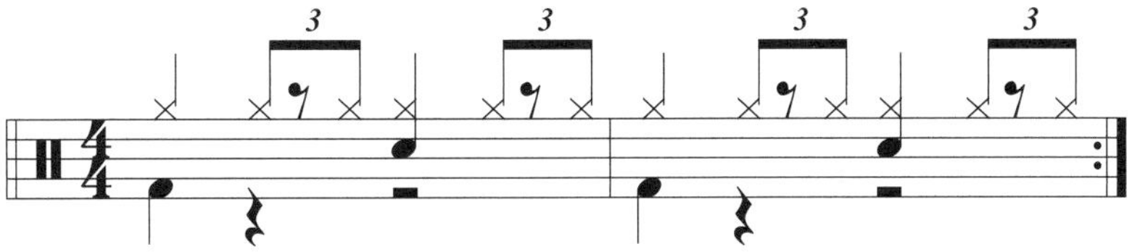

LISTEN! TRACK 38

6.19 Halftime feel

BLUES MASTERS

- Earl Palmer (Little Richard, studio legend)
- Fred Below (Chess Records house band)
- Panama Francis (Atlantic Records house band)
- James Gadson (Bill Withers, Albert King)
- Chris Layton (Stevie Ray Vaughn)

WHO'S DOING IT TODAY

- Steve Jordan (Blues Brothers, John Mayer)
- Chris Parker (Paul Butterfield, Ray Charles)
- Jay Bellerose (T-Bone Burnett, Paula Cole)

Jazz

Like the blues, jazz is a uniquely American art form that has been in existence for nearly 100 years. It was created when African American brass band musicians (primarily in New Orleans) began swinging the "two-beat" feel of march music. This syncopated feel was extremely danceable, and when the first jazz recordings were made in 1917, the music became a sensation.

At the time jazz became popular, the drum set only consisted of a bass and snare drum, with a cymbal and perhaps a woodblock or cowbell. Therefore drummers kept time mainly on the snare drum, using a *press roll* style (Fig. 6.20) that still sounded very much like military drumming. The difference was that the rudiments now "swung."

LISTEN!
TRACK 39

6.20 Press roll pattern

As jazz became more accepted in the 1920s, the size of the bands grew and the arrangements for the horn section became more complex. By the mid-1930s, the Swing era was in high gear, with big bands dominating the pop music scene the way hip-hop and rock acts do today. The hi-hat, which had been invented at the end of the 1920s, became the primary timekeeping instrument for drummers, and a *four-beat* feel on the bass drum would replace the marching-era style two-beat.

Gene Krupa (Fig. 6.21), who exploded on to the scene in 1935 with Benny Goodman's big band, was the very first superstar drummer. He helped make drum solos acceptable, and led his own band for many years. Krupa would remain the best-

6.21 Gene Krupa (top center) popularized the drum solo.

known drummer in the world until he was finally unseated by the Beatles' Ringo Starr, some 30 years later!

Like the blues, the swing feel of jazz is based in triplets. With the evolution of the hi-hat, a particular cymbal pattern emerged that is still at the heart of jazz timekeeping today (Fig. 6.22).

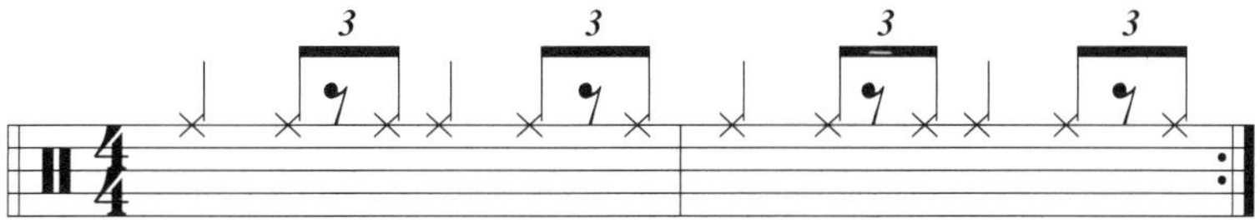

LISTEN! TRACK 40

6.22 Jazz ride cymbal pattern

Figure 6.23 shows a 1930s swing-style groove. Even though the Big Band era ended over 60 years ago, many groups today still play songs that have this feel. If you want to play jazz or swing, make sure you get this one down!

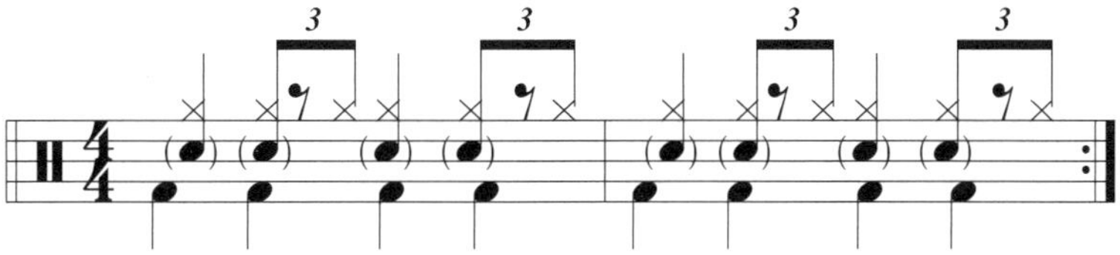

LISTEN! TRACK 41

6.23 1930s swing groove

EARLY JAZZ AND SWING MASTERS

- Baby Dodds (King Oliver)
- Gene Krupa (Benny Goodman)
- "Papa Jo" Jones (Count Basie)
- Buddy Rich (Tommy Dorsey)
- Don Lamond (Woody Herman)

WHO'S DOING IT TODAY

- Jeff Hamilton (Diana Krall, Clayton Hamilton Jazz Orch.)
- John Riley (Vanguard Jazz Orchestra)
- Daniel Glass (Brian Setzer Orchestra, Royal Crown Revue)

Bebop and Straight Ahead Jazz

When World War II ended in 1945, the Swing era came to a close as well. It was replaced by two different genres: rhythm & blues (which we've already talked about) and bebop. Bebop was created by musicians like Charlie Parker and Dizzy Gillespie. They were tired of playing dance music, and wanted to create a new form of jazz that would break away from the restrictions of swing and express a more modern African American musical perspective, which many felt had never been fully recognized due to racism.

6.24 Art Blakey was one of the pioneers of bebop drumming. Notice the small drums compared to those in the photo of Gene Krupa (Fig. 6.21).

Bebop started with a lot of the same ingredients as swing, but often included more complex harmonies and melodies, often played at breakneck tempos. Instead of being a break between melodic sections, improvised solos took center stage. As advanced as any style of classical music, bebop moved jazz away from being dance pop music into a challenging art form, and established the "straight ahead" blueprint we still follow today.

In keeping with bebop's artistic ideals, drummers like Max Roach, Kenny Clarke and Art Blakey (Fig. 6.24) radically changed not only the way they played, but the setup of the instrument as well. First, they shrunk the bass drum—moving from a large, marching-sized shell to one that measured only 18-20 inches in diameter. This enabled them to use the bass drum more like a tom tom than a thuddy timekeeper. Second, they went to the cymbal manufacturers and demanded larger, heavier cymbals on which they could "ride" the time as a more expressive alternative to the hi-hat sound. With this new set up, a bebop drummer could float over the rest of the band, using the bass and snare drums to "comment" on what other band members were playing.

The intricacies of bebop drumming (Figures 6.25–6.27) are too complex to approach in the context of this book, but here are a few basic examples of what this kind of jazz drumming sounds like. In contrast to the previous jazz example, the ride cymbal is now the main timekeeper, leaving the bass and snare drum free to play more melodic ideas.

BEBOP MASTERS

- Max Roach (Charlie Parker, Dizzy Gillespie)
- Art Blakey (Thelonius Monk, The Jazz Messengers)
- Elvin Jones (Charles Mingus, John Coltrane)
- Tony Williams (Miles Davis, Jackie McLean)
- Peter Erskine (Weather Report, Michael Brecker)

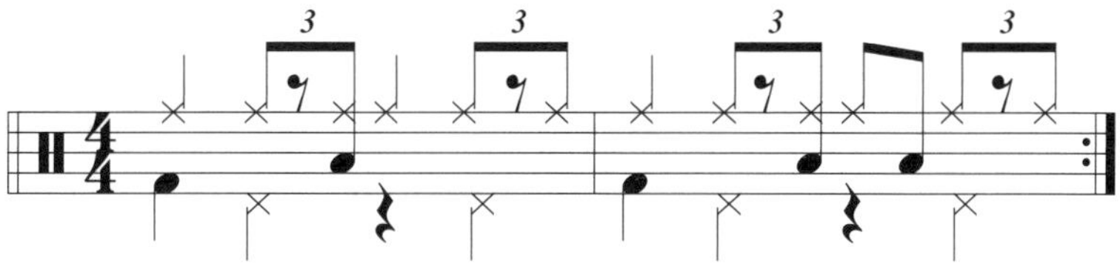

LISTEN! TRACK 42

6.25 Bebop Idea 1

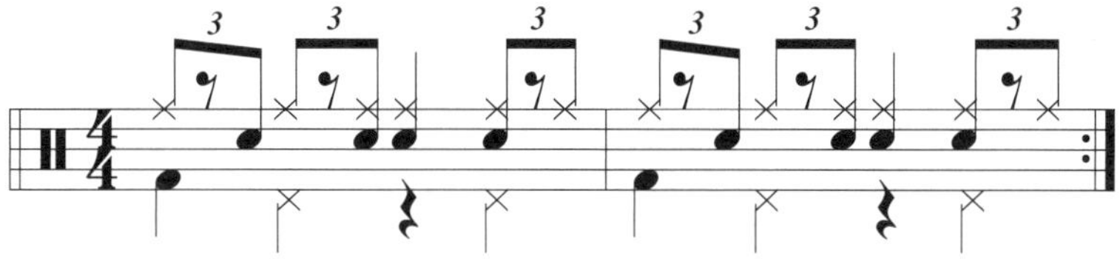

LISTEN! TRACK 43

6.26 Bebop Idea 2

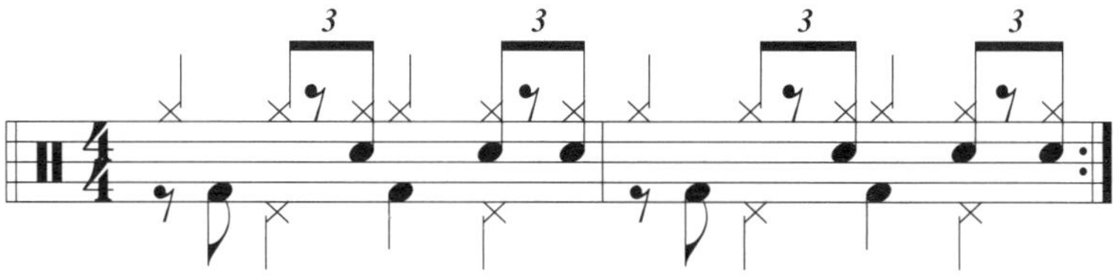

LISTEN! TRACK 44

6.27 Bebop Idea 3

WHO'S DOING IT TODAY

- Jeff "Tain" Watts (Wynton Marsalis, Branford Marsalis)
- Brian Blade (Wayne Shorter, Billy Childs)
- Cindy Blackman (Pharoah Sanders, Joe Henderson, Fig. 6.28)

Soul and Funk

As rock & roll was coming into its own in the 1960s, a fresh set of grooves was also emerging from the African American community. These were the sounds of soul and funk music. Like rock, soul grew out of '50s R&B and gospel music. The driving and danceable grooves of Motown recording artists like the Temptations and the Supremes dominated the airwaves throughout the 1960s, and the Memphis-based Stax

6.28 Cindy Blackman is one of the top straight ahead jazz drummers on the scene today.

6.29 Drummer Al Jackson, Jr. (far right) was the epitomy of a great soul drummer. Jackson was known for his work with Booker T. & the MG's, the house band at Stax Records in Memphis, TN.

label produced some "deep pocket" sounds with the likes of Otis Redding and Wilson Pickett—thanks to a rhythm section anchored by drummer Al Jackson (Fig. 6.29).

By the end of the '60s, James Brown (known as the "Godfather of Soul") was creating a heavily syncopated, high-energy brand of soul that would become known as *funk*. New Orleans funk masters like The Meters and San Francisco Bay-area product Sly Stone would bring the funk tradition into the mainstream, adding elements like slap bass and a tight, syncopated horn section.

Figure 6.30 shows a classic soul feel popularized by the sound of the Motown record label. It's characterized by driving quarter notes played on the snare drum.

A typical James Brown funk groove (Fig. 6.31) "displaces" the traditional two and four backbeat of rock, giving it a delayed kick that's . . . well, downright funky!

LISTEN! TRACK 45

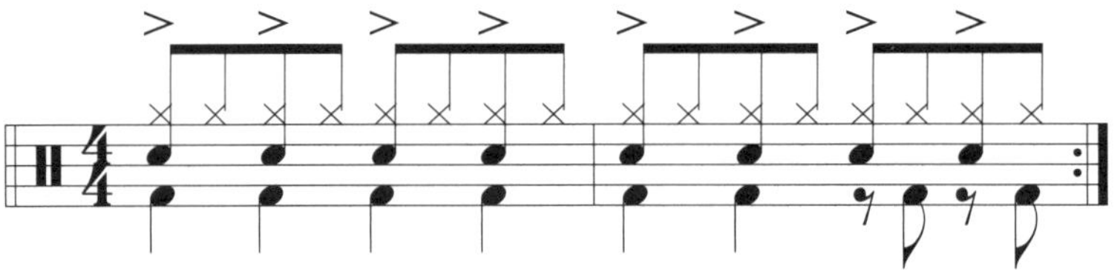

6.30 Motown Feel

LISTEN! TRACK 46

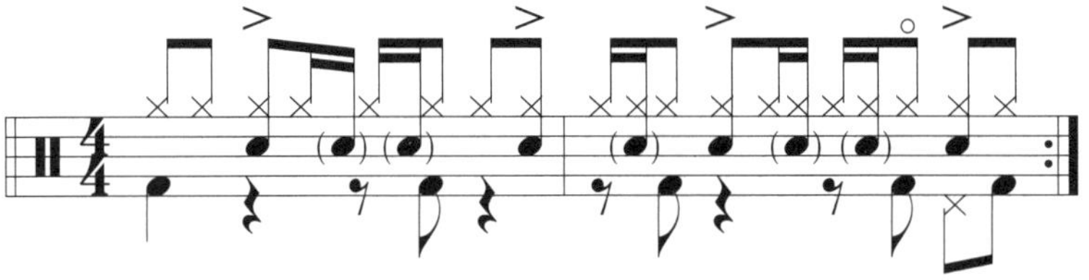

6.31 16th Note Funk

SOUL/FUNK MASTERS

- Benny Benjamin (Motown Records house band)
- Al Jackson, Jr. (Stax Records house band)
- Bernard Purdie (Aretha Franklin, studio legend)
- Clyde Stubblefield (James Brown)
- David Garibaldi (Tower of Power)

WHO'S DOING IT TODAY

- Zoro (Bobby Brown, Lenny Kravitz)
- Chad Smith (Red Hot Chili Peppers)
- Stanton Moore (Galactic, Garage a Trois)

Hip-Hop

Hip-hop emerged in the late 1970s out of soul, funk and disco. It borrowed elements from all these styles, and added the emerging technology of drum machines, sampling and a new streetwise style of storytelling known as rap. Much of hip-hop drumming is very syncopated and based on the half time shuffle feel (see Figure 6.19 above). Typical hip-hop grooves have a very tight, machine-like feel (Fig. 6.32)

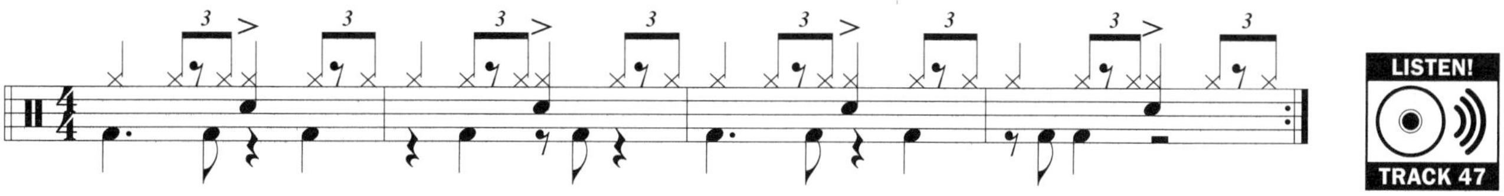

6.32 Hip-hop feel

Hip-hop drummers also utilize a double time feel that is based in the tradition of Gospel music. The up-tempo groove in Figure 6.33 captures the tambourine and hand claps of a joy-filled gospel choir giving praise on a Sunday morning!

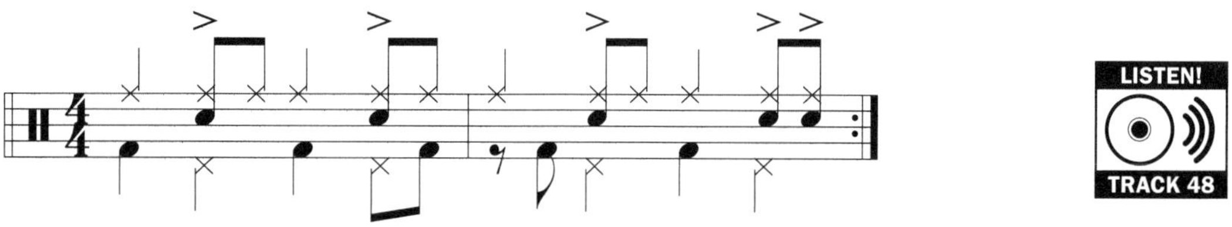

6.33 Gospel feel

WELL KNOWN HIP-HOP AND GOSPEL DRUMMERS

- Ricky Wellman (Chuck Brown and the Soul Searchers)
- Jonathan Moffett (Michael Jackson, Madonna)
- Gerald Hayward (Beyonce, Mary J. Blige)
- Aaron Spears (Usher, Alicia Keyes)

- Ahmir "Questlove" Thompson (The Roots, *Late Night with Jimmy Kimmel*)
- Tony Royster, Jr. (Jay-Z, Joe Jonas)

Fusing Jazz and Rock

Until around 1967, the worlds of jazz and rock were nearly completely separate. In the late '60s, however, two styles known as *jazz fusion* and progressive rock evolved that would start to combine jazz and rock in exciting new ways. Jazz fusion blended jazz harmonies and improvisation with the heavier grooves and electronic instruments of rock and funk. The trend was first popularized by jazz trumpeter Miles Davis in the late 1960s and was solidified in the '70s with groups like Return to Forever, the Mahavishnu Orchestra and Weather Report. Fusion broadened the definition of what might be considered "jazz," and gave jazz musicians the opportunity to showcase their virtuosic "chops" in a more mainstream setting. Top fusion drummers like Steve Smith (Fig. 6.34) are known for their mastery of some of drumming's most complex techniques.

6.34 Legendary fusion drumming veteran Steve Smith

Progressive rock (a.k.a. "prog-rock") evolved as an attempt by rock musicians to elevate their music to new levels of artistic credibility. The mostly British phenomenon suggested that rock was more than just teenagers' music and should be taken seriously as an art form. Prog-rock bands added a variety of new ingredients to the basic rock concept, including classical elements, multiple time signatures, elaborate arrangements and long improvisational jams. Important progressive rock acts include King Crimson, Yes, Genesis, Emerson, Lake & Palmer, and Rush. Figure 6.35 shows a typical progressive rock type beat played in 6/4 time.

LISTEN!
TRACK 49

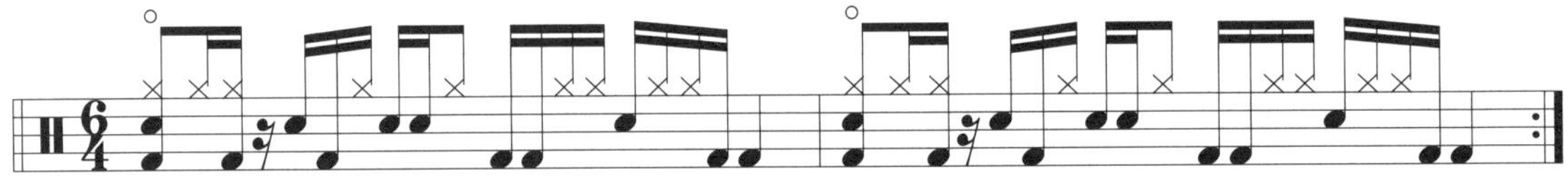
6.35 Progressive rock feel

Today, the blending of jazz with rock, metal, funk and many other styles continues at a furious pace, with new sub-genres emerging all the time. Many of the drummers playing fusion today are incredible virtuosos, whose highly complex, technical approach has created a breathtaking marriage of man and machine.

JAZZ FUSION AND PROGRESSIVE ROCK MASTERS

- Billy Cobham (Mahavishnu Orchestra, Spectrum)
- Bill Bruford (Yes, King Crimson)
- Neil Peart (Rush)
- Terry Bozzio (U.K., Missing Persons)
- Vinnie Colaiuta (Frank Zappa, Allan Holdsworth)
- Dennis Chambers (John McLaughlin, Brecker Brothers)
- Dave Weckl (Michel Camilo, Chick Corea Elektric Band)

WHO'S DOING IT TODAY

- Mike Portnoy (Dream Theater, Adrenaline Mob)
- Thomas Lang (Robert Fripp, Peter Gabriel)
- Mike Mangini (Joe Satriani)

Country

Before it became the high-powered, glitzy style we know today, country music began as folk music, played on acoustic instruments like guitars, banjos, fiddles, and the upright bass. Drums were not initially a part of the country sound, and for many

6.36 Country drumming pioneer Buddy Harman (right), pictured here in the studio with jazz drumming legend Joe Morello. Harman was a left handed drummer—notice the "backward" set up of the drum kit and a traditional grip that's the mirror image of Morello's.

years, the Nashville music industry resisted using them at all.

It was not until the mid-1950s that drums started showing up regularly on country recordings. Nashville drumming legend Buddy Harman (Fig. 6.36) helped to usher in their use with a strong, yet subtle shuffle that was played on the snare drum with one brush and one stick. This so-called *country shuffle* (Fig. 6.37) became Harman's signature, and it can be heard on many of the more than 18,000 sessions he recorded during his career, including Patsy Cline's "I Fall To Pieces," and Tammy Wynette's "Stand By Your Man."

LISTEN! TRACK 50

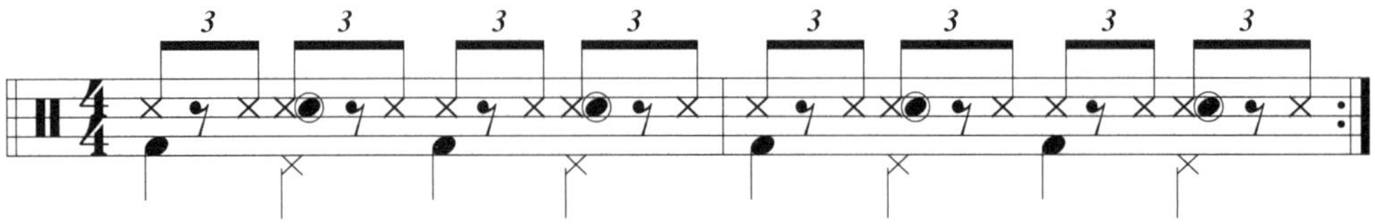

6.37 Country shuffle

Another popular groove found in country music is called the *train beat*, because it imitates the "chugga-chugga" of a train headed down a track (Fig. 6.38). The train beat is played with both hands on the snare, bolstered by a strong "two-feel" in the feet. Although country music today is much closer in sound to other contemporary styles like rock and pop, the shuffle and the train beat remain an important part of the country drummer's vocabulary.

LISTEN! TRACK 51

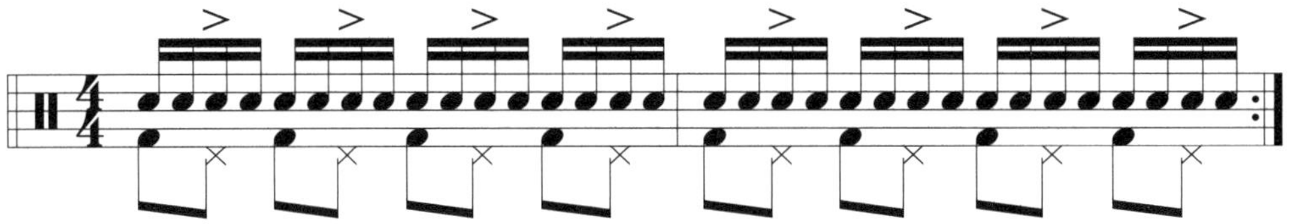

6.38 The "train" beat

COUNTRY MASTERS

- Buddy Harman (Nashville studio legend)
- W.S. Holland (Carl Perkins, Johnny Cash)
- Kenny Buttrey (Bob Dylan, Neil Young)
- Eddie Bayers (Tanya Tucker, Ricky Skaggs)
- Paul Liem (Glen Campbell, Montgomery Gentry)

WHO'S DOING IT TODAY

- Shannon Forrest (Nashville session player)
- Jim Riley (Mark Chesnutt, Rascal Flatts)
- Rich Redmond (Jason Aldean, Trace Adkins)

Latin

6.39 Horacio "El Negro" Hernandez

As you will learn when we explore World Percussion in Chapter 7, traditional Latin American music did not incorporate a drum set. Instead, the rhythms of Cuba, Puerto Rico, Brazil and other Latin countries were played by hand percussionists, who often worked as a section playing tightly interlocking parts. Because of the region's close proximity to the United States, Latin music began to blend with jazz in the early 20th century, particularly in New Orleans, which was a veritable melting pot of cultural integration.

By the 1930s and '40s, Cuban styles like *mambo* and *conga* had meshed with big band and bebop to create a popular new sound called *Latin jazz.* In the early 1960s, it was Brazil's turn, when the *samba* and *bossa nova* became all the rage in the U.S. Along the way, Latin hand percussionists began to integrate more elements of the drum set—like bass drum and floor tom—into their set up. At the same time, jazz drummers began to use the kit to imitate the sound of a Latin percussion section.

Originally from Cuba, Horacio "El Negro" Hernandez (Fig. 6.39) is one of the top Latin drum set players in the world. His breathtaking playing molds Latin hand percussion and traditional drum set techniques in ways that barely seem human. For example, he often maintains a *clave* pattern with his left foot on a cowbell while soloing. Take it from a pro, that's not easy.

It was not long before a tradition of Latin drumset playing was established. In the 1970s and '80s, this tradition would find its way into the mainstream rock and pop sounds of groups like Santana and the Miami Sound Machine. Today, Latin drum set players are some of the best in the world, creating new sounds and techniques to accompany newer styles from *salsa* to *bomba* to *reggaeton.*

Figure 6.40 shows a typical Afro-Cuban mambo played on the drum set. In this

LISTEN! TRACK 52

6.40 Mambo feel

example, the hi-hat plays the *cascara* feel of the timbales; a cross stick on the snare plays a 2:3 *clave pattern*, and the bass drum plays the *tumbao* feel found in the left hand of the piano player.

Figure 6.41 shows a Brazilian bossa nova. The hi-hat part imitates the steady stream of notes from a drum called the *pandeiro*, the snare captures a *tamborim* pattern, and the bass drum plays the part of the *surdo*. (For a complete description and photos of all these Latin instruments, see Chapter 7).

LISTEN! TRACK 53

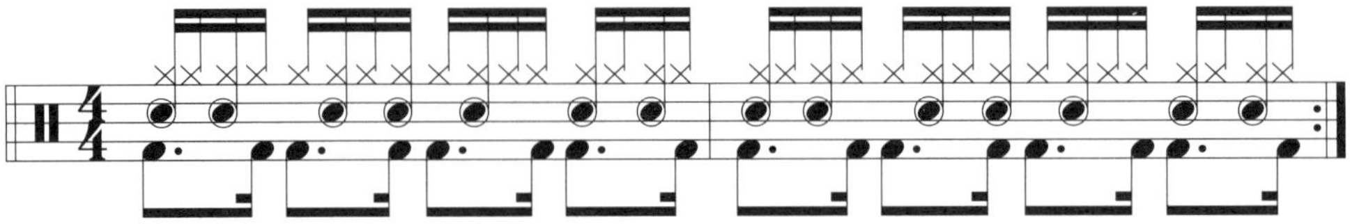

6.41 Bossa nova

LATIN DRUM SET MASTERS

- Walfredo Reyes, Sr. (New York, Afro-Cuban scene)
- Milton Banana (Brazilian samba master)
- Airto Moreira (Return to Forever, Miles Davis)
- Alex Acuna (Weather Report)
- "Sheila E" Escovedo (Prince, Escovedo Family)

WHO'S DOING IT TODAY

- Horacio "El Negro" Hernandez (Santana, Michel Camilo)
- Tiki Pasillas (Mark Anthony, Israel "Cachao" Lopez)
- Jimmy Branley (Gonzalo Rubalcaba, Strunz and Farah)

Reggae

Reggae, one of the most popular styles of music in the world today, hails from Jamaica. Although it has evolved through many forms over the years, reggae has always preserved its unique character through a laid back, danceable groove that you don't find anywhere else.

Like many other styles we've looked at in this chapter, reggae's roots can be found in American rhythm and blues. In the 1960s, R&B was a key element in the evolution of *ska* music, reggae's predecessor. Because their island home is just a few hundred miles from Florida, Jamaicans could tune in to mega-watt stations that broadcast R&B and other American music from Southern cities like Miami and New Orleans. They combined their love of R&B shuffles with traditional Caribbean rhythms like *calypso*, *mento* and *buru* (the ceremonial beat of the Rastafarian religion) and—voila, a new groove was born.

6.42 Lloyd Nibbs is known as the "father of Jamaican drumming."

Drummer Lloyd Nibbs (Fig. 6.42), who played for the influential Jamaican group the Skatalites, was probably one of the first to combine all these rhythms on an American-style drum set. Knibbs and other early ska drummers devised their own

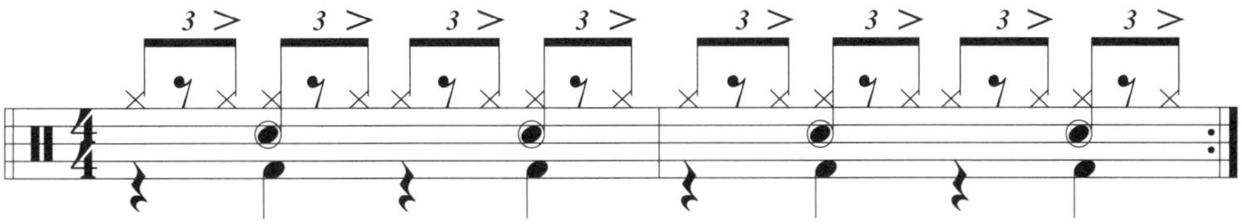

LISTEN! TRACK 54

6.43 The ska shuffle

version of a shuffle (Fig. 6.43), one that differed from the American version in that it accented the cymbal pattern on the offbeats (known as a *skank*), and reversed the bass drum so it played on beats 2 and 4, at the same time as the backbeat.

As ska—a high tempo dance style—morphed into reggae in the late 1960s, the ska shuffle developed a slower, heavier and more grounded feel called the *one-drop* (Fig. 6.44). The name refers to the sparse but bomb-like hits on the bass drum. The offbeat "skank" pattern on the hi-hat became straighter and more pronounced, as

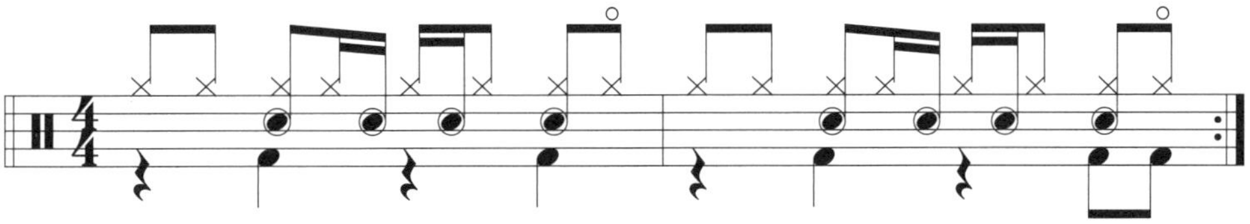

LISTEN! TRACK 55

6.44 The reggae one-drop

did the heavy cross stick/bass drum backbeat. The one-drop was at the core of the reggae sound through its classic '70s period, when artists like Bob Marley, Peter Tosh and Jimmy Cliff became worldwide superstars.

Reggae's influence moved outside Jamaica in the late 1970s, when British bands like the Clash, Police and UB40 made it a core element of their sound. Nearly two decades later, a punk-oriented revival of ska/reggae emerged in Southern California, led by the bands No Doubt and Sublime. Since then, reggae has been blended with rap and hip-hop to produce the "dance hall" style, and with Latin music as part of the modern phenomenon known as *reggaeton*.

SKA AND REGGAE MASTERS

- Lloyd Nibbs (Skatalites, Jamaica session legend)
- Arkland "Drumbago" Parks (Toots and the Maytalls)
- Sly Dunbar (Peter Tosh, Jamaica session legend)
- Carlton "Carly" Barrett (Bob Marley)
- Winston Grennan (Jimmy Cliff)

WHO'S DOING IT TODAY

- Adrian Young (No Doubt, Bow Wow Wow)
- Gil Sharone (English Beat, Jamaican drumming specialist)
- Squidly Cole (Gregory Isaacs, I-Wayne)

7

PERCUSSION AROUND THE WORLD

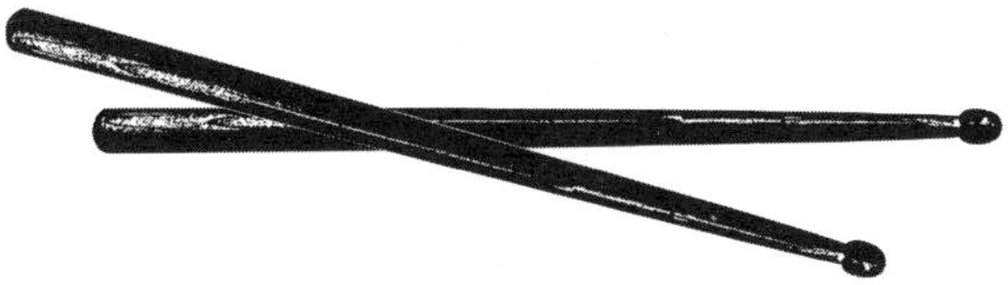

In the introduction to this book, we discussed how percussion instruments are some of the world's oldest. And since it is fairly easy for anyone to pick up an object and use it to create a rhythm, it's probably safe to say that percussion instruments are also the most universal. Virtually every culture around the world uses percussion in some way or another, be it to entertain, dance, fulfill the spirit, celebrate important holidays, or even prepare for war.

In this chapter, we'll take a look at some of the better-known types of world percussion. We'll discover their similarities, learn about their role in various societies, and see how they have influenced our music here in America and the West.

In the last several decades, Western percussionists have come to embrace world percussion with ever-greater enthusiasm and passion. They use these instruments in a traditional way, but are also integrating them more and more into popular musical settings as well.

Once rarely found outside of specialty shops, many of these instruments are now being mass-produced, making them affordable and easy to find at your local music store. This easy access has allowed for the explosion of *drum circles*, and other forums that make it really easy for anyone to participate in playing percussion.

7.1 The world percussion section at the Memphis Drum Shop in Memphis, Tennessee

Percussion: A Common Tradition

Every region of the world has its own tradition of making rhythm, and uses a particular set of tools to create those beats. There are African *djembes*, Japanese *taiko drums*, Brazilian *pandeiros*, Middle Eastern *doumbeks*, and Indian *tablas*, to name just a few. Although these percussion instruments may all look and sound a little different, there are many fundamental similarities among them. Figure 7.1 shows a range of percussion instruments from around the world.

DID YOU KNOW?

... that African drummers could transmit messages very quickly over great distances? Using a series of rhythmic patterns (perhaps similar to Morse code) they could relay a message from drummer to drummer across the landscape at upwards of 100 miles per hour! When the first European explorers visited Africa, they were astounded to find that word of their arrival had spread inland from the coast long before their actual appearance.

First, most drums, whether played with sticks or hands, have a similar sonic palette: a "low" tone, a "high" tone, a "short" tone, and a "long" tone. Some can achieve all these tones on one instrument, while others may require an entire ensemble to do it. On the whole, however, you will be hard pressed to find instruments from any culture that do not incorporate these four basic tonal characteristics.

There are also similarities in the way that cultures around the world use their percussion instruments. For example, we in the Western world (Europe and America) put snare drums, bass drums and cymbals together into a military or orchestral "percussion section." Many cultures around the world organize their percussion in a similar manner. These percussion sections may be led by one individual (kind of like a drum major) who guides the musicians through various phases of a musical piece. Some of these cultures (particularly those based in an African tradition) also add improvisational elements to the percussion section, a person or instrument whose job it is to "solo" over the constant beat of the ensemble.

Probably the easiest way to present world percussion styles and traditions is to organize them by region. And what better place to start than Africa, a continent whose percussive traditions have had tremendous influence the world over.

Africa

The African continent is likely the place where humans first evolved, and it is without a doubt home to some of the earliest percussion as well. When looking at the daily life of Africans, it quickly becomes very clear that rhythm is as much a part of everyday life as eating and sleeping. Traditionally, drums and percussion have been the backdrop to religious ceremonies, holidays and celebrations; they've also been used to transmit messages and stories, and as tools in the making of war.

Although Africa seems like a far away place, most of us have a much closer relationship to its rhythms than we think. As a result of the trans-Atlantic slave trade, African concepts of rhythm and improvisation had a big influence on the development of American pop music styles, ranging from blues and jazz to rock & roll and hip-hop. Many other internationally popular styles, like Brazilian samba, Cuban mambo and Jamaican reggae, can also trace their rhythmic roots to Africa.

7.2 Here in the West, when we talk about an "African drum," we are usually referring to the djembe.

DJEMBE

In West Africa, where it originates, this goblet-shaped hand drum is known as a "healing" drum, and is played at various ceremonies like weddings and funerals. The design of the *djembe* (Fig. 7.2) allows the player to easily pull a variety of different sounds out of it, whether a deep bass tone or a sharp slap. As a result, the djembe is ideal for providing basic rhythmic accompaniment, or creating complex patterns for solos.

DUNUN

Whereas the djembe acts more as a "lead" instrument, the double-headed barrel shaped *dunun* (also sometimes called *djun djun*) functions as a bass drum. It keeps a basic pulse under the djembe's more complex rhythms. The dunun is designed in three different sizes, and can therefore be played by one or a group of drummers.

LOG DRUM (A.K.A. SLIT GONG OR TONGUE DRUM)

The African *log drum* (Fig. 7.3) was one of the main sources of long distance communication in traditional African society. As the name implies, these drums are hollowed out of logs, and have one or more slits (or "tongues") carved into the top. Most drums of this nature have three slits, cut into the shape of an H. Typically, the tongues are various lengths or thicknesses, allowing the drum to produce different pitches. Some ancient versions of log drums were very large (up to nine feet long), and if placed in a strategic spot (e.g. at the top of a hill in a river valley), could be heard many miles away.

TALKING DRUM

In addition to sending messages with drums, Africans also use them to imitate the tone and rhythm of human speech. Witness the "talking drum," known as an *ejin* or a *gangan* (Fig. 7.4). This hourglass-shaped instrument is held under the arm, and squeezed as it is hit with a bent stick. The act of squeezing the drum changes the pitch; the harder the drum is squeezed, the higher the pitch.

UDU

Africans make drums out of various materials, including clay. The *udu* drum (Fig. 7.5), which originated in Nigeria, means "vessel," and resembles a water jug that has two holes. Udu players use their fingers to create rapid-fire strokes against the clay shell; these are matched with a unique low tone, created by striking the hole with the open palm.

GANKOQUI

The *gankoqui* is a metal instrument resembling a cowbell. Unlike its Western counterpart, the gankoqui has two bells (as shown in Fig. 7.6), each of which can provide several different pitches depending upon how the player strikes it.

SHEKERE

Consisting of a dried gourd covered with a net of woven beads, a *shekere* (Fig. 7.7) can produce sound in a number of ways. A player can get a tone by striking the gourd, or create a shaker-like rhythmic feel by "tossing" the shekere between the hands.

AFRICAN XYLOPHONE

Originating in Asia, xylophone-like instruments were introduced into Africa by the 1300s. One popular variety of African xylophone is the *balafon* (Fig. 7.8). Each of the balafon's tuned wooden keys has a gourd placed underneath it that acts as a speaker to help project the sound of the instrument. The resonator gourds can also be treated to produce a buzzing effect.

LISTEN! TRACK 56 to a traditional African percussion section.

MBIRA (A.K.A. KALIMBA OR THUMB PIANO)

This melodic instrument (Fig. 7.9) has been a part of African music for thousands of years. It's made of metal or wood strips that are attached to a resonating box and then plucked with the thumbs or fingertips.

7.3 The African Slit Drum

7.4 Traditionally, the African talking drum was used to dispatch messages between villages, and to pass along various folk tales and prayers. Today, it's mainly used just for music.

7.5 Clay drums like the udu are found in many cultures around the world.

7.6 A skillful player can get a variety of tones out of each of the gankoqui's two bells.

7.7 The African shekere. Gourds are a popular source for making instruments in many cultures around the world.

7.8 The balafon comes from the West African country of Ghana.

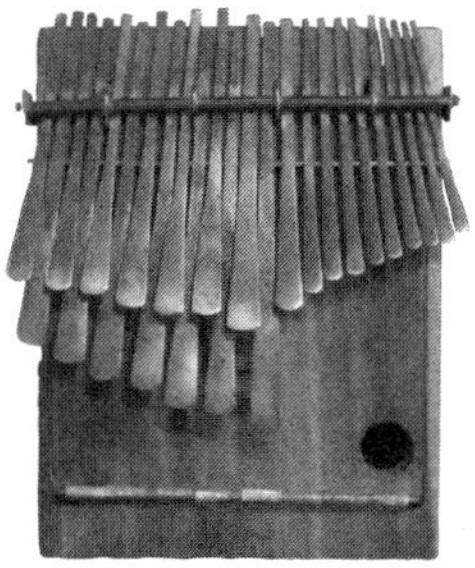

7.9 The Mbira was traditionally played by traveling Griots, African poet/storytellers who would preserve the history of a tribe or village, in entertaining with songs, stories and poems.

Latin and Native American Percussion

When we use the term "Latin" music, we are referring to the sounds that come from "Latin America," an enormous region that includes South America, Central America, Mexico and the Caribbean. These parts of the world were colonized by European countries that spoke Latin-based languages (French, Spanish and Portugese), and therein lies the "Latin" reference.

The trans-Atlantic slave trade that affected the United States from the 17th through the 19th centuries also impacted Latin America (on a much larger scale than in the U.S., in fact). As such, the music that emerged from many Latin American countries is characterized by a mixture of African, European and Native Indian sounds and rhythms.

Today, Latin percussion instruments have become incredibly popular around the world, not only in traditional Latin musical genres, but in Western pop styles like jazz, pop, rock, funk and R&B. Congas, bongos, timbales, shakers, maracas and cowbell are now considered a standard part of every percussionist's arsenal, regardless of what kind of music he or she plays.

DID YOU KNOW?

... that the clave rhythm is used not only in Afro-Cuban music, but in American pop and rock as well? Some well-known songs that incorporate the clave feel include "Magic Carpet Ride" (Steppenwolf), "Faith" (George Michael), and "Desire" (U2).

CUBA

If you've ever watched an episode of *Dancing with the Stars*, or know anything about ballroom dancing, then you've probably heard of *rumba*, *cha-cha*, and *mambo*. All these dance forms, which are also styles of music, emerged from the Caribbean island/nation of Cuba. Despite its relatively small size (about the same as Florida), Cuba has had an incredible impact on the world's music. And despite being ruled under a Communist dictatorship for the last 50 years, it's also managed to produce some of the world's greatest musical virtuosos.

Because of the slave trade, the African emphasis on drums and percussion plays a very important role in the energetic sound and feel of Cuban music. Cuban rhythms are hypnotic, intense, rhythmically complex, and immensely danceable all at the same time.

A typical Afro-Cuban band utilizes drums, shakers and scrapers, all played with tightly interlocking parts that create a seamless rhythmic "machine." The musicians—

7.10 The two-bar clave pattern, around which so much Afro-Cuban music is based. The pattern can be written with either bar first. This version is known as "3:2 Clave," because the bar with three strokes comes first.

both percussionist and non—all base their parts around a repeating pattern known as *clave*, pronounced "cla-vay." Figure 7.10 shows one example of the clave pattern. You can see a number of Latin hand percussion instruments in Figure 7.11.

Claves

The clave pattern is so important that there's an instrument named for it: *claves.* This pair of short, thick wooden dowels play their trademark rhythm throughout a piece. Their bright, clicking tone allows them to be clearly heard above the rest of the ensemble. Although the name "claves," is specific to Latin American cultures, the concept of hitting two sticks together to create rhythm is very old and crosses many cultures. Among the indigenous people of Australia, they are known as *clapsticks*; in

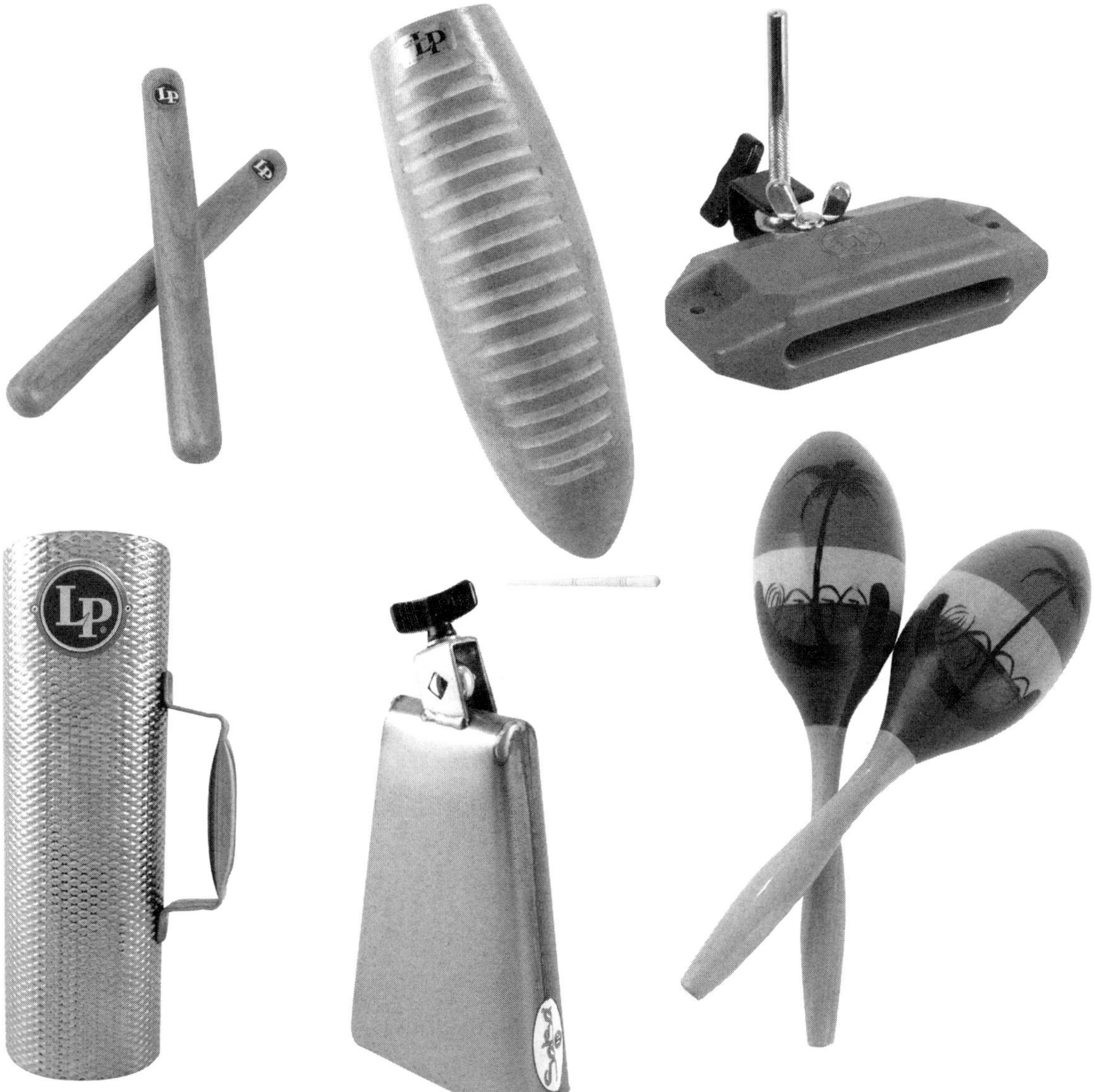

7.11 An assortment of Latin American hand percussion: (top, from left) claves, cuban guiro, jam block; (bottom, from left) merengue guira, "salsa-style" cowbell, maracas

Japan, *shakubyoshi*; in Russia, *treshchotki*.

Cowbells

Afro-Cuban music utilizes *cowbells* of many sizes and shapes, each serving a special purpose and played at a particular part during the song. The most popular types of cowbells include the *cha-cha bell*, the *mambo bell*, the *bongo bell*, and the *songo bell*.

Güiro

The *güiro* is an open-ended, hollow gourd with parallel notches cut into one side. When a stick or metal rod is rubbed along these notches, it produces a hollow, ratchet-like sound.

Maracas

Maracas are hand shakers found in many different cultures across Latin America. Typically played in pairs, traditional maracas are made from a dried gourd or coconut shell filled with seeds or dried beans. Today, they're produced from an endless variety of materials, including leather, wood and plastic. When shaken, maracas

7.12 World-class congueros like Giovanni Hidalgo use various hand and finger strokes to pull an astounding variety of tones and complex rudimental patterns out of the drum.

7.13 An Afro-Cuban percussion “front line.” From left to right: J.C.C.Pérez (congas), Manolito Rodriguez (timbales), Rubén Benítez (bongos).

LISTEN! TRACK 57

to a traditional Afro-Cuban rhythm section. The instruments you're hearing include: claves, conga drums, bongos, timbales, güiro, and maracas.

offer a thick “chucka-chucka” sound that can fill out a variety of rhythms in a very satisfying way.

Congas

The *conga* (Fig. 7.12), a barrel-shaped single-headed drum, is a mainstay in many styles of music throughout the Caribbean. Congas come in three different sizes—the *tumba*, *conga*, and *quinto*—and are often played in sets of two or more drums.

Bongos

Always played as a set of two, *bongos* are smaller and much higher pitched than congas. Played mostly with the fingers, they deliver a sharp, tight tone, which makes them ideal for playing rapid-fire rhythms and solos. The bongo player (known as a *bongocero*) typically holds the drums between the knees, or mounts them on a stand. Figure 7.13 shows bongos along with congas and timbales.

DID YOU KNOW?

... that one of the first “cross-over” uses of maracas in American pop music was by guitarist Bo Diddley in the 1950s? Diddley's band included maraca player Jerome Green, who used the shakers to “fatten up” the sound of many of Diddley's early rock hits.

Timbales

Timbales are a set of two metal drums of different pitches. They look a little like tom-toms, but are tuned much higher. Timbale players (known as a *timbaleros*) keep time primarily on the shells of the drums, playing a clave-based pattern known as *cascara*. Depending on the section of the song, variations on this groove are played on mounted cowbells and woodblock. A timbalero will move to the drumheads when soloing, playing fills, or outlining the transitions between sections of music.

OTHER INFLUENTIAL CARIBBEAN REGIONS

In addition to Cuba, several other Caribbean island nations have also made musical contributions whose importance stretches far beyond their borders.

Puerto Rico

Puerto is famous for originating *salsa*, a hybrid of several Afro-Cuban styles that was established in the 1970s by Puerto Rican immigrants to New York. In more recent times, Puerto Ricans have pioneered the Latin-reggae-rap hybrid known as *reggaeton*. Native styles include *bomba*, which incorporates a short, wide drum of the same name. The bomba drum looks like the Cuban conga, but produces a deeper sound.

The Dominican Republic and Haiti

These two nations on the island of Hispaniola birthed the style known as *merengue*. In the 1970s and '80s, merengue's fast, infectious beat brought it global recognition as a dance craze. A traditional merengue band utilizes two specific percussion instruments: a *güira* (a large, metal version of the güiro) and a *tambora*, a double-headed drum played on one side with a stick and on the other with the palm of the hand.

7.14 Steel drummers can perform alone or in groups, which may include 40 performers or more. Like a vocal choir, a steel band will utilize a variety of different sized drums (from bass to tenor) to cover the full sonic register.

Trinidad and Tobago

In the Southern Caribbean, just off the coast of Venezuela, you'll find the island country of Trinidad and Tobago, home to *calypso* music. The island feel of calypso incorporates a unique percussion instrument called a *steel drum* (also known as a "steel pan"). Originally made from 55-gallon oil containers, one end of the drum is molded into a bowl shape. Then, dents of various shapes and sizes are hammered into its surface. Each surface responds to a note, and when properly tuned, a steel pan can cover about two and a half octaves. Figure 7.14 shows a band of steel drummers.

JAMAICA

Although the island nation of Jamaica is located in the Caribbean Sea, it was a British colony, and is therefore not considered a part of Latin America. That said, like other countries from the region, Jamaica's musical heritage is greatly influenced by the rhythms of Africa (it was also part of the trans-Atlantic slave trade).

One of the musical traditions in Jamaica is *nyabingi* drumming, which is used in the ritual ceremonies of the island's Rastafarian religion. Nyabingi drums are played in a set, and include the *thunder* (bass drum), the *funde* (resembling a small conga), and the *repeater* (the smallest drum, and also the "improvisor"). The rhythms of nyabingi, combined with other Afro-Jamaican styles like *mento* and *burru*, were the basis for reggae, Jamaica's greatest musical export to the world. You can learn more about how reggae grooves are played on the drum set in Chapter 6.

BRAZILIAN SAMBA AND BOSSA NOVA

Like the Caribbean, South America is known for having a tremendously rich musical heritage, as well as a cultural love of dancing. Brazil is the largest country in South America, and is unique in that its national language is Portugese, not Spanish like the rest of the region. Brazil's two most popular musical exports are *samba* and *bossa nova*.

Samba, which originated around 1920, mixes Portuguese, African and native influences. Although it can take on many moods, samba is best known for its role in the annual Brazilian celebration of *carnaval* (carnival). Carnaval is a weeklong party that begins 46 days before Easter—it's a bit similar to the Mardi Gras festivities in New Orleans, but it happens across the whole country and is much bigger.

One of the highlights of carnaval are the huge parades that feature community organizations known as *escolas de samba* (literally "samba schools"). The parades are part of a huge competition, and each school's entry includes literally hundreds of dancers and singers wearing colorful costumes and riding elaborate floats. For musical accompaniment, the samba school incorporates a *baterîa*, a percussion "or-

7.15 The Brazilian baterîa—or "percussion orchestras"—are one of the high points of carnavale.

chestra" that may include upwards of 300 musicians. This is Brazil's version of a marching band, but unlike any you have ever seen or heard before. Here are some of the instruments typically played in a Brazilian baterîa (Fig. 7.15).

Repinique and Surdo

The *repinique* is a high-pitched tom-tom played with a single stick and the hand. Traditionally the leader of the ensemble uses the repinique to solo and direct the other musicians.

The *surdo* fills the role of the bass drum in the baterîa; it maintains a simple, consistent beat that the other players can latch onto. The largest drum in the ensemble, the surdo is worn from a waist belt or shoulder strap and played with a mallet (the free hand dampens the drum). Both drums are shown in Figure 7.16.

7.16 Brazilian drums: the surdo and the repenique

7.17 An assortment of Brazilian hand percussion instruments: agogô bells, afuche-cabasa, caxixi, chocalho, ganza, pandeiro, tamborim, and tri-tone samba whistle.

LISTEN! TRACK 58 to a traditional Brazilian bateria-style rhythm section. The instruments you're hearing include: surdo, tamborim, agogô bells, triangle, and ganzá.

BRAZILIAN HAND PERCUSSION

In addition to drums, Brazilian music uses a variety of hand percussion instruments, shown in Figure 7.17 and described below:

Caixa

The *caixa* is a double-headed snare-type drum that is played with two sticks. It's generally used to produce a variety of interesting cross-rhythms within the baterîa. An interesting fact: unlike the American version of the snare drum, the snare strands on a caixa are mounted across the top head of the drum.

Agogô bells

The *agogô* is a double bell with roots in the West African *gankoqui*, and it has the highest pitch of any of the instruments in the baterîa. Agogô rhythms involve three distinct tones: the sound of each of the two bells, and a clicking noise that is produced when they are squeezed together.

Shakers

The *chocalho* looks a lot like a big, rectangular tambourine, and is the primary type of shaker used in a baterîa (undoubtedly because it is really loud!). Other shakers used in Brazilian music include the *ganzá*, *afuche/cabasa*, and *caxixi.*

Cuíca

The *cuíca* is notable for its unusual construction (it's a single headed drum with a long stick mounted inside the body), and the unusual sound it produces (which resembles the chatter of a high-pitched human voice). The instrument is played by rubbing a damp cloth along the length of the stick, while pressing the head of the drum with a finger or thumb. The closer to the stick the finger is pressed, the higher the pitch of the sound is produced. You might recognize the unique sound of the cuíca from hits like Michael Jackson's "Wanna Be Startin' Somethin'," and Paul Simon's "Me and Julio Down by the Schoolyard."

BOSSA NOVA AND OTHER SOUTH AMERICAN TRADITIONS

In the early 1960s, Brazilian musicians like Juan Carlos Jobim developed a more relaxed version of the Samba called Bossa Nova, which became an international sensation. Bossa Nova uses essentially the same instrumentation as Samba, with an emphasis on the following percussion instruments:

Pandeiro

Although this hand drum (Fig. 7.18) looks very similar to a tambourine, the technique used to play it focuses more on the tone of the instrument than the sound of the jingles (which are actually somewhat muted). Unlike a traditional tambourine, the pandeiro can be tuned, allowing the player a choice of high or low timbre.

7.18 The rocking heel-finger hand motion used to play the pandeiro is very difficult to perfect. A true master not only makes music on this instrument, but spins, twirls and tosses it, bringing to life the festive air of the Carnaval parades. Pictured is percussionist extraordinaire C.G. Ryche.

Tamborim

A small hand drum usually played with a stick or a multi-pronged plastic beater, the *tamborim* plays syncopated accents against the steady rhythmic flow of the pandeiro.

Triangle

Brazilians adopted this instrument from classical music. It offers a lighter, clear tone that fits perfectly with dreamy sound of bossa nova.

One reason the bossa nova became so successful was that its cool sound fit well in a jazz setting. Today, over 50 years later, the bossa nova remains an important part of the jazz musician's repertoire. Jazz drummers found they could replicate the feel of bossa nova by assigning the various percussion parts around the set. The pandeiro and triangle part, for example, can be played on the hi-hat, the surdo pattern on the bass drum, and the tamborim part on the snare. For more on Latin styles of drum set playing, see Chapter 6.

Brazil isn't the only South American country to export percussion instruments and styles to North America. Here are a few other popular examples from the region.

7.19 The multi-purpose cajon, one of the most adaptable of all drums

Peru's Cajon

Originally from Peru, the *cajon* is essentially a hollow wooden box (Fig. 7.19). The player sits astride the cajon while playing it, and gets a sound by hitting the front face (generally thin plywood) with the hands, using many of the same strokes involved with playing a conga drum. In the last several decades, the cajon has become a universal instrument, finding popularity in all styles of music. In the 1970s, for example, it was adopted as part of the standard instrumentation used in Spanish flamenco music. Many drummers have found that the low tone and slap sound produced on the cajon imitate a kick and snare remarkably well. As such, the cajon is now used as a stripped down (and more portable) substitute for the drum set in many styles of music. The cajon can also be played with light sticks or brushes, and can be adapted to work with a bass drum pedal, leaving the hands free to explore other percussive options.

Columbia's Tambora

This double-headed drum, played on one side with a stick and on the other with the palm of the hand, is featured in *cumbia*, a popular style of music and dance that comes from the South American country of Colombia.

7.20 The huehuetl drum of Mexico

MEXICO

Traditional Mexican percussion can be traced back to the ancient civilizations of the Aztecs and the Mayans. Music and dance in these cultures was closely linked to spirituality and nature. The most commonly used percussion instruments were drums, shakers, rattles and shells.

Huehuetl

The *huehuetl* (Fig. 7.20), which means "old," is a family of drums of three different sizes. Each has an upright tubular design that is open at the bottom and stands on three legs

7.21 Mexican dancers in Aztec dress, wearing leg bands made from ayoyote seeds

cut from its base. A huehuetl can be beaten by hand or wood mallet.

Ayoyotes

These are leg bands and bracelets (Fig. 7.21), made out of thick leather strips and covered with the large seeds from the ayoyote plant. In Aztec music and dance, their sound is designed to resemble a rattlesnake or the rain.

Rainstick

This unusual instrument originated in Mexico and South America. The long tubular shaped design is filled with pellets, which sound like rain when they run from one end to the other.

20th Century Mexican Styles

Contemporary Mexican styles are influenced by the large numbers of German and Polish immigrants who came to Mexico in the 1800s. *Banda* music, for example, places the upbeat two-beat feel of polka music into the setting of a marching band. Various brass and woodwinds are featured, along with traditional polka instruments like the accordion.

Banda groups typically include two "marching style" percussionists, one who plays bass drum and mounted cymbal, the other who plays *tarola*: a snare, timbale and cymbal setup that functions in many ways like a drumset. The tarola player may also use various Latin percussion elements like congas, cowbell and woodblock. This same percussion instrumentation is also featured in other contemporary Mexican pop styles like *norteño* and *tejano*.

DID YOU KNOW?

... that percussionists use a variety of special sticks and mallets? You can see a few examples in Figure 7.22.

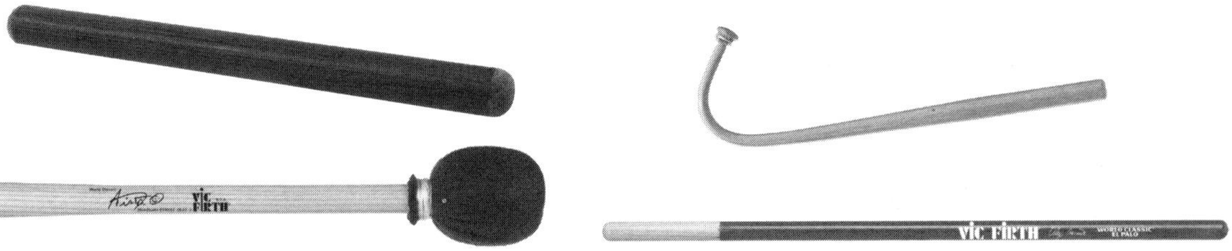

7.22 Tools of the Trade. Clockwise from top left: Cowbell beater, talking drum beater, timbale stick, surdo beater.

NATIVE AMERICAN PERCUSSION

The music of North America's indigenous people is based in singing and chanting, almost always with some kind of percussive accompaniment. Traditionally, both drums and rattles were believed to have great power, and were used for both ceremonial and social purposes. In general the rhythms in Native American music are very straightforward—1/2 notes or 1/4 notes used mostly for timekeeping, but the feel is unusual.

Membrane drums

Native Americans used many kinds of *membrane drums*—hollowed-out logs covered with an animal hide (Fig. 7.23). At intertribal gatherings, drummers often sit around a single large drum, all playing it in unison while chanting. Indians of the Pacific Northwest will do the same, but with a log or a special board.

7.23 Native American dancers and their drums

Water Drum

These are membrane drums, which are made of wood, clay or metal. As per the name, *water drums* all contain some amount of water, which gives them a distinctive sound.

Frame Drum

These shallow, single-headed drums are common in many cultures around the world (other examples include the Irish *bodhran* or the Arabic *tar*). They can be played with the hand or a stick, and are capable of producing a tremendous amount of nuance and sophistication.

Box Drum

Found among the Native peoples of the Pacific Northwest and Alaska, these huge, resonant drums literally look like a wooden box that's open on one end.

Rattles

Native Americans use a variety of rattles and often dance with anklets and bracelets covered with deer hooves.

Asian and Middle Eastern Percussion

As with Latin America, it's impossible to do any more than scratch the surface when looking at the rich and ancient musical heritage of Asia. Music was closely bound with both nature and spiritual beliefs, including Buddhism, and many percussion forms developed in these vibrant cultures.

CHINA

China's civilization extends back 5,000 years, and its music and drumming greatly influenced the other countries around it. The Chinese believed that making instruments from different materials would help express the relationship between nature and spirituality. As a result, traditional Chinese instruments are often categorized by the materials from which they're made. Here are a few examples.

Wood: Temple Blocks

Also known as *muyu* (Fig. 7.24), these pitched wooden blocks were used in Confucian temple ceremonies. Their intricately carved surfaces and bright painted exteriors gave them the nickname "wooden fish" or "dragon mouths."

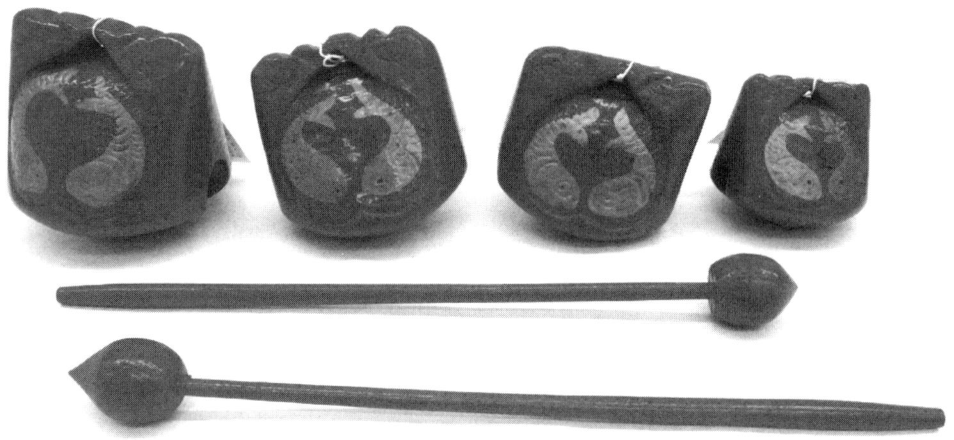

7.24 Muyu, chinese temple blocks

Metal: Gongs

The gong (Fig. 7.25) is the most important metal instrument in Far Eastern cultures. It was considered to be an object of power, and was therefore used in various cultural activities, in the making of war and for transmitting messages. Because of their widespread usage in Chinese culture, there are many different types of gong. The *chau*—also called a tam-tam—is large, flat, and looks like a bullseye (this is the type commonly found in Western symphony orchestras). In classical Chinese opera, gongs that descend or ascend in tone are used to introduce major characters. A *nipple gong* has a central raised bell; as opposed to the chau, it has a distinct pitch, and is used in Chinese temples for worship.

DID YOU KNOW?

... that the epic rock songs "Dream On" (Aerosmith) and "Bohemian Rhapsody" (Queen) both end with the explosive roar of a tam-tam?

Metal: Cymbals

China has a long history of cymbal making, and the unique quality of their cymbals sets them apart from the European or Turkish varieties we've already looked at. The outer rim of a Chinese cymbal (Fig. 7.25) turns up in the reverse direction from the rest of the cymbal. This shape gives it an abrasive, cutting sound that might best be described as "trashy."

The unusual sound and explosive character of Chinese cymbals have made them a favorite with drum set players for more than 100 years. While other early elements of the kit have faded, the "China cymbal" remains an integral part of the drum set, and is used in many styles from jazz to rock.

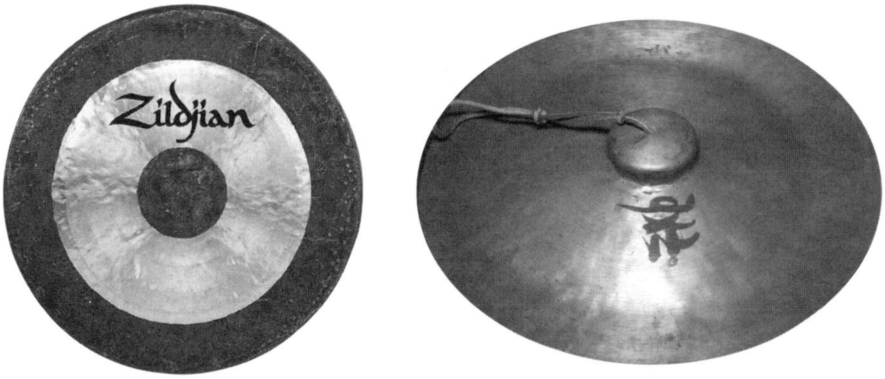

7.25 A gong (left) and a traditional Chinese cymbal (right). The raised bell in the middle of the cymbal was designed as a handle, so they could be played as a set, similar to marching or orchestral cymbals.

Stone: Chimes

Known as *bianqing* (Fig. 7.26), this ancient instrument consists of a set of L-shaped flat stone chimes, each of which has its own tone. The chimes were hung in a wooden frame and struck with a mallet. Along with the bronze bells called bianzhong (Fig. 7.27), the bianqing were an important instrument in China's ritual and court music going back to ancient times.

7.26 Bianqing, Chinese stone chimes

7.27 Bianzhong are a set of tuned brass bells used in the Chinese court music.

This ancient instrument looks like a giant, decorative box made of pottery (Fig. 7.28). It may have been used as a container, but also creates a beautiful tone when struck with a stick.

7.28 The fou drum looks more like a piece of art than a musical instrument.

Pellet Drum

This fun little drum (Fig. 7.29) is used in countries throughout Asia, including China, Japan, Korea, Tibet and Mongolia. Traditionally, it was designed for use in religious rituals, but today, it is generally sold as a children's toy or noisemaker. The "pellets" hang from the body of the drum, which is attached to a vertical rod. When the pole is spun back and forth, it causes the pellets to strike the heads of the drum, creating a wonderful effect.

7.29 Asian pellet drum. Did you have one as a child?

JAPAN

Traditional Japanese performing arts—which include theater styles like Noh and Kabuki, as well as the classical court music called Gagaku—developed slowly over many centuries and have changed very little. In these settings, visuals are extremely important. All movements by the musicians are refined, controlled and beautifully displayed.

Traditional Japanese Percussion

When it comes to making rhythm, the Japanese have a unique and stylized approach. Unlike most styles of music, traditional Japanese rhythms are not something you can easily tap your foot or clap along with. The music is designed to reflect the feeling of nature, and therefore the use of silence and pauses is important. As a result, rhythm does not flow in a way that we are used to. It also means that percussion is used sparsely. Figure 7.30 shows a number of of the percussion instruments more commonly found in traditional Japanese settings including:

Hourglass Drums

These instruments include the hip drum, or *suzumi*, and the *kotsuzumi* (shoulder drum). These instruments make up the backbone of the orchestra that accompanies the Noh and Kabuki theater artforms.

Tsuri-daiko

An ornately painted drum, the *tsuri-daiko* is hung from a stand and played with a padded stick. Along with the *shoko* (a small gong) and the *shakubyoshi* (clappers made from a pair of flat wooden sticks), the tsuri-daiko makes up the percussion section in the orchestra of the traditional court.

Shime Daiko

This medium-sized two-headed drum is used widely as an accompaniment in all types of traditional music.

Odaiko

A larger barrel-shaped drum, the Odaiko is typically mounted on a stand. It's often used in shrine music.

7.30 Gagaku (defined as "elegant music") is a type of Japanese classical music that has been performed at the Imperial Court in Kyoto for several centuries. The percussionists in the front row are playing (from L-R), the shoko, the tsuri-daiko and the suzumi hourglass drum.

Mokugyo

The mokugyo is a woodblock similar to a Chinese temple block.

Taiko Ensemble Drumming

In Japanese, the word *taiko* literally means "drum." When we talk about taiko drums today (in Japanese, *kumi-daiko*), we are generally referring to a category of larger, barrel shaped instruments that have their roots in feudal Japan. Like military drums in other cultures, these taiko were used to motivate troops, set a marching pace, and call out orders. Taiko also refers to a popular style of ensemble drumming that was established after World War II. For the first time, drummers began to play several taiko drums at once, which brought a new flair to the instrument. Taiko drumming groups are known for their precision, discipline, power and virtuosity. The most popular of these, like Kodo, tour all over the world today.

The rhythms of taiko ensembles (Fig. 7.31), who play with sticks called *bachi*, are based on the simple patterns of shrine drumming. This allows for nearly any person with an interest in taiko drumming to play along. As a result, taiko drumming has become popular in many countries outside of Japan.

7.31 A taiko drumming ensemble performing in Japan. The giant drum in the back has a diameter of nearly 8 feet, and is just about as long. It weighs about 3 tons, and was carved out of a single piece of wood from a 1200-year-old tree.

KOREA

The Korean peninsula has a strong tradition of energetic and visually exciting drumming. Many Korean drumming styles incorporate movement, meaning that the drummer not only accompanies dancers and other performers, but is often part of the dance as well.

P'ungmul (a.k.a. Nongak)

P'ungmul (Fig. 7.32) is a Korean folk tradition that comes from village harvest festivals, and includes joyful drumming, dancing, and singing. The principal rhythm maker in p'ungmul is the *changgo*, a double-headed hourglass drum, worn by the

7.32 The high energy Korean dance style of P'ungmul

dancer/drummer around the waist. Other dancers play small hand held drums called *sogo*, sometimes while twirling their heads so as to produce long spirals with white ribbons attached to the crown of their hats.

Samul nori

Samul nori is a more contemporary Korean tradition that evolved out of p'ungmul. It literally means "to play four objects"—the four objects being percussion instruments (two gongs and two drums of different sizes). Samul nori is played sitting down, but still manages to a be very physical and exciting style to watch.

Samgo-Mu is a traditional Korean drum dance, which originally began as a Buddhist ritual. Typically, it is danced/played in a group, with each performer standing before one or more drums hung in a frame. Like ice skaters or synchronized swimmers, the samgo-mu drummer/dancers work their way through elaborate routines, often flying between the drums with acrobatic grace (Fig. 7.33). These drummers can create many different sounds beyond hitting the drums themselves. These include: clicking the sticks together, striking the frame the drum is hung in, and scraping the stick along the edge of the drum to get a rasping sound.

7.33 Performers of samgo-mu dance while drumming, matching acrobatic movements in perfect precision.

7.34 The beautiful instruments of a Javanese gamelan orchestra

INDONESIA

The sound of Indonesian music is epitomized by the *gamelan orchestra*, which consists primarily of percussion instruments made from metal and wood. Interestingly, the instruments in a gamelan (Fig. 7.34) are a distinct entity; they are built and tuned to stay together as a set, and are generally not interchangeable with instruments of other orchestras.

The overriding sound in a gamelan orchestra is metallic. Metal xylophone-type instruments called the *saron* and the *slenthem* form the backbone of the ensemble, playing the main melodies. Other instruments in the gamelan include two different kinds of tuned gongs, a gong-like set of metal bowls called *boning*, and wooden drums known as *kendang*.

INDIA

Indian drumming first made an impact on the West in the late 1960s, thanks in large part to the Beatles, who added Indian instruments and spiritual elements into their music.

Indian music in general is very focused on rhythm, and the system for dividing up and counting rhythmic patterns—known as *tala*—is much more complex than our concept of meter. Drummers will often "sing along" with the parts they're playing using a series of mnemonic syllables, known as *bol*. Each syllable represents a different kind of stroke, and there are at least 20-30 altogether (two examples are "Ga" and "Tin"). Singing these syllables helps the drummer to get through the long and complex combinations of the tala.

Tablas

India has many different drums and drumming traditions. The most well known to us in the West are the *tablas*, which are one of the primary instruments in Hindustani classical music. Tablas (Fig. 7.35) are typically played as a set; the smaller drum

7.35 A set of Indian tabla drums, made up of the dayan (L) and the bayan (R). The dark circles on the head affect the tone. They're made from a paste derived from cooked rice!

(or *dayan*) is made from a piece of hollowed out wood, and can be tuned to suit the player's needs. The larger, bowl-shaped *bayan* can be made of clay, metal, or wood, and has a deeper tone that's similar to that of a kettledrum. The tabla player uses combinations of fingers and palms to create a wide variety of different sounds, reflected in the counting system of bol as described above.

DID YOU KNOW?

... that I once attended an Indian music concert that had only a few songs on the program, but lasted for over four hours? Take that, Bruce Springsteen!

Carnatic Music

The classical music of South India is known as *carnatic*. Percussion instruments used to accompany carnatic music include the *mridangam* (a double-headed hand drum), the *kanjira* (a frame drum that sometimes has jingles) and the *ghatam* (a clay pot-type instrument similar to the African udu).

Kathak Dance

In our discussion of various cultures in this chapter, we've mentioned how the line between percussionist and dancer can sometimes become blurred. In the classical Northern Indian dance form known as Kathak, this is definitely the case. Part of the Kathak dance performs a series of complex compositions with the feet—stamping out rhythms that are accentuated with the jangle of ankle bracelets. These rhythms are sung using bol syllables as described above, and mimicked by the tabla player in the orchestra.

ARABIC

Arabic music is typically played across a large region that includes the Middle East, North Africa, and parts of Eastern Europe. Many of the instruments used in Arabic music date back thousands of years to ancient Mesopotamian and Egyptian cultures. In general, Arabic cultures place a very strong emphasis on rhythm (as opposed to harmony), and percussion is used extensively.

The three instruments shown in Figure 7.36 are found in both popular and classical Middle-Eastern music; they are generally played together in an ensemble.

7.36 Arabic percussion instruments. Clockwise from top: a tar frame drum, a riqq tambourine, and three different doumbek hand drums.

Doumbek

The *doumbek* (which is also sometimes called a *darbuka*) is one of a family of hand drums that are shaped like a goblet. It can be made of clay, metal, or wood, and has a very thin, responsive drumhead that helps it produce a distinctively crisp, resonant sound. The doumbek is played with the fingers and fingertips, using a much lighter touch than with other hand drums like the African djembe or the Cuban conga.

Tar

A *tar* is an ancient frame drum that comes from North Africa and the Middle East. The tar is held in one hand and played with the other (although both hands contribute to the overall groove). It has an open tone, and can be used to accompany other instruments or in a tar ensemble.

Riqq

A *riqq* is a type of tambourine (also considered a frame drum) and plays an important role in Arabic folk and classical music. Traditionally, the riqq is composed of a wooden frame, jingles, and a thin, translucent head made of fish or goat skin.

Polynesia

Polynesia is a region located the South Pacific that includes the islands archipelagos of Hawaii, Samoa, Tonga, Tahiti and New Zealand. Each of these cultures has its own distinctive musical heritage, but they all come from a similar origin. For the purposes of this book, we'll focus mostly on Hawaii.

HAWAII

Hawaii's biggest cultural contribution to the world is a dance form known as *hula*. Although we often associate hula with the ukelele and Hawaiian steel guitar, these attributes were only added after the arrival of Westerners to Hawaii in the late 1700s. Ancient hula, called *kahiko*, was performed before Western encounters with Hawaiians. Unlike modern hula, it is accompanied only by chanting and various percussion instruments.

7.37 The Hawaiian pahu drum

Pahu Drum

The most common drum used in ancient Hawaii is called a *pahu*. Some of these drums are as small as coconut shells, others are ornately carved from large tree trunks (Fig. 7.37).

7.38 Various Hawaiian percussion instruments: Clockwise from top: ipu, pu'ili, kala'au, ili'ili and uli'uli

Ipu

The ipu (Fig. 7.38) is a hollowed gourd that is beaten with the hands and on the ground by the dancers and chanters.

Hand Percussion Played by Dancers

As in other cultures, certain Hawaiian percussion instruments are played by the dancers themselves (Fig. 7.38). These include *uli'uli* (a feathered gourd with rattles that are shaken), *pu'ili* (bamboo slats used to slap against each other or the body), kala'au (rhythm sticks) and *ili'ili* (small flat rocks that are struck together).

Other islands in the South Pacific have their own percussion traditions. Here are two examples.

To'ere

A *to'ere* (Fig. 7.39) is a log drum from Tahiti, which is used to play the very upbeats rhythms in Tahitian dancing.

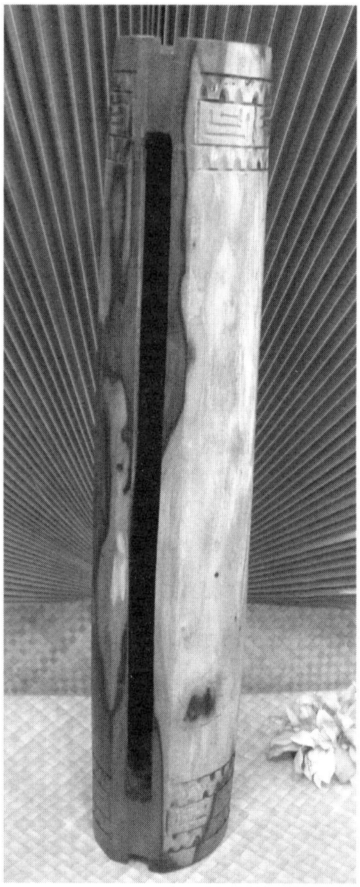

7.39 A to'ere log drum from Tahiti

Body Percussion

The Maori people of New Zealand do a dance called *kapa haka* that uses the body itself as a percussion instrument (Fig 7.40). The aggressive dance style includes slapping of the chest and thighs, foot stamping, and facial grimace in an attempt to appear as menacing as possible.

7.40 The Maori kapa haka dance style utilizes "body percussion."

Moving On

The most exciting thing about "world" percussion is that it allows drummers to experience different cultures through both the sounds of their drums and the styles of their drumming. Exploring the drumming world is a really fun way to learn and practice new techniques.

8

8

ELECTRONIC PERCUSSION

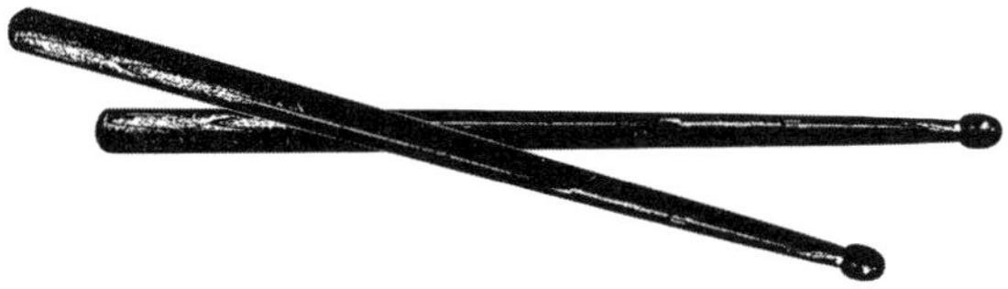

Most historians agree that the existence of percussion predates recorded civilization. And yet, technology has helped percussion instruments evolve into some of the most sophisticated and diverse musical tools of the modern era. Today, you'll find machines that can play drum parts with a precision beyond human ability, software that can mimic the performance of a live player, and pads and triggers that put thousands of sounds at the disposal of drummers and hand percussionists. These innovations are not only available to professional performers. Thanks to computers and even musical video games, every percussionist today has more ways to learn and practice their instrument than ever before.

Rhythm Machines, Synths, and Electronic Music

Electronic percussion may be modern, but it's not new. Inventors created hand operated or clock-like percussion machines centuries ago. But it was the wider availability of elctricity in the later 19th century that paved the way for the first devices we might now call "drum machines." As with many industries, if a machine could replace a musician, money would be saved. During the silent film era, movie theatres installed "photoplay" machines, mechanical orchestras "controlled" by a keyboardist who pulled various knobs and levers that operated various percussion instruments to accompany the action onscreen.

Modern electronic drums trace their roots to the 1930s and a device called the *Rhythmicon* (Figure 8.1), which was able to create complex rhythms beyond the scope of what a musician could play. In 1959, Wurlitzer designed the first commercial rhythm machines, which created backing rhythms for organ players.

8.1 The Rhythmicon, the world's first "drum machine"

In the 1960s, a new type of instrument emerged: the synthesizer. These purely electronic instruments didn't have strings, reeds or drum heads, but used electrical signals to make sounds. Synthesizers were also outfitted with a series of controls that could be used to alter the electronic sounds they produced in a nearly infinite number of ways.

Some of the first synthesizers used by ordinary musicians were invented by an electrical engineer named Robert Moog, who created a now legendary line of products that bear his name. The Moog synthesizer (Figure 8.2) was influential in developing a new genre of music called "electronic," which explored the musical potential of the instrument. Around the same time, companies started to build portable rhythm machines that could play back preset patterns. One of the most popular was called the Rhythm Ace (Fig. 8.3). The company that built the Rhythm Ace would evolve into the Roland Corporation, an important maker of electronic percussion.

In the mid 1970s, the pioneering German band Kraftwerk explored the potential of synthesizers with their landmark album *Autobahn*. Synthesizers also spread rapidly into more traditional musical genres like pop and rock (particularly progressive rock), and influenced the hybrid sounds of jazz-fusion.

DID YOU KNOW?

... that the Moog synthesizer had its first commercial breakthrough in 1968 with the Wendy Carlos recording *Switched-On Bach*? The album imitated the sounds of an orchestra and became one of the highest-selling classical music recordings of its era. Carlos also used synthesizers to create the scores of several legendary films, including 2001: A Space Odyssey, A Clockwork Orange, and The Shining.

8.2 A pair of Moog synthesizers

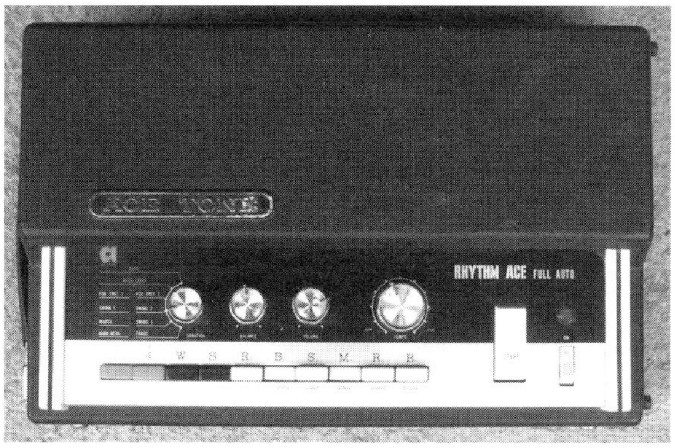

8.3 The Rhythm Ace, an early drum machine

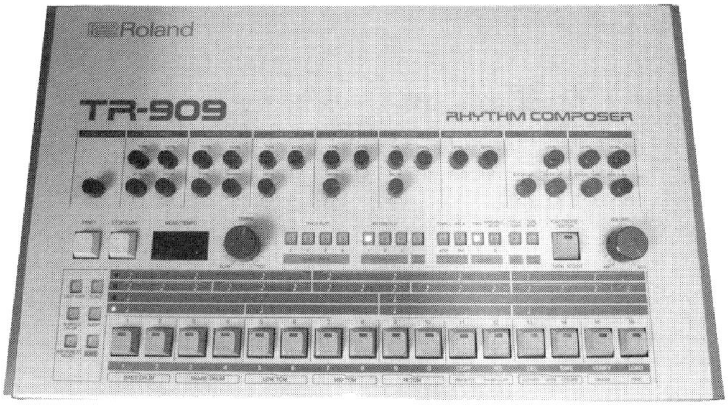

8.4 The Roland TR-909 shows the evolution in pattern and sound control.

The Rise of the Drum Machine

In the 1970s, a dance craze called *disco* emerged. In order to create the steady beat favored on the dance floor, people started to record to a metronome, or click track. The idea was to "tighten up" the groove and make the final production sound more perfect. Drum machines, notably the Roland TR-808 and TR-909 (Fig. 8.4), began to become popular because they were able to play at an exact tempo, and, unlike human drummers, never got bored playing the same beat over and over!

By the early '80s, computer-based digital technology began to replace purely electronic analog instruments. These digital devices sounded much more realistic and had many more features. Drum machines stopped being experimental instruments used in one or two genres and became a force in all of popular music. People started using devices called *sequencers* to record drum and instrument sounds. Sequencers, which are still used today, trigger sounds in electronic instruments; they don't actually capture any audio. Because of this, a drum's tone, note placement, and even the tempo can be corrected and changed after the fact—as long as the music is recorded onto a preset grid.

As a result, click tracks became a mandatory part of many recording sessions, and drum machines began to be used more frequently to actually replace human beings as timekeepers. In emerging styles like hip-hop, it became standard to create all rhythm (a.k.a. "beats") using drum machines, as well as prerecorded loops and samples. For the first time, people were making radio-ready dance music without having to go into a studio to record a full band.

Sometimes the decision to take the drummer out of the equation was financial, as opposed to creative. With a drum machine, an artist did not need to pay for a large studio space and countless microphones to create a solid, well-recorded groove. Often, non-drummers (typically keyboardists) became specialists in programming drum parts.

For drummers of the 1980s, negotiating this new world of digital technology presented a whole new set of skills and challenges. Being "under the microscope" in a recording studio was stressful enough, but now, rather than relying on his or her internal sense of rhythm, a drummer was expected to lock in with the unrelenting perfection of a click track.

8.5 Simmons was one of the first companies to produce electronic drum sets in the late 1970s.

In previous eras, slight ebbs and flows in the time feel—brought on by emotional highs and lows in the music—were often considered an asset. A gradual increase in tempo, for example, could add excitement; maybe even give the song a certain "magic" quality that would make it a hit.

In the world of the click track, however, time fluctuations were not only considered impractical, they were frowned upon. If a drummer sped up or slowed down even slightly, it could cause him or her to lose the click, meaning that the band would have to stop and begin the take over again. For many drummers, trying to play catch-up in this environment was difficult and frustrating.

If drummers were not being completely replaced by machines, they often had to play their parts on electronic drum pads like those made by the Simmons company (Figure 8.5). Although these pads were positioned in much the same way as a typical drum set, they were crude and unresponsive compared to real drum heads, and they allowed for very little player expression.

Rather than fight the trend, many drummers adapted by getting accustomed to working with click tracks, often using portable drum machines. These devices were designed as practice tools, and for many drummers today, the click track is an indispensable part of every practice session. Like the old-fashioned metronome that came before it, a click will help you develop a stronger sense of time. And that's important, because in many settings today—whether in the studio, or playing live with samples, loops or backing tracks—playing along with a click track is simply "part of the gig."

The Nuts and Bolts of Electronic Percussion

Since digital technology and electronic instruments are so much a part of music today, here are some basic terms that you might encounter when negotiating the world of electronic percussion.

DRUM MACHINES

A drum machine is a mechanical device or computer software that can be programmed to create rhythms (Figure 8.6). These days, drum machines come in many shapes and sizes. They can be mounted into a rack, carried as a portable device, or built directly into audio production software like Apple's GarageBand. There are even drum machine apps available for smart phones (these are great for practicing).

8.6 The Alesis SR-16 drum machine was the industry standard in the 1990s.

SEQUENCERS AND DIGITAL AUDIO WORKSTATIONS (DAW)

A digital audio workstation (DAW) is a device that can play and record both audio and MIDI. Today, most DAWs are built around computers. Popular software applications include Avid ProTools, Roland|Cakewalk SONAR, Steinberg Cubase, and Apple Logic, but you can also find these features built into keyboards, standalone recorders, and even mobile apps.

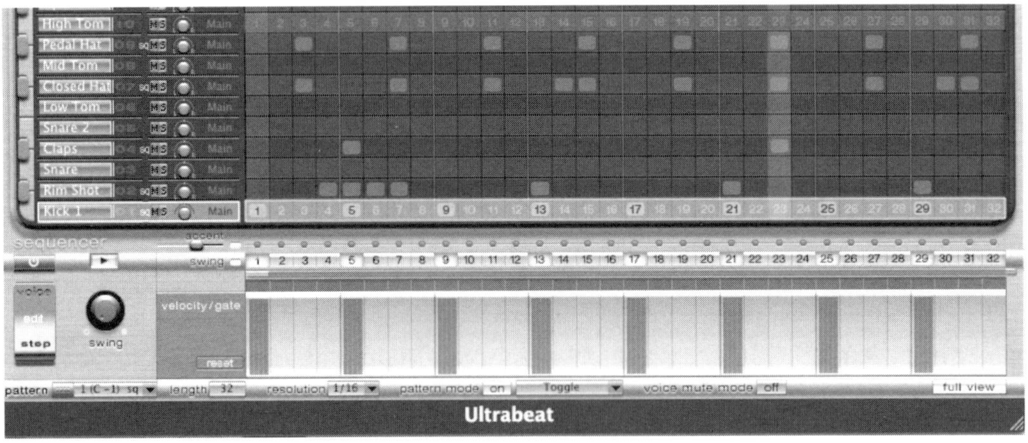

8.7 In grid-style drum machine programming, each square in the center of the image triggers a drum sound.

PROGRAMMING

Programming has two meanings related to drum machines and electronic drum sounds. First: to create and store a percussion part (or a series of them) on a drum machine or similar device, as shown in Figure 8.7. As you can see, the pattern is laid out in a grid, with various electronic drum sounds active or inactive at different times in the pattern.

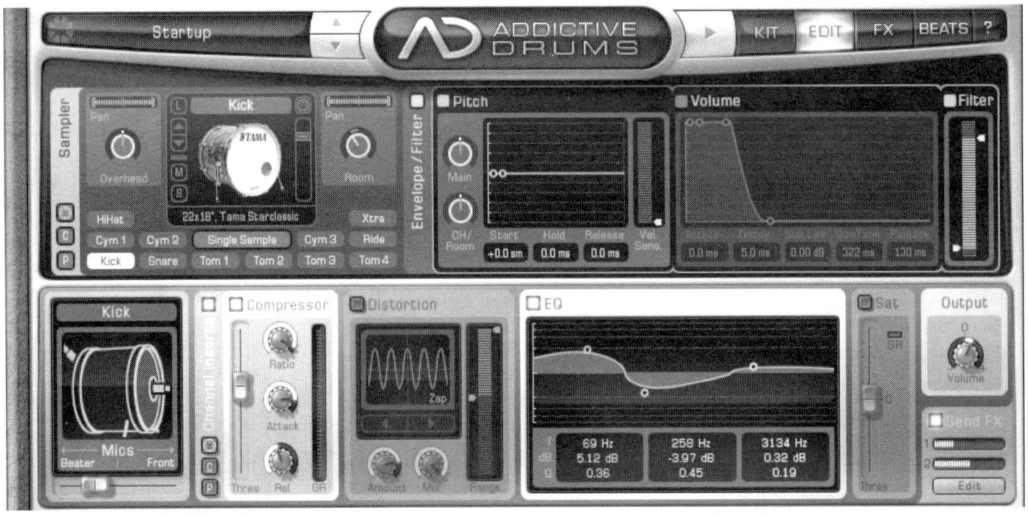

8.8 Addictive Drums' editor window shows settings for the kick drum, including pitch, volume and more.

The second definition of programming is to alter the sounds produced by the drum machine that's playing the pattern. For example, changing the pitch or decay of an electronic snare drum. This second kind of programming also applies to electronic drum kits and any other electronic instrument. Figure 8.8 shows how this is done on a software program called Addictive Drums, which lets users choose the type of drum for each part of the kit as well as set up various sonic characteristics.

CONTROLLERS AND TRIGGERING

One of the biggest differences between electronic and acoustic instruments is the way they separate the act of playing and the sound the instrument makes. With a snare drum, you hit the head and it vibrates. With an electronic drum, you hit the "head" and it sends a signal to another device, which then produces the sound. The head is just a *controller*, and the receiving device, sometimes known as a *slave*, could produce any number of sounds from that signal. With drums, the controller is often called a *trigger*.

Using a digital language known as MIDI, a controller can be connected to a wide variety of slaved sound modules or other devices. Because they're completely separate, the sound module doesn't care what form the controller takes, as long as it sends the right MIDI signal. Therefore, keyboard controllers, pads, and even wind and guitar controllers can be used to play electronic percussion. At the same time, drum pads can be used to trigger any sound—not just percussion but also strings, brass, loops—anything the sound module has in its memory banks!

SAMPLING

Sampling is a digital technology in which short audio recordings (or *samples*) are stored so that they can be triggered by a controller. A sample can contain any kind of sound: a single note played on an instrument like piano, flute, violin or drum, a groove played on a drum set, a section of music played by a whole band, people speaking, sound effects and more. A *sampler* is a device used to store, organize, and play back these sounds. Typically, each sample is assigned to a key on a keyboard (or a pad on a drum machine). When you press that key (or hit that pad), the sampler plays the pre-assigned recording. Modern drum machines rely heavily on samples, as does software such as the Addictive Drum program we looked at in Figure 8.8.

In the 1980s, the first hip-hop DJs started sampling drum breaks from existing songs (like James Brown's "The Funky Drummer") and looping them or rearranging the beats to create a new groove altogether. Then, they would lay other samples or instruments over these loops to build a completely new song. Today, many devices,

DID YOU KNOW?

... that the single "Amen, Brother" released in 1969 by the soul group the Winstons contains a four-bar drum break that is one of the most sampled grooves of all time? The "Amen Break," as it has come to be known, lasts only six seconds, but it became one of the staples used for creating "breakbeats," a process by which DJs heavily edit drum breaks by slicing up the beats digitally and rearranging them to form new variations.

from drum machines to programs like GarageBand, come with their own built-in collections of such loops. You can also purchase independent libraries of samples that provide you with thousands of other sound options to choose from.

Loops

A loop is a recorded sound that repeats. It can be any sound, but usually when people talk about loops, they're talking about short musical passages, one- or two-measure drum beats, bass lines or riffs. In musical terms, a loop would be a measure with a repeat sign on each end. There's a whole industry for loop-based music, and producers can use loops of different types to "construct" tracks, which can form part or all of a song or arrangement. This type of production is especially popular in dance music, hip-hop, R&B and electronica, but it's also an element of more traditional genres. Rock songwriters, for example, might use a pre-recorded loop for a drum part, and then record guitar, bass and vocals over it.

Figure 8.9 shows the same drum part depicted in three different ways: in standard musical notation; as a MIDI drum loop used in a sequencer, and as an audio drum loop.

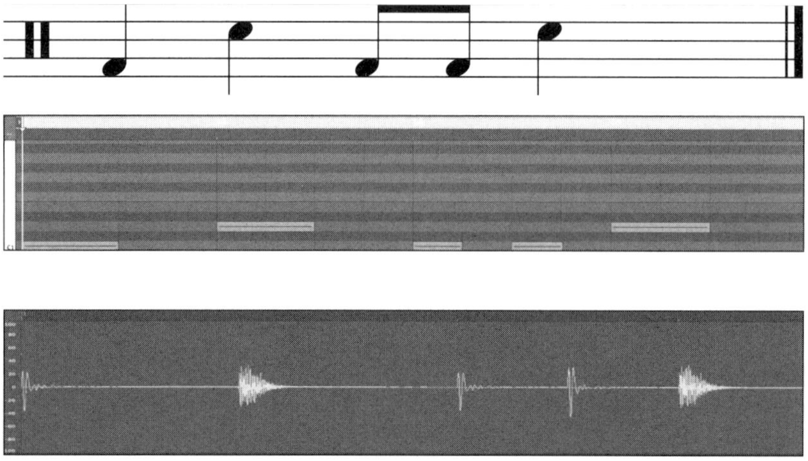

8.9 Here's a simple kick and snare pattern as it appears in (from top) written notation, a MIDI sequencer, and as an audio waveform in a DAW.

How Do Drummers Fit Into the Digital Music World?

Today, drum machines, click tracks, sampling and other forms of programming play an important role in the creation of music, particularly in pop-oriented styles like rock, hip-hop and modern country. DAWs allow the engineer to alter a drummer's recorded parts in any number of ways, making them sound and feel as "perfect" as something a drum machine might play. With this being the case, you might be asking yourself the following question: If rhythms can be manufactured, altered and "perfected" using digital technology, what's the point of learning to play an instrument at all? To rephrase the question, is there still a place for drummers and percussionists in today's musical world? The answer is a resounding "Yes!"

Remember, the ability to program a machine doesn't automatically make someone a musician; nor does it provide an understanding of how music fits together, or how to make a song appealing to a listener. Understanding musical fundamentals and knowing how to use them creatively is still important! Some of the top music producers of the last 30 years (among them Narada Michael Walden, Sly Dunbar, and Questlove from the Roots) started as drummers, and there's little doubt that their success in the production field comes as a result of having mastered their instrument first.

And for those who fear that percussionists may be replaced for good with all this, remember that technology is just a tool. If we think of it as something that can be added to what we already do as musicians, technology can open up vast new frontiers that will only help us to do our jobs more effectively.

LISTEN! TRACK 57 to a traditional Afro-Cuban rhythm section. The instruments you're hearing include: claves, conga drums, bongos, timbales, guiro, and maracas.

Controllers

Electronic drums have opened up a new world of sounds from drummers. Yes, you can use them to "play" traditional percusison and drum set instruments, but you can also use them to do things drummers never even dreamed about in years past. Want your snare drum to sound like a timpani—or an explosion? You can now do that with the push of a button. And you don't have to program these sounds either; you can use controllers designed just for drummers.

ACOUSTIC DRUM TRIGGERS

Triggers are devices that mount onto acoustic drums (typically the rim as shown in Figure 8.10). When the drum is struck, the trigger translates the resulting vibration into an electric signal, which is converted to a digital signal by a device known as the "brain," which may or may not generate sounds of its own. Drummers typically use triggers for two purposes: to augment the natural sound of the drum with the sample that is being triggered, or to replace it altogether.

8.10 The acoustic trigger clamped onto the rim of this drum generates an electronic signal when the drum is struck.

ELECTRONIC DRUM SETS

When it comes to electronic drum sets, technology has advanced significantly since the first generation prototypes of the late 1970s. More than ever, today's electronic sets (Figure 8.11) look and feel like the real thing, with pedals, drums and cymbals all positioned the way they would be on an acoustic setup. The pads on these kits are incredibly sensitive, allowing for greater musical expression on the part of the player, and they produce almost no noise when hit, giving drummers the added benefit of being able to practice quietly, using headphones to hear all the generated sounds.

The most popular electronic drum sets on the market today include the Yamaha DTX series and Roland V-Drums. Both of these are capable of simulating a variety of acoustic kits, from jazz to metal, and within each kit setting, it's possible to select the tuning, size and material of the drums and cymbals to be used. Effects like muffling, microphone position and ambient acoustic can also be simulated.

8.11 A modern electronic drum set. The model on the left is the "brain."

Unlike the generic rubber pads used in earlier eras, today's electronic sets feature unique drum, cymbal and hi-hat pads that are composed of highly sensitive materials like mesh or textured silicone. Each pad is equipped with multiple triggers to mimic the subtler functions of the instrument being imitated. For example, the snare and tom pads have impact zones for both the head and the rim, allowing for strokes, rim shots and more exotic sounds like shell tapping. Cymbal pads include separate zones on the edge, bow and bell, and are even designed for a player to create a "choke" type sound. Another major benefit of modern electronic sets is that menus and various settings can also be accessed or adjusted by tapping various pad surfaces with a drumstick. This gives drummers the flexibility to make these changes without having to stop playing.

MIDI CONTROLLERS FOR PERCUSSIONISTS

The drum set is only one platform for triggering electronic drums with realistic performance techniques. Drummers can find a huge array of pads in many shapes and sizes, which can be played with sticks, hands, or even fingers. Many of the devices listed below can be used to trigger both internal sounds or exteral sound modules via MIDI.

Multi-pad Controllers

The Alternative Mode company specializes in designing controllers for drummers and percussionists. Their products include the MalletKat (Figure 8.12), in which the pads are arranged like the bars on a vibraphone or marimba), the PanKat (set up like a steel drum) and the TrapKat (which includes 24 programmable pads aligned in a very accessible layout). Roland makes a similar product called the Octopad (Figure 8.13). All of these products can be used with trigger pedals, so the feet can get into the action as well.

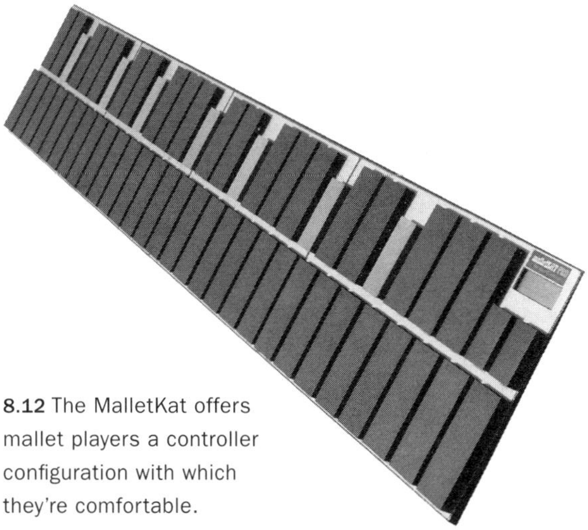

8.12 The MalletKat offers mallet players a controller configuration with which they're comfortable.

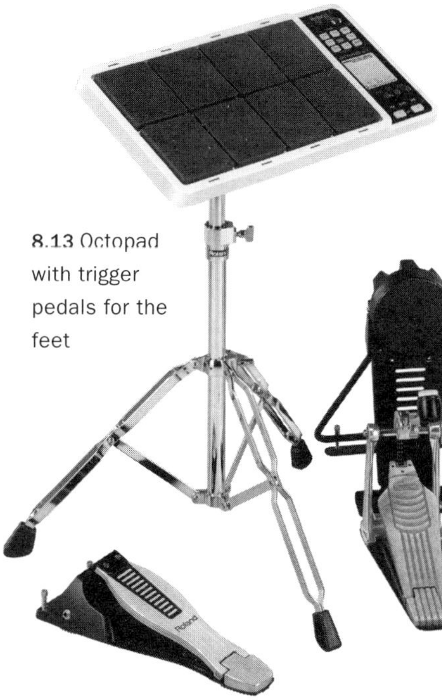

8.13 Octopad with trigger pedals for the feet

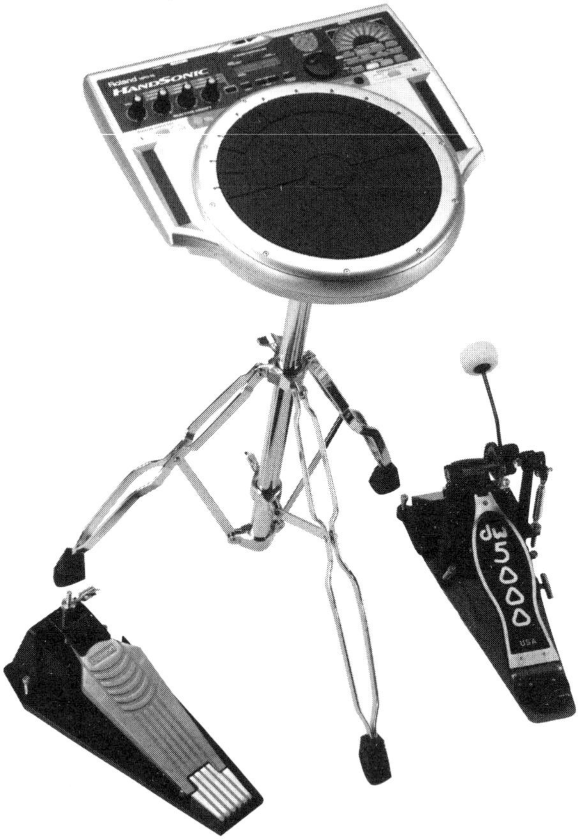

8.14 The HandSonic controller, designed for conga players and other hand percussionists.

Hand Percussion

Roland's HandSonic line (Figure 8.14) is an electronic hand percussion multi-pad that allows conga players and other hand percussionists to play up to 600 realistic acoustic and electronic percussion sounds.

Controllers for Marching Drums

Devices like the Roland RMP-12 (Figure 8.15) are portable electronic marching percussion instruments that can go with you out onto the field. These devices incorporate mesh head technology, which makes them lighter than a standard marching

8.15 The Roland RMP-12 Rhythm Coach

drum and allows drummers to practice longer with less stress and fatigue. They also include a built-in "Rhythm Coach" that helps drummers work on timing, evenness of strokes and other skills.

Electric Cymbals

Zildjian's new line of AE Cymbals (Figure 8.16) are real acoustic cymbals that sound and respond just like a traditional cymbal, but play at less than a quarter of the volume. A dual microphone system and sophisticated digital signal processing enables the player to enhance and alter the natural sound of each AE Cymbal in up to 20 different ways, all without the use of sampling or MIDI.

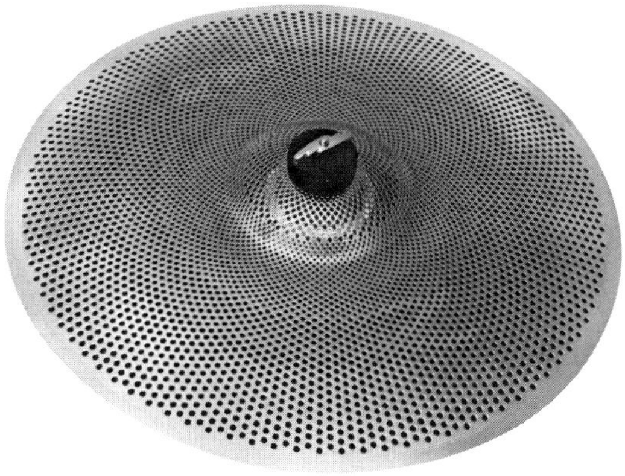

8.16 Zildjian AE cymbal

CONTROLLERS FOR STUDENTS

Although electronic drums and high-end pad controllers were initially designed for professionals, they have become an important tool for students and recreational percussionists. Not only do they allow you to practice without disturbing family or the neighbors, they can also be used with educational tools like Roland's HD-1 Drum Tutor software, which lets students using a drum controller play along to a computer track, do exercises and analyze their timing. Even a video game like Rock Band, when paired with a controller like the ION Drum Rocker, can become an effective practice tool.

Other Approaches to Rhythm in a Digital Age

As we move further into the 21st century, percussionists continue to combine traditional instruments and digital technology as both a learning and performance tool.

MIMIC THE MACHINES

In the early days of programming, drum machines and other digital technology were used to imitate the sound and feel of actual human percussionists. After three decades, however, the language of programmed rhythms has become sophisticated enough to take on a musical vocabulary all its own. As a result, the last few years have seen some drummers open new doors by figuring out how to imitate the machines. Players like Jojo Mayer, Zach Danziger, and Johnny Rabb have all developed ways to mimic the mechanical and decidedly "inhuman" feel of styles like techno, house, ambient and drum & bass. They're able to do this using mostly traditional, acoustic drum sets, although they often enlist the help of samples, loops and certain electronic controllers.

Pre-recorded loops by famous drummers—there are dozens of libraries available—can also be useful teaching and learning tools. Try practicing along with a groove until you can match its tempo, feel and dynamics. This is especially good if you want to get beyond the metronome and learn various grooves. Ironically, in this case, the digital technology can help you learn some very "human" drum styles!

SCRATCHING AND BEATBOXING

Two other ways in which musicians put a human spin on digital technology is through scratching and beatboxing. While these art forms are not just for percussionists, they offer a world of possibilities for anyone interested in rhythm.

Scratching

Scratching is a technique used to produce distinctive sounds by moving a vinyl record back and forth on a turntable. The needle creates a "scratching" sound that can be used as a building block to create all kinds of rhythmic ideas. The technique was developed in the late 1970s by pioneering hip hop DJs like Grand Master Flash, who transformed the turntable from a device that played records into an instrument all its own. In the last two decades, artists from across the spectrum (including rockers like Linkin Park and Beck) have integrated scratching and other DJ techniques into their sound. Today's MIDI DJ controllers (Figure 8.17) are outfitted with digital turntables. The digital rigs are not only more portable than their predecessors, they actually allow DJs to scratch without the need for records or CDs.

Beatboxing

Beatboxing is a form of vocal percussion involving the art of producing drum beats and other musical sounds using your mouth, lips, tongue and voice. Like scratching, the term "beatboxing" comes from the early days of hip-hop, when people began to mimic the first generation of drum machines, then known as beatboxes. Beatboxing is a true testament to the creativity of the human voice; there is no limit to the incredible sounds that beatboxers have been able to come up with. In addition to creating beats, many beatboxers also involve singing, vocal imitation of a turntable, and the simulation of bass, horns, strings, and other musical instruments.

8.17 A MIDI DJ controller, complete with "turntables" for scratching

THE "UNREPLACEABLE" PERCUSSIONIST

Whether we like it or not, programmed technology like drum machines, samples and loops are here to stay. However, we should not assume that these technologies are poised to put the percussionist out of business completely. When it comes to styles of music not based on a solid, repetitive groove—for example, jazz, marching and orchestral music—programming technologies are very limited in their ability to produce the subtle nuances required to make the music sound authentic. Along similar lines, although electronic drum sets are infinitely more sensitive than they were 30 years ago, they are still not able to truly reproduce the exact feel and sonic richness of an acoustic kit.

Finally, when it comes to the concert stage, just about every attempt to do away with the live drummer has failed. Even top rap and hip-hop artists, who almost exclusively program or sample their beats in the studio, still use a full band when they hit the road. Essentially, there's just no replacing the energy, showmanship and excitement that a live drummer or percussionist can provide.

Moving On

Modern technology will continue to offer percussionists more sounds, more ways to learn, and more tools for expressing themselves. You don't have to be a technical expert, but every drummer can benefit from a basic understanding of drumming technology.

9

A PERCUSSIONIST'S LIFE: TAKING IT TO "THE NEXT LEVEL"

In the first eight chapters, we covered a lot of territory and helped you discover many fascinating percussion styles, instruments and techniques. Hopefully, those chapters have inspired you to pick up a percussion instrument and begin exploring the magical experience of rhythm yourself. If you're already a musician, I hope you've picked up some ideas that will take your music to the next level.

In this chapter, we'll look ahead and dig much more deeply into the nuts and bolts of what actually comprises a percussionist's life. We'll cover some fundamental skill sets that every percussionist needs to know about—practicing, performance, showmanship, etc.—and we'll explore some of the options open to you if you hope to make music your career. Whenever possible, I'll share experiences from the 20-plus years I've spent as a professional musician. Hopefully, some of the wisdom I've gathered during that time help make your percussive life as fulfilling as possible.

A Golden Age of Percussion

If, as I mentioned above, your goal is to take your love of percussion to the next level, you've picked a marvelous time to do it. The 21st century can truly be considered a "golden age," in which percussionists and other musicians have access to more instruments, techniques and technology than ever, all of which can help them to explore their potential to the fullest.

The existence of the Internet means that we live in an ever-shrinking world. Borders matter less and less. Information is easier to find than ever before. Say you were interested in the African udu drum, which we discussed in Chapter 7. In the space of a few minutes, you can learn about the history of the udu, watch it being played by an African master, find 10 different online locations that sell it, discover an udu teacher in your area, and maybe even track down a local drum circle where you can immediately put your new instrument to use.

As a 21st century percussionist, you have options for learning about and creating music that someone in your position 20 years ago could never have dreamed of. These options include:

- Turning your bedroom in to a fully functional recording studio.
- Practicing at any hour of the day or night using an electronic drum set or other type of controller.
- Working with an electronic practice "tutor" that can analyze your timing and other basic skills with laser-like precision.

Even with these incredible tools at your disposal, however, there are still many traditional skills that you will have to develop in order to become better at your instrument, perform well on stage and work effectively with other musicians. The following sections cover some of those skills.

Practicing

Every field has a few true geniuses—people whose talent boggles the mind and who seem to perform superhuman feats effortlessly. Such people are rare, however. Even someone as talented and successful as the great inventor Thomas Edison had this to say: "Genius is one percent inspiration and ninety-nine percent perspiration." Simply put, even among the greatest of the greats, few achieved the status of "genius" without putting in a lot of hard work. There's no way around it; if you want to be a better musician, you've got to practice.

DID YOU KNOW?

. . . that a growing percentage of the private lessons I teach take place online? It seems amazing, but web-based communication platforms like Skype or iChat make it possible for me to work with students from all over the world, many of whom I've never met in person.

For some musicians, practicing comes naturally. They can't wait for any opportunity to pick up their instrument, and will spend hours working on a technique or coming up with creative ideas. For others, however, practicing is a dirty word; it's the downside to learning an instrument. "Too hard," "a chore," "boring," "like homework"—these are words that many musicians (especially beginners) often use to describe the repetition and discipline associated with learning the fundamentals. For many, the negative association with practicing becomes so great that they give up playing music altogether.

PRACTICING THE FUN!

Too often, the idea of practicing is presented in the same light as "homework"; namely, as a dreary, repetitive task that's not supposed to be fun, interesting or inspiring. Take it from me, it doesn't have to be that way.

Here's my philosophy when it comes to practicing: Practice = preparation with a purpose. Practicing can be fun if you have a goal while you're doing it, something to work toward. Think back to what it was that first inspired you to take up an instrument. Maybe it was to be the lead snare drummer in marching band, maybe it was to enter a talent show, maybe it was to be the fastest double bass player on the planet. Keep that in mind every time you enter the practice room (Figure 9.1). You may not always be able to draw a direct link between every exercise and your final goal, but by staying close to your passion, practicing will be less of a bore.

9.1 Here's the practice space I use in New York City. A bit grungy, but it gets the job done.

PRACTICE TIPS

The following are some things to think about when you head to the "woodshed" (a musician slang term for the practice room). These tips will make your practice time more effective, allowing you to accomplish a greater amount in a shorter period.

Warm Up

If you've ever played sports, you know that every workout starts with a series of warm-ups. Warming up is critically important, because it prepares the muscles and joints to work at their peak, and helps to keep you from getting injured. In the case of practicing an instrument, a good-warm up can also center the mind, allowing you to stay focused during your practice.

Here's my patented warm-up regimen: Start by jamming, playing anything you want, for about 10 minutes. Get it all out—just go for it and have fun. Then, for the next 10 minutes, do just the opposite. Play a very simple exercise very slowly. As you do so, let all thought go out of your mind. Just focus on what the body is doing in the moment. At first, this may seem difficult, uncomfortable, or not terribly interesting. But if you can get through it for a mere 10 minutes, it will start to get easier, and you will increase your potential to be a good practicer.

Don't "Perform" in the Practice Room

We often waste a lot of practice time by jumping from one random idea to another, rather than focusing on the actual material we're trying to learn. To make it easier for you to cut down on the distractions, set up only what you actually need. For example, if you're a drum set player working on a funk groove, literally remove all the parts of the kit—toms, crash cymbals, etc.—that are not essential to that groove. It's like being on a diet; if you're trying to avoid desserts and snack foods, don't stock them in the fridge. The urge to "cheat" will be too tempting!

Don't "Practice" in the Performance Space

In the same way that we sometimes waste practice time by playing as though we're onstage, we often lose focus in a performance because we try to throw in too many new ideas that we're really still practicing. Like a big meal, it takes the body a while to digest and internalize new material. Chances are that if you just learned a new pattern or fill yesterday, you won't be able to reproduce it, especially in the pressure-filled environment of a performance. It's like trying to write a paper at 3 a.m. the night before it's due: It wont be your best work. If you practice regularly, what you work on in the practice room will eventually show up in your playing on its own, without you even having to think about it!

Make Lots of Mistakes

Yes, you heard right. The time to make mistakes is when you're practicing! Remember, you're learning something new, so expect to blow it now and again. The issue is not the mistake itself, but how you deal with it. Lighten up, have fun with your mistakes. Laugh about them. Become friends with them! And most importantly, play right through them. This will make them seem a lot less ominous. In fact, if you're not making any mistakes at all, you're wasting time working on things you already know.

Don't Beat Yourself Up

Making a mistake is not a reflection on who you are as a person. Too often, I've worked with students who apologize every time they make a mistake, or spend a lot of time trying to tell me how "bad" they are. You're not a bad player: You just made a mistake! Think of it this way. When you're talking with a friend and you accidentally mispronounce a word, do you bring the conversation to a screeching halt and apologize? Of course not. You keep right on talking without even mentioning the mistake you just made. Musical mistakes should be seen in the same light: They are tiny bumps in the road that may trip you up momentarily, but in reality, they're no big deal.

Use Click Tracks and Other Practice Tools

As I said back in Chapter 1, keeping good time is a percussionist's "job number one." Practicing with a metronome or click track is an obvious way to help you reach this goal. By locking in with the steady pulse of a click, you will strengthen your own internal clock, and increase your ability to maintain a particular tempo for longer periods of time (the length of a song, for example). Click tracks are also a standard part of many live and studio situations, so it makes sense to use your practice time to become more comfortable with them.

In addition to a click track, you can also play along with existing recordings as a form of practice. This gives you the chance to "sit in" with other musicians, and feel the music from their perspective. As opposed to the rigid perfection of a metronome, working with songs (especially ones recorded in the era before click tracks) will help you experience a wide variety of human time feels, and make you more flexible when it comes to working with other musicians.

9.2 The Commandments of Early Rhythm and Blues Drumming

Many instructional books these days come with accompanying play-along tracks that are specifically designed to help you improve these abilities. For example, my 2009 book *The Commandments of Early Rhythm and Blues Drumming* (Figure 9.2) comes with a CD featuring 11 tracks. Included are two versions of each track: one with drums, and one without the drums, allowing you to "sit in" with the rest of the band.

Develop Your "Concentration Chops"

Obviously, one of the main reasons we practice is to improve our technique. But I also like to use my practice time to develop what I call "concentration chops" ("chops" is musician shorthand for "your ability on your instrument"). Having strong concentration chops will improve your listening skills and help you stay focused on the music for longer periods of time.

One way to develop your concentration chops is to play along with a particular song many times in a row. The first step is to learn the basic groove. Then, play along with the song until you are able to stay locked in from start to finish. Next, shift your focus to other aspects of the song. For example, see if you can learn the bass part, or memorize the guitar solo, or figure out all of the drummer's fills. By learning the song from many different angles, you'll have a much better understanding of how music functions in general.

Work on What Scares You

When I was in music school, I asked one my teachers—a fantastic musician—what he practiced. His answer was insightful, but a bit surprising. "I work on what scares me, what I'm the worst at," he said. I never thought that a musician of his confidence and experience would be scared of anything! But he was right. Too often, we only end up working on what we already know, and the stuff that "scares us" gets shoved into a closet, only to grow into a giant hairy monster of anxiety every time we think about it.

If you start by acknowledging the elements of music that make up your hairy monster—maybe it's reading music, or working with a click—and start to devote even a small amount of practice time toward confronting them, they will gradually become less scary. In the end, you'll be a more confident musician, open to a wider variety of ideas and able to better cope with the more stressful elements of music, such as performance and auditions.

Learn the Benefits of Practicing Slowly

Students often ask me, "How do I learn how to play fast?" After all, if someone can play fast, that means they're good, right? I answer by telling them in order to play fast, you have to practice slow. Although it doesn't seem quite as glamorous, playing patterns and fills in a slow, controlled manner will give you a much clearer understanding not just of the notes, but of the space between them. When you speed up the tempo, your understanding of that space will give the faster version of the groove much more clarity, and it will be easier to play. Trust me, it works!

Record Your Practice Sessions

Recording your practice sessions (using either audio or video) can be incredibly helpful. Recordings reveal exactly what the rest of the world hears, which may be very different from the way your hear yourself in your head. Studying these recorings will help you discover your strengths—and where you need to improve.

Make the World Your Practice Room

Part of my "preparation with a purpose" philosophy means that we no longer need to define practicing as something that can only be done at a specific time and place. Practicing will seem less scary, boring or otherwise negative if you make it a part of your everyday life, and turn the world into your practice room. Practice on a pad while watching TV; practice foot exercises while riding in a car, on the phone, or sitting at your desk at work or school (just make sure your teacher or boss can't hear you). If you're learning to read music, carry your book around and "sing" through the exercises for five or ten minutes during your lunch break. I live in New York City, which means that I often walk to gigs, rehearsals, or appointments. During my walks, I always bring a pair of sticks so that I can work on stick twirls, finger strengtheners, and other "portable" kinds of exercises along the way (Figure 9.3).

Playing With Other Musicians

Generally, unless you are in the practice room or doing a solo gig, a big part of life as a musician is spent interacting with your fellow players. We musicians spend hours rehearsing, performing, traveling to shows and just hanging out and listening to music. In a professional situation that includes a lot of touring, you may find that you're actually spending more time with bandmates than with your own friends and family. Even though everyone in a group generally shares a common love of music, the occasional inter-personal dispute over how to handle various situations is bound to crop up.

GENERAL DO'S AND DON'TS

To keep those sorts of issues at a minimum, here are some common sense basics that should apply whenever you're working with others. All of them are based around the same principal: Show courtesy and respect for your fellow musicians (and everyone else, for that matter).

9.3 I often practice the "stick on stick" technique that I use onstage while walking through New York City.

Be on Time

In the professional music world, being on time for meetings, rehearsals and especially performances counts for a lot. So much so, that it's often said that "90 percent of success is showing up on time." As the drummer or percussionist in a group, you will likely have more gear than the others, so try to get there a little early. Believe me, in addition to showing courtesy to others, you'll save yourself a lot of extra stress.

Acknowledge Others' Ideas

Musically speaking, a group can only be successful if its members all "agree" on a common direction in which to go. The group won't sound good if the members aren't listening to each other on a rhythmic, harmonic and melodic level. The same rules apply when it comes to making non-musical decisions: where to play, what time to rehearse, what material to cover, etc. Unless everyone is okay with one person making all these decisions, a certain amount of give and take is necessary. Remember, these kinds of logistical decisions are minor in the bigger picture of having fun and making music—so don't invest too much energy in trying to be "right" every single time.

Don't "Noodle"

There's nothing more annoying at a rehearsal than a "noodler," someone who never stops playing, even when other members are discussing song arrangements or other musical details. Your standing will go way up among your fellow musicians if you curb your impulse to noodle, and play only at the appropriate time.

THE RHYTHM SECTION

As a drummer or percussionist, you are considered part of what is called "the rhythm section"—the part of the band whose primary job is to provide the groove over which a singer or lead instrument performs the melody. In addition to the drummer and/or percussionist, a rhythm section typically includes a bass player, as well as a chordal instrument like a guitar or keyboard (Figure 9.4).

Your Role as an "Accompanist"

Whether you're in the school concert band, a rock combo or a broadway pit orchestra, your role as a rhythm section player is, by nature, more of a supportive one. As a result, you may receive less time in the spotlight than the singer or soloist. While this may seem somewhat unfair (after all, isn't everyone working equally hard to make the music sound great?), your ability to truly shine as an "accompanist" is what will make you a successful (and in demand) percussionist. Sometimes, this can mean that you won't get to use the flashy techniques you've developed in the practice room—epecially if they drown out the other instruments.

Onstage Skills: Performing and Showmanship

Once you've spent some time learning an instrument and rehearsing with others, the next logical step for most musicians is to go out and perform. Live performance

9.4 When it comes to "locking down" the groove, look to your partners in the rhythm section. Pictured is the rhythm section in my band Royal Crown Revue: guitarist Mark Cally and bassist Veikko Lepisto.

can be an incredible rush—after all, there aren't many jobs in the world where you receive applause for doing good work. But performing is definitely a very different animal than practicing, recording or otherwise making music for your own personal pleasure. A performer not only has to be concerned about playing well, but how he or she is presenting the music to the audience. By putting yourself out there as a performer, you are also asking that audience to "judge" you via their response. This may not seem like much of a big deal if you're part of a 120 member marching band, but if you are performing a set of your original material in a coffee house, a rousing round of applause from the crowd (or the lack of it) can make all the difference in the world.

No doubt about it, to be a musical performer you've got to have a pretty thick skin. If you plan to succeed in the long term, it's important to keep your ego in check, and think of each performance as a learning experience that's part of a much bigger picture. There will be successes and failures, but you can't get too hung up on either. As I like to remind myself when I have a particularly unmemorable night on stage, "Out of all the gigs I've ever done, that was one of them."

SHOWMANSHIP

If you haven't spent much time on stage, you might have some questions as to how you're supposed to perform. Do you jump around like Mick Jagger, or act cool like Snoop Dogg? Do you smile or frown? Make eye contact with the audience, or gaze at your shoes?

The answer is, there's no right answer. Too often, people think they should perform a certain way because that's how their favorite star does it, or because they are trying to make a particular impression on the audience. In my experience, however, an audience can smell a "poser" a mile away. If you want my advice, keep it real! Your performance should be a natural expression of who you are as a person, and how you are affected by the music that you're playing (Figure 9.5). It's all good, as long as it's authentic!

NERVES AND STAGE FRIGHT

Some musicians can't wait to get on stage. And when the lights go down, they come to life and play their best. Others—including many stars—are terrified by the very

9.5 The author, performing with guitar legend Brian Setzer

idea of performing in public. This fear can take the form of physical symptoms like a pounding heart, sweaty palms, upset stomach—even an inability to play one's instrument.

If you've ever experienced stage fright, don't worry. For the majority of musicians, it's merely a phase they overcome once they learn to be comfortable in front of an audience. But there are chronic sufferers for whom the battle with stage fright is ongoing, sometimes lasting an entire career. Unchecked, this kind of anxiety can take its toll, even causing someone to turn to drugs, alcohol or other addictions as a means of "coping" with the stress. Such substance abuse never solves the problem, and it can cause far more serious ones.

But stage fright doesn't have to turn performing into a completely miserable experience or end a musical career. In fact, many household names suffer from such anxiety, but they've learned to manage it in a healthy way so no one is aware of the issue. Here are a couple of ways to overcome a case of the nerves.

Work on It Onstage

You've probably heard the classic suggestion given to someone who suffers from stage fright: "Just imagine the audience members are all sitting in their underwear." Silly as it sounds, there's some truth to that statement. If being in front of an audience scares you, then shut them out and focus on the music. When rock legend Rod Stewart started his career, he was so frightened that he sang from behind a curtain. Some people perform with their eyes closed. Again, as long as the performance is authentic, there is no "right way" to do it.

Work on It Offstage

Jogging, playing a team sport, pilates, yoga, and other forms of physical activity help calm the mind (and the nerves). Consider a longer warm-up before you get onstage, or take a few quiet minutes to review the material you'll be playing. Finally, you might consider seeking out counseling from a professional. Often, the anxiety that comes with performance stems from traumas or other negative experiences we've suffered in life. If you can get to the root of these experiences, you may lose the stage fright as a consequence.

REMAINING CALM IN THE MIDDLE OF A STORM

Even if you don't suffer from stage fright, sometimes a mishap will occur in the middle of your performance that can provoke plenty of anxiety. For example: you break a drumstick; the sound system suddenly goes out; you can't hear the bass player; you forget which part of the song comes next.

Take if from a pro, these kinds of things happen all the time. Often they are not our fault, but the results can still feel embarrassing. Short of stopping in the middle of a song (a last resort only!), what can you do to get through it?

Be Prepared

First, think about potential problems before you ever get on stage. Check your gear and replace worn out parts, sticks or heads that are on their last legs. Second, make sure you've got the material down cold. There will be many potential distractions to deal with once the show begins, don't let the music itself be one of them. If you need to, bring cheat sheets or charts onstage to remind you what's coming next.

Don't Focus on the Problem

What's done is done. There's nothing you can do to change it—so let it go and try to get back on track. If you've had a gear malfunction, see if you can find another way to keep the groove going. If you need to, simplify your part until things are once again under control. Developing your "concentration chops" as described earlier will help you to recover more quickly and get back to what matters most: playing the music.

Pretend It Didn't Happen

The most important thing to remember is that as bad as things may seem to you, chances are that no one in the audience had any idea that something awful just happened. It's a proven fact that audiences generally remember the beginning and ending of a song, but not so much what happens in the middle. As long as you don't make a big deal out of problems or mistakes, they probably won't notice. Just keep the time going, and don't stop. Remember, "the show must go on," is more than a phrase, it's a way of life!

A Career In Music. Is It for You?

For most people, playing music is a hobby, something they do for fun. But it's also possible to have a career in music. There are many different approaches you can take toward this end: You can be a performer, teacher, musical scientist, composer or recording engineer. You can use music to heal others, or you might create a career that involves some combination of all these things. If getting paid for doing something that you love sounds pretty good, you probably have some questions: How can I go about becoming a music professional? What kinds of careers are possible? How much money can I make? This section will help explore some of the answers to these questions.

SOME WORDS OF ADVICE

Let me begin by being completely frank: Playing music is a wonderful, exciting and satisfying way to make a living. It allows you to experience the world in a way that few people have the opportunity to do. That said, music can also be an extremely tough career path to follow, especially if you want to be a full-time performer. Performing artists are often presented in the media as having glamorous lives; they seem to write hit songs effortlessly, or create killer grooves without even thinking about it. But the reality is usually less about glamour and more about hard work and a sincere dedication to your craft. It's not easy, and most of those who do try to make a living as performers give up pretty quickly in favor of a job that demands less of them and provides more security.

I say all this not to shatter your dreams or stop you if you are determined to make it as a professional musician. For me, the litmus test of whether you've "got what it takes" can be distilled into one basic question: Are you so passionate about music that it's the only possible career option you see for yourself? If so, what are you willing to do to make that happen?

I didn't make the decision to commit to a life in music until I was 22 years old. By that point, I had looked at some other options, and realized that there was nothing more I'd rather be doing than following my passion. Once I made the decision to jump in head first, music became my full-time obsession. Everything I did was geared toward developing my career. Every non-musical job I took only existed as a temporary stepping stone toward my greater goal of becoming a full-time musician. Through tenacity, creativity and perseverance, I made it happen, and I've now been a professional for more than two decades.

BREAKING DOWN THE PROS AND CONS

Is a career in music for you? Let's look at some of the benefits and drawbacks; being aware of these points might help you to make a more informed decision.

The Pros

- You get paid to do what you love.
- Your routine varies from day to day, which keeps things fresh.
- A life in music offers a wide and rich variety of experiences like travel and interaction with all kinds of interesting and creative people who are also pursuing their passion in life.
- If all goes well, you could parlay your talents into fame and fortune.
- You never have to "retire" from this job—making music can be a lifelong pursuit that will keep you feeling young well into your golden years.

The Cons

- Certain jobs in music follow a typical nine-to-five scenario, where you put aside your work when you "clock out," and don't think about it until the next morning. However, in many musical careers (especially those involving freelance work), you are essentially in business for yourself. This means that in addition to practicing, performing, writing and otherwise doing the things that an artist does, you are also responsible for promoting yourself, pursuing new clients, and creating all your own sources of income. It's a pretty big commitment, because if you don't generate work, you don't get paid. As a result, you may have less time for fun, friends and down time in general.
- Your lifestyle may differ from most folks. You may have to work at night, on weekends and on holidays. If you're a touring musician, you may be away from home for long periods of time. This can put a certain amount of stress on relationships, particularly with loved ones who don't share your timetable.
- If you don't have a salaried job (like a music teacher), your income as a professional musician can vary dramatically from month to month, and sometimes you have to live with a certain amount of financial insecurity. This may not be a big deal when you're young, but can become more of a challenge when you take on responsibilities like a mortgage, a family, etc.

MY EXPERIENCE AS A PROFESSIONAL MUSICIAN

Although I've certainly dealt with many of the drawbacks listed above during my career, I find that after two decades as a professional, I'm just as passionate about music as I ever was.

One of the ways I've remained inspired is that I've never stopped being a student—not only in terms of improving my technical abilities, but also as far as studying the history and tradition of my instrument. That's one of the reasons I'm writing this book!

Another way I've stayed inspired is by trying to remain humble and grateful about what I do. In any career, a person may feel that after spending a certain number of years "paying dues," or "climbing the ladder," they deserve a certain level of success or financial reward simply because they've put in the work. Unfortunately, life doesn't always provide a direct link between work and reward, and that can be especially true in the life of a musician.

That said, I always try to remind myself that regardless of how much reward or success I've experienced—I've been extremely lucky to be able to follow my passion and get paid for it. Maintaining this positive outlook can be a challenge at times, but it keeps me grounded and helps me continue forward on my musical journey.

Examples of Some Careers in Music

The list below offers a more detailed description of some professional options available to musicians. In many cases, a successful career will combine several of these options. This is certainly true for me. As a performer, I play everything from club dates and large tours to weddings, corporate events and theater shows. In addition to performing, I do recording sessions, produce my own instructional CDs, DVDs and books (like this one), and have an active teaching career (both privately and as a clinician). It's a very busy life, but that's the name of the game if you want to make a living in music.

PERFORMING ARTIST

Many people first pick up an instrument because they are inspired by the pop stars they hear on the radio and see on TV. According to the traditional definition, a star is someone who sells millions of records, makes millions of dollars and leads a glamorous and exciting life. While that may be true for a select few, the vast majority of performing artists trying to make it in the rock and pop world never earn a penny from their labors. It's an incredibly competitive field, and often elements beyond musical talent (image, fashion, current musical tastes, and even luck, for example) factor into success and failure. Even if your band does get signed to a record deal and has a million-selling single, there's still no guarantee that you'll actually walk away with much money. And today's music business favors "one hit wonders," so your odds of having a long, multi-CD career are slim.

9.6 Royal Crown Revue, featuring the author behind the drums

Still, plenty of artists do get signed, and a certain percentage of them go on to become stars—or at least make a good living. With enough talent and hard work, there's no reason why that person couldn't be you. Royal Crown Revue, my band of the last 18 years (Figure 9.6), was signed to Warner Brothers records for most of the 1990s. And although I wouldn't say we were rock stars, I had the chance to tour extensively, rub elbows with some big names, and generally experience the "rock & roll lifestyle." We had fun, but believe me, it's not all it's cracked up to be.

That said, the odds of becoming a rock star are kind of similar to winning the lottery. I suggest that while you pursue your dreams of stardom, take a more practical approach as well. Study music business, learn how to teach, discover how to utilize social media, develop your fan base, learn to read music, familiarize yourself with as many different styles of music as you can, and get good enough so that other musicians want to hire you. In short, do whatever it takes so you can earn your income from behind a percussion rig rather than a desk.

FREELANCE MUSICIAN

A "freelance" musician works for many different employers at different times, rather than being permanently employed by one entity. Although it may not be as glamorous as being a rock star, freelancers have many more opportunities to actually making a steady and well-paid living from music. In my capacity as "hired gun," I may do a jazz gig on Monday, a classic rock date on Tuesday, a big band session on Thursday and a Broadway show on Friday. And occasionally I hit the road with bigger acts, such as guitarist Brian Setzer's big band (even if you're not a rock star, there's nothing that says you can't tour with one!). While some freelancers maintain a full-time career, there are also plenty of "weekend warriors" out there who supplement their "day jobs" with musical work.

SHOW PERCUSSIONIST

This kind of work is based around theatrical shows that incorporate live music. Theater shows typically have a rigid schedule (on Broadway, it's eight performances per week), and are based in a single location. You could also be part of a touring company, which sets up shop in various cities for several weeks at a time. In addition to being a well-rounded musician, requirements to being a show percussionist include

9.7 The Street Drum Corps

excellent reading skills and the ability to work with a click and to follow a conductor. As opposed to the freelance scene, show work can be a full-time job, and may include health benefits and other perks. The downside is that this kind of work can be very repetitive, because you generally do exactly the same show every single night.

Opportunities as a show percussionist include the following: musical theater productions, circus work (either the traditional variety like Ringling Bros. and Barnum & Bailey, or the nouveau kind like Cirque Du Soleil), shows that have an emphasis on percussion (like *Stomp* and *Blue Man Group*), and cruise ship show bands. There are also percussion-based performance groups like Southern California's Street Drum Corps (Figure 9.7). Their presentation can be described as "rock-band-meets-performance-art," and they mount shows of various sizes all over the world.

ORCHESTRAL PERCUSSIONIST

Being a percussionist in a major symphony orchestra is probably one of toughest careers to break into for a young player. Symphonic musicians generally have a very high degree of technical expertise, and nearly all have studied music performance at a college conservatory. The hiring process for a symphony usually involves a series of rigorous auditions that involve months of preparation, and candidates often compete against hundreds of others for just one or two spots.

If you enjoy playing classical music, but such a rigorous audition process is beyond the scope of what you're prepared to do, there are also numerous community orchestras across the country, ranging from regional professional or semi professional orchestras to local amateur ensembles. For more on orchestral percussion, see Chapter 4.

STUDIO PERCUSSIONIST

In this job, you are hired for your exceptional skills in the recording studio. Your assignments may include playing backing tracks on an artist's CD, making music for commercials, performing on the scores for films, television shows and video games, or even recording loops for a sound library. Studio musicians (sometimes called "session musicians") can also be featured in front of the camera; shows like *American Idol* and *Dancing With the Stars* feature live bands that back up the action every week.

In addition to impeccable reading skills, great sound and dynamics, a vast knowledge of musical genres, superb timing, and the ability to play with a click track, a great studio musician must be able to instantly create parts that fit seamlessly into songs and blend with the other musicians.

With today's recording technology, many session musicians record their parts individually (in their own studio space), and then send the resulting tracks to the producers. This is ultimately a cheaper way to produce music than having everyone play together in one room, but it requires that you learn some engineering skills in addition to playing your instrument.

MILITARY PERCUSSIONIST

If you want to travel all over the world, playing a wide variety of music in many different settings, there aren't too many opportunities better than the military. Every branch of the U.S. Armed Forces employs its own musical units: wind ensembles, jazz combos, big bands, marching bands and pop/rock outfits. Being a musician in the military is a full-time job, and it's a great way to gain valuable professional experience while getting a salary, benefits and the option to receive financial assistance if you continue your musical training later in life.

CHURCH PERCUSSIONIST

Many churches hire live bands as part of their services and other functions. In addition to being spiritually fulfilling, working in a religious setting can be quite a solid career option as well. Many congregations employ full time music directors and players, and being a part of your church community can lead to many other opportunities such as joining a gospel, R&B or Christian rock band.

ACCOMPANIST

Like drumming, dancing employs a strong focus on rhythm. As such, dance schools will often employ drummers and percussionists to accompany their classes (particularly modern and ethnic dance). Working in this setting can be fun and exciting, because you are interacting one on one with the dancers, and the job may involve a lot of improvisation. Broadway theaters also typically hire drummers as accompanists (partnered with a piano player) when in the early phases of rehearsing a new show.

Other Options

If your passion for music does not include the desire to perform, or if you want to mix performing with other kinds of work, there are many other career options to choose from.

MUSIC EDUCATOR

Many musicians teach at some time in their careers—and that includes some of the world's best known artists. As with performing, teaching can take on many different forms and be done in a variety of settings.

School or Other Institution

If you are musically gifted and love working with people, you cannot find a more rewarding, enjoyable profession than as a school music teacher. A teacher's day can often be long, starting quite early in the morning and ending in the evening, especially if there are concerts or rehearsals to attend. But the satisfaction one can get from helping students learn and understand the beauty and power of music can carry a teacher through the toughest schedule.

School teachers must be college trained in both music and in teaching. Most music education programs require that you learn a variety of music skills, not just those in your area of expertise. At the elementary and secondary levels especially, you have to be flexible and competent on a number of instruments as well as vocal techniques in order to reach a broad range of students.

Those who reach advanced levels of study in music (usually in the form of a post-graduate degree like a masters or a doctorate) may also go on to teach at colleges and conservatories. These places can also be a haven for experienced professionals who may want a break from touring or recording—as long as they also know how to teach!

Private Teaching

Many performing musicians supplement their incomes by teaching privately. Others see private teaching as full-time occupation. How you set up your teaching practice is up to you, but most private teachers charge per lesson (or per hour). Many private teachers have their own studios or teach in their students' homes. Some will teach out of a music store or private music school that employs in-house private instructors. This has its advantages for the teacher, because it means the store usually provides the students. However, it also means the store takes a cut of the teacher's fee.

Working With a Marching Ensemble

If you've grown up in the world of marching, you know that life as a performer generally comes to an end in your early 20s, when you "age out" of drum corps eligibility or graduate from college. However, if you just can't stay away from the rudimental drumming scene, there are plenty of groups out there looking for a good instructor. Independent drum corps and drum lines—especially those that compete—place a premium on good instruction. In addition, schools at every level, communities across America, police and firefighter leagues, and many other organizations field marching bands. In recent years, theatrical shows that feature corps-style presentation have also become popular. These include *Street Drum Corps*, *Drum Line Live* and the "Jammitors," who roam the streets of Disneyland and Disneyworld performing on trashcans and other "junk" in ways you've never seen before.

Danny Raymond (Figure 9.8) is one rudimental drumming veteran who has made a career out of working with various drum corps, including the Santa Clara Vanguard. You can hear Danny perform a rudimental drum solo on the CD-R that comes with this book. Learn more about marching percussion in Chapter 3.

9.8 Danny Raymond (center), pictured with the Santa Clara Vanguard at the 2009 DCI championships

Clinician

If you become an expert in your particular area of percussion, you can be hired to teach at events called *clinics*. These are special educational presentations done in front of a larger group or sometimes just a few participants (in which case they're called *master classes*). Clinics give the audience the chance to know the presenter better, and to get a more personal insight into their particular specialty. I began doing clinics about eight years ago (Figure 9.9); my presentations usually focus on the evolution the drum set and traditional styles of drumming (for more on these topics, check out Chapters 5 and 6).

ETHNOMUSICOLOGIST

Ethnomusicology is a profession that looks at music from a cultural and historical perspective. Ethnomusicologists often focus their research and teachings on non-Western or ancient music traditions (like some of those discussed in Chapter 7). They might also do comparisons between various different cultures to see how their musical practices might be related.

MUSIC THERAPIST

Music Therapy is an established profession in which music is used to heal, provide comfort, or to aid in other types of therapy. Its goals are similar to that of standard

9.9 The author conducts a drum clinic in Albany, New York

"talking" therapy, except that the treatment of patients involves music. Music therapist is a credentialed degree (meaning you can get a Master's or a Ph.D in it), and work opportunities include institutions (like hospitals, schools, or health agencies), as well as private practice.

Music therapy is generally most helpful for those who find it difficult to express themselves in words (for example, children, developmentally disabled people, or stroke and accident victims). Treatments include singing, moving to, and/or listening to music. Many music therapists use drums and percussion in their work, because it's easy for a patient to get a sound out of these instruments right off the bat. There are also proven health benefits to playing percussion, which we'll learn more about in the next section.

Recreational Drumming

If you enjoy playing music just for fun, you might be interested in a new phenomenon known as *recreational drumming*. Recreational drumming (which actually incorporates percussion of all kinds) includes a variety of activities designed to promote general health and wellness. Like other musicians, people who participate in recreational drumming develop various skills like time-keeping, improvisation and ensemble playing. But the benefits of recreational drumming extend far beyond the musical; they prove that drumming can reduce stress and promote self-expression and community connection.

DRUM CIRCLES

The best-known type of recreational percussion setting is the *drum circle* (Fig. 9.10), a kind of jam session in which groups come together and play various drums and hand percussion. The circle can range in size from a handful of players to hundreds of participants.

9.10 A facilitator (center) leads a drum circle

A drum circle may include people of all ages; it offers equality because there is no head or tail. As opposed to other group settings like a percussion ensemble or a marching band, the members of a drum circle are not rehearsing for anything in particular, nor are they trying to become more technically proficient performers. Rather, their goal is to share rhythm, get in tune with each other and begin to work together as a musical community.

With more research pointing to the physical benefits of recreational drumming, drum circles have begun showing up in all kinds of settings, from corporate executive retreats to prison programs and agencies working with the developmentally disabled. Drum circles are often led by *facilitators*, trained teachers who uses inspirational leadership techniques to turn a mixed group of people into a fully functioning and exciting improvisational ensemble.

DID YOU KNOW?

. . . that Remo makes a product related specifically to health and wellness called the Aroma Drum (Figure 9.11)? It combines the benefits of drumming and aromatherapy in one package.

9.11 Remo "Aroma Drum"

One reason for the recent growth of drum circles is the availability of usable instruments. In the past, congas, djembes, doumbeks, tars and bodhrans had to be created one at a time by a master craftsman. Today, companies like Remo, Latin Percussion and Toca are mass-producing all of these instruments, along with new ones designed specifically for use in drum circles

(Figure 9.12). These new variations are inexpensive, easy to find at your local music store, and often made from recycled and other environmentally friendly materials. The upshot means that whatever your level of interest, ability, or finances, it's easier than ever to jump in and start participating as a percussionist.

VIDEO GAMES

Yes, believe it or not, it's possible to improve general timing and other motor skills by playing rhythmically oriented video games. While titles are bound to change, current examples include *Taiko Drum Master, Donkey Kong Jungle Beat*, and *Rock Band*. Many of these games come with controllers that are designed to look and feel like actual drum sets. However, don't think that you're going to become a master percussionist simply by sitting behind a video game controller. The technology is simply not yet sophisticated enough to capture the subtlety of a real instrument.

The Beat Goes On

One of the great things about music is that it always changes, but it never really breaks with its past. By the time you read this, new genres, instruments, and technologies may appear. Tastes may change. Teaching methods may evolve. But no matter what, the basics that have been driving percussion since long before recorded history will still be there, and percussionists will be keeping time with them for many centuries to come. I hope the basics you've learned on these pages will help you find your own path on this neverending musical journey. Happy drumming!

9.12. The drums in this photo were specifically designed for use in a recreational percussion setting.

ALSO AVAILABLE FROM DANIEL GLASS

DVDs:

■ *The Century Project: 100 Years of American Music From Behind the Drums* (2012, DrumChannel.com)

■ *TRAPS: The Incredible Story of Vintage Drums* (2012, DrumChannel.com)

BOOKS:

■ *The Roots of Rock Drumming* (2013, Hudson Music)

■ *The Commandments of Early Rhythm and Blues* Drumming (2009, Alfred Music Publishing)

■ The *Ultimate History of Rock'n'Roll Drumming* (2005, DanielGlass.com)

■ *The RCR Drum Transcription Book* (2002, DanielGlass.com)

PHOTO & DISC CREDITS

Vic Firth: Sticks and mallets, p. 35; Rudiments Poster, p. 42 and CD-R; Sticks and mallets, p. 57; Sticks and mallets; p. 76; Cindy Blackman, p. 105 (photographer unknown); Steve Smith, p. 108 (photographer unknown); Sticks and mallets, p. 132.

Latin Percussion, Inc.: Afuche/Cabasa, Guiro, "Shake It" shaker, p. 2; Tambourine, p. 8; Djembe, p. 119; Udu drum, p. 121; Assorted hand percussion, p. 123; Giovanni Hidalgo, p. 124; Afro-Cuban ensemble, p. 125; Surdo and Repenique, p. 128; Assorted hand percussion, p. 129.

Pearl Corporation: Shekere, p. 2 and p. 121; Drum set, p. 5; Cowbell, p. 8; Snare drums, p. 32; Snare drum, p. 52; Tambourines and woodblocks, p. 56; Pedal, p. 74; Horacio Hernandez, p. 111; Tamborim, p. 129; Cajon, p. 131.

Roland Corporation: Electronic drum set, p. 69; TR-909 drum machine, p. 149; Drum Trigger, p. 155; Electronic drum set, p. 156; Octopad controller, p. 157; Handsonic controller, p. 158; RMP Rhythm Coach, p. 158.

Drum Workshop, Inc.: Drum Set, p. 6; Snare drums, p. 32; Drum set, p. 69; Double bass drum pedal, p. 80.

Aquarian Drumheads: Drumheads, p. 92.

Remo, Inc.: Frame drums, p. 2; Drumheads, p. 8; Drumheads, p. 92; Talking drums, p. 121; Drum circle, p. 184; Aroma Drum, p. 184; Health Rhythm drums, p. 185.

Zildjian, Inc.: Splash cymbal, p. 9; Piatti cymbals, p. 54; Zildjian Factory, p. 73; Gene Krupa, p. 77; Gong, p. 135; AE electronic cymbal, p. 159.

Adams Musical Instruments: Percussion rack, p. 9; Timpani, p. 51; Bass drums, p. 53; Xylophone, p. 59; Marimba, p. 59; Chimes, p. 61.

AA Meinl: Rain stick, Nino egg shakers, p. 2.

Courtesy Alfred Music Publishing: Cover photo: The Commandments of Early Rhythm and Blues Drumming, p. 167.

Courtesy Ludwig Corporation: Theater "trap drummer," p. 75.

Reloop: DJ midi controller, p. 161.

Alternative Mode: MalletKat controller, p. 157

Boss Corporation: Metronome, p. 20.

Alesis Corporation: Metronome, p. 20; SR-16 Drum machine, p. 151.

TreeWorks Chimes: Wind chimes, p. 2.

Redmedea: Balafon, p. 121.

Zanzambira: Mbira, p. 121.

The Early Music Shop: Tabor, p. 31.

Evans Drumheads: Snare Drum, p.7

William P. Gottleib Collection/Library of Congress: Buddy Rich, p. 12; Lionel Hampton, p. 60; Max Roach, 82.

Courtesy of the Hogan Jazz Archive, Tulane University: Congo Square, p. 28; Papa Jack Laine, p. 69; Congo Square, p. 71;

Jose Altonaga: Chinese tom-tom and Chinese cymbal: p. 74; Low boy, hand sock cymbals, p. 78; Drum set, p. 85; Chinese Cymbal, p. 135; **Jim Pettit, Memphis Drum Shop:** Tam-tams, p. 55; Buddy Harman, p. 109; World percussion, p. 118; **Scott "Harry" Friedman, Horn Trader Music:** Early drum set, p. 71; **Ed Hartman, The Drum Exchange:** Greeko cymbal, p. 73; **Courtesy Stan and Jerry Keyawa, Professional Drum Shop:** Bob Crosby band, p. 77; Louis Jordan, p. 83; Count Basie band, p. 100; Gene Krupa band, p. 102; Booker T, p. 106; **Smithsonian/Folkways:** Baby Dodds, p. 72; **Billy Vera:** Chick Webb, p. 81; **Courtesy Louie and Francine Bellson:** Louie Bellson, p. 79.

Michal Manas: Turkish drummers, p. 26, p. 51; **Gregory F. Maxwell:** Orchestra bells, p. 58; **Daniel Glass:** Drum Set, p. 91; Practice space, NYC, p. 165; **Alex Rodriguez Cruz:** Daniel Glass, p. 169; Royal Crown Revue rhythm section, p. 171; **Chris Marchan:** Royal Crown Revue, p. 177; **Richard Uhl:** Daniel Glass, p. 35; Matched grip, p 36. and p. 40; Traditional grip, p. 41; Daniel Glass, p. 183; **Marco Soccoli:** Daniel Glass, p. 64; **Axel Breutigam:** Daniel Glass/Brian Setzer/John Hatton, p. 172; **Terry Dame:** Pots and pans drum set, p. 69; **Tim Barcus:** Truman State Percussion Ensemble, p. 62; **Jim Callaghan:** Evelyn Glennie, p. 65; **Marsyas:** Early Greek cymbal, p. 34; **Estonian Foreign Ministry:** Symphony Orchestra, p. 50; **Seth Tisue:** Harry Partch Instrument, p. 63; **Christina Faist:** Sitting Position, p. 90; **Jackie Jordan:** Drum tuning, p. 93; **Jean-Luc:** Keith Moon, p. 98; **Kristen Woo:** Street Drum Corps, p. 178; **Kamal Asar:** Danny Carey, p. 99; **Heinrich Klaffs:** Art Blakey, p. 104; **January Jones:** Lloyd Knibb, p. 112; **Peter Selmayr:** Rhythmicon, p. 148; **Mark Hyre:** Moog Synthesizer, p. 149; **Bombay Sweets:** AceTone drum machine, p. 149; **Ben Franske:** Simmons drum set, p. 150; **Courtesy Danny Raymond:** Santa Clara Vanguard, p. 182; **Pymouss:** Steel drum orchestra, p. 126; **Fabio Gouveia:** Brazilian drummers, p. 128; **Courtesy C.G. Ryche:** C.G. Ryche, p. 130; **Mexican Art Dealing:** Huehuetl drum, p. 131; **Danza Azteca Palmecac:** Aztec Dancers, p. 132; **Freddythehat:** Gankoqui Bells, p. 121; **Zhangmoon618:** Chinese stone chimes, p. 135; **Calton:** Chinese brass bells, p. 135; **Kevin Spencer:** Fou drum, p. 136; **Echard Pecher:** Gagaku orchestra, p. 137; **Chris 73:** Taiko drummers, p. 138; **Vero Villa:** P'ungmul drummers, p. 139; **Brian Negin:** Samgomu dancers, p. 140; **Giovanni Sciarrino:** Gamelan Orchestra, p. 140; **Barghava's Music:** Tabla drums, p. 141; **Ben Marlin:** Arabic Percussion, p. 142; **Hula-Instruments.com:** Polynesian percussion, pp. 143-144.

Sid Unser: Boston Crusaders and Vegas Vanguard, p. 30; Jersey Surf, p. 34

Public Domain: Civil War Military Band, p4; Civil War-era drummers, p. 26; Traditional Scottish Band, p. 27; John Phillip Sousa, 1893, p. 27; African American Marching Band, p. 29; Revolutionary War drummer, p. 40; Buddie Gilmore, p. 71; Native American drummers, p. 133; Maori Kapa Haka dancers, p. 145.